# Game Narrative Design and UX Fundamentals

Game narrative and UX share a deep, interconnected relationship. This book explores the connections between narrative and UX to develop a framework for creating player-centric stories in games by covering best practices in both crafts using a unified language.

Games are beautiful motivation engines, and there are three primary gears that power these engines: Context, Action, and Emotion. Each of the three sections of this book will lay out the elements of narrative and UX that lead to a coherent experience, guiding the player through the game world while teaching them the systems and actions of the gameplay.

This is very much intended to be a reference book emphasizing fundamentals, but also offers a deep dive into the best practices and methodologies. It will appeal to aspiring and current game narrative designers, UX designers, researchers, writers, developers, students at the graduate level, or anyone interested in expanding their understanding of player centricity or world-building.

# Game Narrative Design and UX Fundamentals
## Tools for Player-Centric Storytelling

Abigail Rindo

**CRC Press**
Taylor & Francis Group
Boca Raton  London  New York

CRC Press is an imprint of the
Taylor & Francis Group, an **informa** business

Designed cover image: Shutterstock Images

First edition published 2025
by CRC Press
2385 NW Executive Center Drive, Suite 320, Boca Raton FL 33431

and by CRC Press
4 Park Square, Milton Park, Abingdon, Oxon, OX14 4RN

*CRC Press is an imprint of Taylor & Francis Group, LLC*

© 2025 Abigail Rindo

ISBN: 9781032379982 (hbk)
ISBN: 9781032372532 (pbk)
ISBN: 9781003342977 (ebk)

DOI: 10.1201/9781003342977

Typeset in Times
by codeMantra

# Contents

# Acknowledgments

When I was approached at GDC to write a book about game narrative and UX, I couldn't quite believe it, so I'd like to start by thanking Celia Hodent, who invited me to speak at the UX Summit, making the talk that inspired this book possible. Celia also should be lauded for what she has done for the UX design craft not just at GDC but in games in general. There are so many game developers like her who share their learnings and wisdom, and I feel very fortunate to be a part of an industry that is so open, creative, and passionate. Game developers, I salute you!

I wouldn't be in this industry without the support of my mentors Mary Hillstrom, Matt Brunner, and Kenny Shea Dinkin, who have all helped guide me along my career path with patience, wisdom, and brilliance. This book was a journey, and I was fortunate enough to have some early readers who gave incredibly helpful feedback—Madhumitha Venkatesh and Signe Jorgenson. Thank you for your thoughtful insights and edits. To my parents Pam and Mike Rindo and my cousin Marc Seriff—thanks for being my cheerleaders during the writing process.

Throughout my years of working in games, I have had the great pleasure of working with many remarkable individuals, but I'd like to thank the Writer's Room at King, the amazing designers in GDW, my sister Rachel Rindo, Paul Stephanouk, Sara McPherson, Nana Li, Anna Brandberg, Desiree Brathwaite, Patricia Gomez Jurado, Paula Ingvar, Paul Hellier, Bob Bates, Christopher Ory, and Rachel Ansell for their continued inspiration and support as I navigated imposter syndrome, burnout, creative block, and the many other hurdles so many of us find on our path to making games and writing. I wish I could thank every dev I've had the pleasure of working with but unfortunately I don't have the room. Know that if you and I have worked together in the past, however, I am thinking of you fondly as I write these words.

Lastly, to the love and light of my life—Joseph Kane, you make my world brighter. Thank you for your brilliance, humor, and support.

# Author Biography

**Abigail Rindo** is an award-winning developer who has worked on games ranging from educational to mobile free-to-play. She has had the pleasure of working in many disciplines (production, marketing, art, design, narrative), on many platforms, and with many worlds and IPs. She has collaborated with many talented developers on more than 50 titles and regularly mentors people from around the world. She currently resides in Sweden with her brilliant husband and fluffy cats while working as VP of Creative for King.

# Introduction

## *The Close-Knit Relationship between Game UX and Narrative*

Video games, as a medium, defy simple definition. Unlike cinema or literature, which present narratives to passive audiences, games implore interactivity and action. They don't just tell stories—they enact complex systems of rules, procedures, and mechanics that players navigate, manipulate, and internalize. **Games are beautiful motivation engines**. When players plant a digital crop or match a set of similarly colored tiles, they participate in the beauty of the everyday. Games have a unique capacity to render life's trivialities as significant, teaching us to pay attention and marvel at the minutiae. They can be platforms for reflection, tools for empathy, or vehicles for political and philosophical critique.

In his book *A Theory of Fun for Game Design*, Raph Koster argues that games are inherently narrative in nature since they directly involve the player in a story or experience. Narrative designers support the game by creating narrative context, reinforcing action through storytelling, and using design and storytelling tools to evoke player emotion in the game experience.

Game narrative is about more than just crafting a compelling story. It involves weaving that story into the very mechanics and interactions of the game. It's about ensuring that every quest, character, and environment coheres, making the story intrinsic to gameplay. Metaphors and world-building take the complex systems under the hood and translate them into established mental models (the internal models we create in our minds to help us understand how things work) and actions that guide the player through their goals and challenges.

This understanding is where UX design plays a pivotal role. UX designers ensure that the player's interaction with the game is smooth, intuitive, and enjoyable. They also analyze player behavior, pinpointing areas of friction and refining game mechanics to enhance the overall experience. This allows the narrative to unfold seamlessly, ensuring that story elements aren't hindered by gameplay incongruences.

DOI: 10.1201/9781003342977-1

While game narrative and UX are ostensibly different in their objectives—the former focuses on the story and the latter on the player's interaction with the game—these disciplines share a deep, interconnected relationship.

In essence, while narrative design gives a game its soul and heartbeat, UX design ensures that this heart can beat without interruption.

These disciplines share **goals**. Both endeavor to plan and map out the player's journey, guiding the player through the game's actions and experiences.

These disciplines share **tools**. UX designers create wireframes and flow maps to visually represent this experience, and narrative designers create storyboards and story maps.

These disciplines share **methodologies**. Research is a vital step for both disciplines, and experienced designers know that it must start early in the process.

As we explore the connection between these disciplines of game development, we'll explore the fundamentals while digging deep into these shared goals, tools, and methodologies.

# NARRATIVE RULES ARE GAME RULES

In their book *Rules of Play: Game Design Fundamentals*, Katie Salen and Eric Zimmerman describe several key concepts for designing games and game-based systems. One of their key principles is that game narrative should support and communicate game **goals** while keeping the player interested in achieving those goals. Narrative designers are active advocates for the gameplay experience, structuring and connecting goals around emotion, events, and character. Whether the player is receiving thanks from a grateful character (NPC), unlocking a doorway to a new area, or simply clearing a board of falling shapes, their progress through the game's goals should be reflected in the game's world. A well-crafted game narrative does this in a variety of ways:

1. Reinforcing, teaching, and supporting game rules
2. Challenging the player and giving them feedback on progress
3. Acting as a vehicle for player agency, identity, and interaction

## Game Rules and Feedback

Game narrative should reinforce, teach, and support game **rules**. The rules of the game are what create the structure for *how* it is played—the boundaries or constraints that reinforce that structure and the consequences of the player's actions. The narrative of the game should help the player understand *why* they are doing these things. In the Western children's game of *Capture the Flag*, the game rules dictate and constrain the number and size of the teams competing, the boundaries of the field, and the way that the flag can be captured. *Capture the Flag*'s narrative of battle, while abstract, reinforces these constraints by relying on established mental models associated with taking territory and resources to help explain why hordes of children are running around a field with pieces of fabric. We'll talk more about creating constraints through conceits and world-building in Chapter 3 and best practices for choosing foundational verbs that act as a bridge between the player and the game rules in Chapter 4.

Game narrative should **challenge** the player and give them **feedback** on their progress. As the player progresses through the game, they should feel like they are impacting the world around them. This can happen through a variety of story structures and narrative systems that mirror the player experience, taking them on an emotional journey as they overcome obstacles. In *Capture the Flag,* the challenges of the game are contextualized through the concepts of "jail" and "territories." We'll discuss the story structures and systems in Chapter 7.

# UX RULES ARE GAME RULES

UX designers support game **rules** by guiding the player's experiences and interactions. They reinforce and support the *how.* Teaching the player how to play the game by helping them form new mental models and reinforcing existing ones is a key component of creating a seamless and fun player experience. By conveying the game's affordances (actions) through well-designed signifiers, designers create intuitive experiences. Additionally, by creating game loops that leverage neuroscience and psychology to apply the established principles of forming new ideas, designers can quickly deliver the player to the fun. We'll discuss creating intuitive designs through metaphor choice and actions in Chapters 3 and 4 and how to teach and reinforce those actions in Chapter 5.

The player experience should support and communicate game **goals** while keeping the player interested in achieving those goals. The UX designer creates a timeline of these goals that take the player on an emotional journey. As the player navigates the world, they should be able to easily access and understand what is expected of them and how to achieve it. We'll discuss how to guide the player on these goals in Chapter 5, how to understand what motivates players in Chapter 6, and how to map those motivations in Chapter 7.

The player experience should **challenge** the player and give them **feedback** on their progress. Because every player has a different background and skill level, some players will be more challenged by games than others. Good user experience designers recognize this and build flexibility into the game's features to ensure enjoyment for a wide audience. We'll further discuss understanding players and their needs in Chapters 2, 6, and 7. To help players understand where they are in the game and what they need to do to progress, the player experience needs to provide them with appropriate feedback. We'll discuss intuitive and diegetic ways to indicate and reinforce this feedback in Chapters 4 and 5.

The player experience should act as a bridge for **player agency** and **interaction**. By creating an intuitive experience that takes the player's needs into account, user experience designers reduce friction and let the player do what they came to do, which is play. We'll discuss interpreting player actions and interactions through game verbs in Chapter 5, and we'll explore opportunities for creating player agency by building intuitive systems through storytelling in Chapters 7–8.

# WHAT THIS BOOK IS AND ISN'T

- It is:
  - A reference book on the fundamentals of game narrative and UX that includes information on...
    - The connections and relationships between narrative design and UX
    - Methodologies, systems, and techniques
    - Case studies and examples
    - Best practices
  - Meant to inspire, not prescribe
- It isn't:
  - A book to be read cover to cover that provides how-tos or...
    - Detailed tool tutorials
    - Engine or platform specifics
    - Procedural or machine learning (ML) methods
    - How to write for games or design wireframes
    - How to get a job in the industry

# HOW TO USE THIS BOOK

A player-centric system for narrative games

When exploring the parallels between narrative and UX design, I've determined three key pillars that form the foundation of a player-centric system. This book has, therefore, been divided into three sections: **Context**, **Action**, and **Emotion**. These are the gears and pistons that power our motivational engine (Figure 1).

**FIGURE 1**   Games are beautiful motivation engines, and the primaru gears that move that engine are context, action, and emotion.

**Context** explores the foundational narrative decisions we make when crafting a game world to help guide and reinforce the player experience.

**Action** explores the verbs, inputs, and systems the player leverages to overcome the game world's challenges and rules.

And **emotion** explores how we craft the game's stories and interactions to motivate and guide the player on their journey.

## DIFFERENT AUDIENCES, DIFFERENT METHODS

This is very much intended to be a reference book. While it emphasizes fundamentals, my sincere hope is that any game developer, aspiring or veteran, will get something out of it. If you are an aspiring designer, are early in your career, or are exploring a new craft, I recommend starting with the introductions in Chapter 1, which will give some background and foundational information for each discipline. Be warned, we'll go through a lot of information, and this chapter is dense! Once you feel you have a good grasp of the foundational principles, move on to the chapters you are most interested in based on that initial study.

If you are established in the industry, I suggest browsing through the text and finding the subjects you really wish to dig into. I've attempted to organize the text in a way that facilitates this kind of perusal through headers, breakout sections, and bold text. My sincere hope is that this book becomes one of those you keep close at hand to peruse when looking for inspiration or a nugget of insight.

# WARNING! THAR BE SPOILERS AHEAD!

**FIGURE 2**   This book talks about narrative, and therefore has spoilers! Look out for this icon to avoid them.

This is a book about narrative and UX fundamentals. Therefore, I will be talking about stories. Lots of stories, both within games and outside of them. Spoilers have therefore been appropriately flagged, and I encourage you to skip spoilers for the games you haven't played so you can experience them for yourself. If you play them to learn more about the concepts in this book, so much the better!

# PART 1

# Context

# Introduction to Game Narrative and UX

**1**

---

## INTRODUCTION

---

User experience design and storytelling go hand in hand for many reasons—these disciplines in game development share similar tools, player-centric philosophies, and design methodologies. But before we dig into the interplay and connectedness of these areas, it is essential to build a foundational understanding of each discipline both inside and outside of the medium of games. Get ready, we're going to go through a whirlwind tour of the foundational principles of each of these disciplines!

### What You Will Learn in This Chapter

- What differentiates game narrative and UX design from other media
- Different roles for game developers in game narrative and UX
- Traditional forms of narrative and UX fundamentals
- Differences between forms and methodologies
- Examples of games that emulate these forms and fundamentals

---

## GAME NARRATIVE IS DIFFERENT

---

Storytelling is a long-established craft in the lens of human history. Stories have been told in games since before the first battle strategy metaphor was used to describe the more than 4,000-year-old game of *Go*. Veteran game designer Sid Meier is often quoted as saying, "A game is a series of interesting choices," and it is this ability to choose that truly sets our medium apart from other forms of storytelling. **Game narrative is not**

DOI: 10.1201/9781003342077-3

**plot, it is experience**. And in order to maintain an immersive experience, the game world must be cohesive, intuitive, and coherent. Narrative designers often joke that we are "Chief Coherence Officers." Does that mean movie script writers and novelists can't work on game narratives? Absolutely not. However, anyone who creates stories for games has to understand the essential differences and challenges that this key component of "experience" causes.

## Player Agency, Identity, and Interaction

Game narrative should act as a vehicle for **player agency** and **interaction**. Games are beautiful motivation engines. Before you begin building the game's world, you need to have a strong understanding of the player's goals and motivations. This will help you guide players through the game while crafting stories with emotional arcs and cliffhangers that keep them playing. Narrative sets the stakes for what rewards they will get if they achieve their goals, and what the consequences will be if they do not. In *Capture the Flag*, there are several identities that occur—flag holding player, jailed player, rescuing player, etc. These identities create strong motivations around social competition, and the goals and narrative reinforce these by creating high-impact moments associated with capturing and freeing objects or players. We'll have a deeper discussion of guiding the players with goals in Chapter 5, along with player motivations in Chapter 6.

Players have a level of agency within a game that they rarely have in books or films. We'll discuss identity and agency throughout this book, but for now, it is helpful to break down these concepts into three categories: expression, interaction, and responsibility.

**Expression** refers to the player's ability to craft and customize their own experiences. This can happen by impacting the environment around them, making choices about what to create, or choosing how to represent themselves. We'll discuss player identity and expression extensively in Chapters 6–8.

**Interaction** refers to the player's ability to use action and connection to solve problems within the game world. By creating stories that seamlessly integrate with game actions or verbs (the words to describe those actions), narrative designers elevate the player from being a passive viewer and consumer to an active participant. We'll discuss immersive storytelling through player verbs in Chapters 4–6

**Responsibility** refers to a player's sense of ownership over the characters, world, or choices within a game. When the player feels ownership over their own choices and decisions, they become more invested in the game world. We'll discuss narrative systems that facilitate and reinforce player choices in Chapters 3 and 6–8.

### NARRATIVE DESIGN, GAME WRITING, AND UX WRITING

Narrative design, game writing, and content design are disciplines of game design that often have overlapping roles and functions but also have important distinctions. These disciplines often work closely together or are combined in various ways across game studios. All three have a significant impact on the player's ability to understand and enjoy the game and its story, so it's helpful to gain an understanding of the different levers of the game each of these disciplines pulls.

**Narrative design** focuses on integrating the game's story into the actions, interactions, and systems within the game. This can include characters, environments, story arcs, quest design, or crafting. Narrative designers often have to work closely with designers from other disciplines, and they focus on creating coherence across the entire gameplay experience.

**Game writing** focuses on creating documentation that supports the game's story, whether or not that documentation is player-facing. This encompasses character dialogue, cutscene scripts, flavor text, world lore, and backstory. The goal of the game writing discipline is to create an exciting story that is enjoyed and understood by both the player and the teams who work on the game.

**UX writing** focuses on the game's non-narrative content and how it is conveyed through text. It is also often referred to as content design. Whether they're writing a full tutorial or simple button text, the UX writer's goal is to make sure the player can find the information they need to understand what the game expects of them. They focus on using written content to ensure player comprehension and limit friction in the player's experience.

# A BRIEF OVERVIEW OF TRADITIONAL NARRATIVE STRUCTURES

As I said before, game narrative isn't plot, it is experience. In their 2014 Game Developers Conference (GDC) talk "Death to the Three Act Structure," Tom Abernathy and Richard Rouse amusingly conclude that "game stories are not structure." However, knowledge of traditional story structures can help you make decisions about your game narrative, so it is helpful to have a basic understanding of these structures before taking a deep dive into game structures and examples in our later chapters (particularly Chapter 7).

# LINEAR NARRATIVE STRUCTURES

**Explicit** or **linear** narrative refers to a traditional narrative structure in which the player is taken on a journey paced and designed to fit the story. This doesn't, however, require all linear stories to begin at the beginning. Many stories told in the three-act or epic poem forms (which will be discussed later in this chapter) begin *in medias res*, or in the middle. While some argue that this strategy is non-linear, I would argue that for the sake of a definition for game designers, it is more important to consider aspects of agency, choice, and affordance when defining linear structures in the context of games.

I define linear narrative games as those that tell **specific stories the player cannot significantly deviate from**. Most linear games supplement this overarching explicit narrative with subplots, branching choices, or quests, but there is almost always a point at which the player returns to the main storyline. These games typically follow what is considered a traditional story arc and have a cinematic feel. Let's look in detail at a few traditional narrative structures and some examples of how they are emulated in games. Be warned there are lots of spoilers ahead, so look out for the spoiler icon!

## Joseph Campbell's Hero's Journey

The hero's journey has been used in storytelling for centuries. It traces the journey of a hero as they face challenges and obstacles in their quest to achieve their goal. This structure was popularized by Joseph Campbell in his book *The Hero with a Thousand Faces*, and it is often used as a framework for creating epic stories that resonate deeply with audiences. The hero's journey has 17 stages divided into three sections: Departure, Initiation, and Return (Figure 1.1).

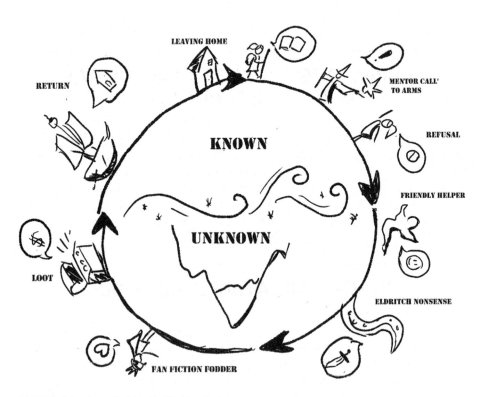

**FIGURE 1.1**    Joseph Campbell's Hero's Journey

- Departure
  - **Call to Adventure:** The hero receives a call to journey into the unknown. This is often represented by a distant kingdom, secret location, tall mountain, or even an abstract experience such as a dream or journey of self-reflection.
  - **Refusal of the Call:** The hero refuses the summon for adventure, either through original obligations, entropy, fears, or insecurity. This stage is often used to introduce new problems to the story. It also can add depth and background for the hero.
  - **Supernatural Aid:** The hero commits to the quest and receives aid in the form of a mentor, magical item, or extreme event. They are able to make significant progress toward their goal.
  - **The Crossing of the First Threshold:** The hero journeys forward and comes up against their first obstacle as they enter an unknown and dangerous world.
  - **Belly of the Whale:** The hero separates from the safety of the known world and enters into a new world, which surrounds and immerses them. This experience begins to transform the hero in a profound way.
- Initiation
  - **Road of Trials:** The hero undergoes a series of trials, often occurring in sets of threes. These trials are arduous and test the hero's resilience and fortitude. As they undergo these trials, they evolve and change.
  - **Meeting with the Goddess:** Someone powerful reveals the main goal and trial to the hero. The hero then receives items that will help them in future trials.
  - **Temptation** (originally called "Woman as Temptress," but I can't write that without rolling my eyes): The hero faces physical or material temptations that may lead them to abandon or stray from their goal.
  - **Atonement:** The hero confronts a powerful entity, and that confrontation becomes a fulcrum point in their journey.
  - **Apotheosis:** The hero's perception changes and their resolve strengthens. They regain their fortitude and drive to endeavor on the most difficult part of their quest.
  - **The Ultimate Boon:** The hero achieves the goal of their quest and receives a boon for completing it.
- Return
  - **Refusal of the Return:** The hero has triumphed in the distant land they journeyed to and is hesitant to return home with their boon.
  - **The Magic Flight:** The hero has to escape the distant land, often receiving magical help to evade foes.
  - **Rescue from Without:** The hero receives help from a guide or rescuer to return them to their everyday life.
  - **The Crossing of the Return Threshold:** The hero returns to find that their home has changed in their absence.

- **Master of the Two Worlds:** The hero finds balance, either in abstract or literal aspects of their life.
- **Freedom to Live:** The hero finds peace and can live in the moment.

The *Uncharted* series (Naughty Dog) is a classic example of the hero's journey in modern storytelling. It follows the story of Nathan Drake, a charming treasure hunter who travels the world in search of ancient artifacts and lost cities. At the beginning of the fourth game, *A Thief's End,* the player experiences the call to adventure in a flashback scene of Nathan and his brother Sam infiltrating a jail while on the search for clues leading to hidden pirate treasure. His refusal occurs when Sam is shot and presumably killed. Nathan retires and hangs up his adventuring hat until Sam comes back (a clever twist on "Supernatural Aid") and convinces him to do one last job. Nate crosses the first threshold by lying to Elena about taking on a scavenging job in Malaysia.

The brothers enter the belly of the whale in Italy, where they attempt to steal an idol during an illegal and high-stakes auction. The idol leads them on a road of trials until they discover the location of fabled pirate haven Libertalia in a hidden temple in the Scottish Highlands. As they are about to depart, they are confronted by Elena, who has discovered that Nate has lied not only about the job but also about his brother. This plot twist is a clever take on the "Meeting with the Goddess" and "Temptation" phases, as it combines elements of the two to emphasize the conflicted choice Nathan has between his brother and his wife. Eventually, they reconcile, overcoming obstacles together and returning home with some treasure and self-reflection, emulating the last of the phases of the Hero's Journey through the climax and epilogue of the game.

The gameplay in the *Uncharted* series does a great job of supporting the obstacle stages of the journey, allowing the player to drive the moment-to-moment action. This does not, however, grant them agency. Like a theme park ride, the *Uncharted* series takes the player on a journey that is "on rails." In other words, the player is involved in the action but has not been granted the ability to enact change. Games based on the hero's journey rarely have significant choice or emergence, mainly due to the rigid structures of the sequence. Stakes are raised, but the player must meet those stakes with skill and effort rather than creativity and choice.

## Maureen Murdock's Heroine's Journey

In an alternative take on the hero's journey, Maureen Murdock, a student of Campbell's, wrote *The Heroine's Journey: Woman's Quest for Wholeness.* It is a female-centric approach to the traditional journey (Figure 1.2):

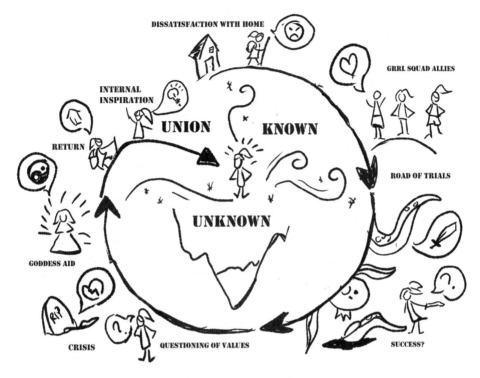

**FIGURE 1.2**  Maureen Murdock's Heroine's Journey.

- **Heroine Separates from the Feminine:** Here, Campbell's "Call to Adventure" arises from unresolved trauma or dissatisfaction with the status quo. The call is internal, rather than external. The heroine begins to distance herself from what she deems as feminine. This could be based on her feelings of inferiority, her relationships, or her position in society.
- **Identification of the Masculine and Gathering of Allies:** The heroine seeks out and embraces a new way of life, rejecting traditional frameworks. She finds new allies that help her better understand herself.
- **Road of Trials:** Very similar to Campbell's stage of the same name, the heroine encounters obstacles and trials on the way to achieving her goal. This often takes the form of antagonistic relationships that try to pull the heroine back to her initial trauma or societal position.
- **Experiencing the Illusory Boon of Success:** The heroine overcomes the obstacles, but she betrays her own values in the process. Rather than feeling a sense of freedom (like in Campbell's journey), the heroine feels estranged and oppressed.

- **The Descent and Meeting the Goddess:** A crisis befalls the heroine. She may lose a loved one, become injured, or lose her own sense of identity. A mentor appears and helps her find her way.
- **Yearning for Reconnection:** The heroine attempts to return to her original state, the one she was in at the beginning of the cycle. This may take the form of trying to reconcile a relationship or return to her place in society.
- **Reconciliation:** The heroine realizes she must understand all parts of herself to be fully free. This is a period of self-reflection.
- **The Union:** The heroine understands that the world is not binary and integrates the different perspectives she has gained. She finds a state of balance and, in turn, creates balance in the world around her.

Because the heroine's journey is less rigid and based more on introspection and personal growth, it often allows for more expression of player identity and agency than the traditional hero's journey. *Life is Strange* (Dontnod) is a choice-based branching narrative game that mirrors the heroine's journey. Branching narratives give the player choices— or, rather, the illusion of meaningful choice. In these games, players choose actions or dialogue options reminiscent of a Choose Your Own Adventure story. Often episodic in nature, these games present an interesting counterpoint to traditional story structure. Due to the nature of the digital medium, they have the capacity for more complex experiences than the dog-eared novels of our (or at least, my) youth.

*Life is Strange* follows the journey of Max Caulfield, a teenage girl who discovers she has the ability to rewind time. Max's call to adventure begins when she receives a vision of a tornado destroying her hometown, Arcadia Bay. This vision propels Max to hone her newly discovered powers so that she can prevent the disaster from happening.

Throughout the game, Max goes through a series of internal struggles and challenges as she tries to come to terms with her powers and the consequences of her actions. The game features a range of archetypes that are found in the heroine's journey, including the mentor (her photography teacher, Mark Jefferson), the mother (her best friend Chloe's mother, Joyce), and the wise woman (Chloe's mysterious friend, Rachel Amber). These characters play important roles in helping Max navigate her journey, and she reflects upon her own feelings while empathizing and growing with her new friends. She also navigates complex relationships with her friends and family and confronts unresolved traumas from her past.

*Life is Strange* uses choice-based narrative mechanics to make Max's personal growth more meaningful as she faces a series of tough choices that have far-reaching consequences for herself and the people around her. The game emphasizes Max's emotional and psychological growth as she learns to trust herself and make difficult choices. As the choices become more difficult, they emphasize and reinforce for Max the importance of using her powers to create positive change in the lives of those around her rather than simply using them for personal gain. The game achieves this by showing the consequences of her actions. The player also has some agency in determining the reconciliation and union stages, making the ending impactful and memorable.

# Gustave Freytag's Three-Act Structure

The three-act structure is a narrative framework that has been used in storytelling for centuries and is widely recognized as a standard format for organizing a story. It is believed to have its roots in ancient Greek theater, where plays were structured into three parts: the prologue, the main body, and the epilogue. This structure was later popularized in the nineteenth century by French playwright and screenwriter Gustav Freytag, who described it in his book *Technique of the Drama*.

In film and television, the three-act structure is often used to divide the story into three distinct sections, each with its own set of obstacles and challenges that the protagonist must overcome. It provides a clear and straightforward framework for organizing a story and helps to ensure a clear and cohesive narrative structure.

*Journey* (thatgamecompany) makes use of the three-act structure to convey its story through player action and exploration. The game follows the journey of an anonymous robed figure who travels across a vast and beautiful desert with the ultimate goal of reaching a distant mountain.

In the first act, the player is introduced to the world. A tall mountain can be seen in the distance, beckoning them. The goal and theme are clearly set through the environment's shapes and structures, which guide the player through the structure of the levels and the composition of the landscape. This act is characterized by exploration as the player learns the game mechanics and how to navigate the area. The second act begins when the player faces dangerous creatures and more treacherous terrain. This act is characterized by trials and tribulations as the player overcomes difficulties to progress toward their goal. They can work with another player to overcome these obstacles, creating a connection that deepens as tension rises and challenges become more difficult. Gameplay mirrors the arc of the story structure, and the emotional journey is well-mapped to the difficulty and challenge.

The player reaches the climax of their journey at the base of the no-longer-distant mountain. This act is characterized by resolution as the player experiences a sense of accomplishment and closure as the game culminates in a powerful and emotional finale.

## *Freytag's pyramid*

"Freytag's Pyramid" is a framework for analyzing and understanding the structure of a three-act story. It focuses on setting context, creating conflict, increasing the stakes, and finding resolution. It can be a helpful model to use when the lengthy steps of the hero's and heroine's journeys feel too prescriptive. The pyramid consists of five stages: exposition, rising action, climax, falling action, and resolution (Figure 1.3).

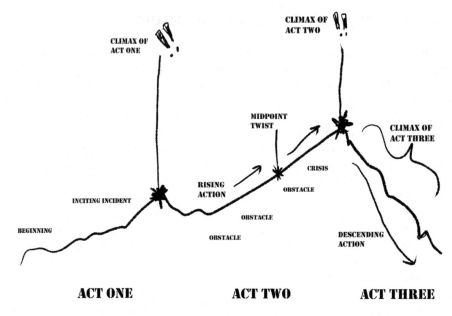

**FIGURE 1.3** Three-act structure.

- **Exposition:** This stage establishes the story's setting, characters, and premise (if too much is revealed at once, we call it an "exposition dump"). We are introduced to the world and the story's main conflict. A clear goal or objective is presented, and a call to action is raised.
- **Rising Action:** The characters face challenges and obstacles as they work toward their goal. The central conflict is further developed, and the stakes are raised to increase tension and engagement.
- **Climax:** The conflict reaches its climax and the stakes are raised to their highest point. The characters face a difficult decision or choice, and the outcome of their actions determines the direction of the story. By this stage, we are at the edge of our seats, fully invested in the characters, world, and story.
- **Falling Action:** The characters deal with the aftermath of the climax, resolving the remaining conflicts. Characters may self-reflect or have a period of growth as they process the events that have taken place.
- **Resolution:** The characters either achieve their goal or the story reaches its resolution, and there is an overall sense of closure. There is a clear ending to the narrative arc.

It is not difficult to find examples of Freytag's pyramid in games, but *God of War* (Sony Santa Monica) is a classic case. The game's exposition introduces Kratos, the game's protagonist, by setting the tone and stage of the world shortly after the death of his wife, Faye. In this compelling sequence, the player—who is accompanied by his son—chops down a tree that is used for the funeral pyre.

The rising action consists of a series of quests and battles that Kratos and Atreus undertake to spread Faye's ashes at the highest peak in the land. These quests build tension and introduce new conflicts, such as the Norse gods who attempt to thwart their journey and the revelation that Atreus is a demigod. Gameplay becomes more difficult as the tension rises, increasing the player's engagement along with the story.

The climax occurs during the confrontation between Kratos, Atreus, and Baldur, one of the game's primary antagonists. This battle is the culmination of the rising action and provides the game's most intense and dramatic moment. The battle is notoriously difficult, creating an elation of release when Baldur is defeated. The falling action focuses on the strained relationship between father and son, as well as Atreus's growing powers in the wake of Baldur's defeat. At the resolution, Kratos and Atreus complete their journey to scatter the ashes, ending the narrative arc of their quest to grant their wife and mother a peaceful rest. While the game ends with a twist that sets up the possibility of a sequel, the overall story arc is resolved with the characters completing their final goal.

## Linear Poetry

Many poetic structures follow a linear structure while using meter, rhythm, and imagery to enhance the narrative. In epic poems such as *Beowulf* or Dante's *Divine Comedy*, we often see parallels with the hero's journey. However, introducing complex rhyme schemes offers a layer of abstraction that leaves the source material open to wider interpretation than in many other narrative forms.

Epic poems often use repeating epithet motifs to add rich variety to their characters and environments, such as "resourceful Odysseus" or the "rosy-fingered dawn," explicitly stating attributes with flowery language and imagery. Because they are written in verse, epic poems also allow a character's internal emotions and thoughts to be stated more literally. The reader, who often has more information than the characters within the poem's narrative, takes the form of an intimate observer.

 *Child of Light* (Ubisoft) is a game with dialogue written almost entirely in rhyming ballad form, with occasional iambic (meter) flourishes added for flexibility and impact. The game's collectibles, known as Confessions, are delivered in sonnet form. While the rhyming feels somewhat forced at times (and I imagine created logistical nightmares for localizers), it reinforces the game's fairy tale quality and the themes associated with a young girl who grows up to become strong and independent. This game also loosely follows the heroine's journey, similar to the way that many epic poems mirror the hero's journey.

 *Shadow of the Colossus* (Team ICO) follows the story of a young man who seeks to resurrect a young woman by defeating a series of giant stone beasts. Each colossus the player defeats can be viewed as a stand-alone stanza of an epic poem, with each battle following a distinctive motif and rhythm. Rather than being granted specific names,

each beast is numbered according to when the player encounters them, evoking the feeling of numbered sonnets or stanzas. Overall, the game's imagery is evocative without being explicit, allowing room for interpretation and reflection.

 As the main character in *Hellblade: Senua's Sacrifice* (Ninja Theory) ventures deeper into the Norse underworld to rescue her deceased lover, the game's sound and imagery change to reflect her internal struggles with mental illness. As Senua becomes more distressed over time, the game's visuals become more distorted and the audio becomes more chaotic, creating a sense of disorientation and confusion. Senua hears voices in her head, which are represented in the game with a unique approach to audio design that makes the voices sound like they are whispering directly into the player's ear. Like the chorus in a Greek epic or a monologue in a Shakespeare play, the voices serve as a constant presence throughout the game, providing commentary on Senua's actions and offering both encouragement and criticism. This serves to immerse the player in Senua's experience and to evoke a sense of empathy and understanding for her struggles.

## Opera and Musicals

Opera and the modern musical are both forms of musical storytelling that combine music, drama, and stagecraft to create a powerful and emotional experience for the audience. The basic principles of storytelling in opera and musicals are similar to those used by other narrative forms, but with some unique features. For instance, they are usually divided into several acts, with each act consisting of scenes that move the story forward.

- **Overture:** The overture is a musical introduction that sets the tone.
- **Act 1:** The first act introduces the characters and sets up the story, including the conflict or problem that the characters must resolve.
- **Act 2:** The second act develops the story, including the relationships between the characters, the rising tension and conflict, and any twists or surprises.
- **Act 3:** The third act is the story's climax. The conflict reaches its peak and the characters face their greatest challenge.
- **Finale:** The finale is the story's conclusion. The conflict is resolved and the characters either achieve their goals or suffer the consequences.

While there are similarities to the three-act structure, the addition of music allows for abstraction, much like linear poetry. The music's motifs often convey specific themes, and characters often sing what is on their mind. The powerful combination of music and staging is used to convey the emotions of the characters and the story, making it a powerful and immersive form of storytelling.

 While not many games follow this structure (take note, designers), there are a few notable examples. In *Transistor* (Supergiant), the game's overall action and plot points are emphasized by the soundtrack, composed by Darren Korb. Red, a performer who has lost her voice, has to navigate and fight her way through a robotic army with the Transistor, a talking sword who acts as the narrator. The game uses voice as a common theme to parallel the conflicts and relationships within the plot. While the characters do not sing outright, Red sings some of the soundtrack's songs to narrate her inner monologue as she overcomes the dramatic obstacles in her path. It is not until the finale that she fully regains her voice and sings to another character.

*PaRappa the Rapper* (NanaOn-Sha) is a rhythm game designed by musician Masaya Matsuura. It consists of six different songs that the player taps out in time on their controller. At the beginning of the game, a musical cutscene sets the tone and details the player's goal. It has a classic boy-meets-girl, straight-out-of-Broadway plot where players help PaRappa prove he has what it takes to get the attention of the sweet Sunny. The fun and friendly songs each feature a different rap master who teaches PaRappa new skills through unique challenges (or obstacles, if you will), all the while emphasizing his repeated key motif: "I gotta believe!" The game ends with an explosive finale of PaRappa rapping on stage with his teachers and impressing the girl of his dreams. Like most rhythm games, *PaRappa the Rapper* puts the player in control of the music, giving audio and visual cues to indicate how well they're completing the skill-based directions. The game narrative mimics the player's progression; as the player becomes more skilled at the game's mechanics, PaRappa's musical prowess increases.

*Stray Gods* (Summerfall Studios) adapts the musical model more literally, using songs as the primary vehicle for the narrative's major branches in three distinct acts. As the main character, Grace, tries to solve the mystery of a murdered muse in a world of modern Greek gods, the player influences the other characters through the types of songs she sings. Like musicals, the songs reveal unknown information or the characters' inner thoughts and feelings. The music's tone, rhythm, and even genre change based on the player's choices, which impact the story.

As I mentioned before, there are not currently a lot of games centered around music themes and storytelling structures. But with music's rich history as well as its ability to convey emotion, it is a design tool that we can and should use more frequently.

# NON-LINEAR NARRATIVE STRUCTURES

Games are excellent at conveying stories through systems due to the agency and interaction available to the player. As Sid Meier has aptly said, "The ability of players to exert free will over their surroundings rather than obediently following a narrative—is what sets games apart from other media." Non-linear storytelling methods allow game makers to transform their complex mechanics and spreadsheets into engaging engines that reflect and reinforce the player's choices.

## Kishotenketsu

Kishōtenketsu is a traditional narrative structure often used in East Asian literature. Examples of the Kishōtenketsu story structure include the classical Japanese novel *The*

*Tale of Genji* and the Kabuki play *Kanadehon Chūshingura*. These stories are notable for their non-linear structure, allowing them to explore multiple perspectives and providing a more complex and nuanced view of the story's events than a linear narrative would allow.

The structure is often noted for its lack of conflict and resolution. Instead, the focus is on creating a sense of completeness and closure through a series of subtle narrative shifts and contrasts. Unlike the three-act structure, which includes a clear and straightforward beginning, middle, and end, the Kishōtenketsu structure is characterized by its four distinct stages: introduction, development, twist, and conclusion (Figure 1.4).

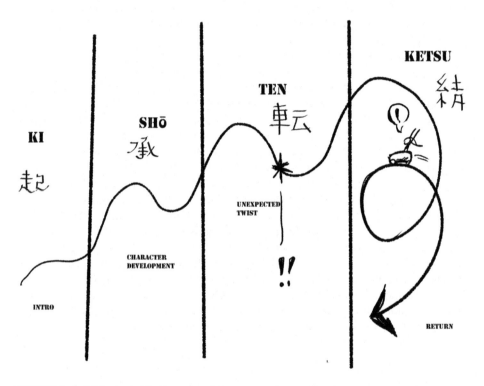

**FIGURE 1.4**   Kishotenketsu.

The term Kishōtenketsu is an amalgamation of four Japanese characters that represent the four stages of the narrative structure:

- **Ki:** The setting and characters are introduced, and the story's premise is established.
- **Shō:** The story is fleshed out. As the story is developed, the audience learns more about the characters and their motivations.
- **Ten:** The story takes an unexpected turn, introducing a new and surprising element that changes the course of the plot.
- **Ketsu:** The story reaches its resolution, and the audience is provided with a sense of closure.

While the "Ketsu" aspect of Kishōtenketsu is directly stated as an ending or resolution, it's worth noting that this narrative structure is often considered non-linear because twists will often happen in succession, and there isn't necessarily a final conclusion that ties up all the loose ends. While the story provides a sense of closure around one of the main twists, the focus is primarily on how the characters grow and change, not on what they accomplished or completed.

*Odin's Sphere* (Vanillaware) represents this narrative structure in both its story, which follows repeating loops from different character perspectives, and the combat levels themselves, which operate on a circular rotation where the beginning of the level connects directly with the end.

In *Nier: Automata* (Platinum Games/Square Enix) the player experiences a circular story pattern that follows the same sequence of events through the perspective of three different protagonists. As they see the story from these different viewpoints, their perception of the truth evolves and their understanding of the overarching story changes. The choices they make in each loop impact the future loop, and in the end, the final Ketsu.

Live service games that regularly update their content could also be compared to Kishōtenketsu. With each season, DLC, or regular update, the game adds an additional twist that shifts the story, rather than creating an arc with dramatic rises and falls.

## Indigenous Stories

Similar to Kishōtenketsu in some ways, many indigenous stories may not have a clear beginning, middle, and end, or a traditional climax or resolution. Instead, they may be cyclical or circular, with themes and motifs repeating throughout the story. They may begin with the ending or start in the middle, and they may continue for a lifetime. This creates stories that often emphasize the importance of context and background, rather than simply moving the plot forward. Storytelling themes often emphasize the interconnectedness of all things and highlight the relationships between humans and the natural world. This is often in contrast to Western storytelling, which often focuses on individualism in general and the triumph of the individual over the environment specifically.

Understanding indigenous storytelling structures and traditions can help you as a storyteller and game maker craft deeper non-linear narratives that are centered around the player experience. Indigenous storytelling is often passed down orally through generations rather than through written text. This frequently occurs in song, which is the most rigid story form. Indigenous storytelling also tends to prioritize communal values and collective well-being over individual gain or achievement. This means that stories often emphasize the importance of community, cooperation, and respect for others. And because tribal values and cultures change over time, the stories evolve and change with them. As a result, the stories are subject to change depending on the storyteller and the audience; therefore, they are more fluid and adaptable. For instance, Inuit storytellers will have audience members lay on the floor with their heads forming a circle so they can experience the resulting dreams together.

The *Haudenosaunee Thanksgiving Address,* a communal prayer for the Six Nations (Mohawk, Oneida, Cayuga, Onondaga, Seneca, and Tuscarora), is a beautiful example of indigenous storytelling, emphasizing the interconnectedness of all things and using repetitive circular structures to tell the tale of the cycles of life. The story does not have a clear climax or resolution; rather, it emphasizes the importance of acknowledging and honoring all elements and beings in the natural world. It is cyclical and circular, with themes and motifs repeating throughout the story. And it does not focus on a single protagonist or conflict. Instead, it focuses on the interconnectedness and interdependence of all things in the natural world.

Many systems-driven games follow non-linear structures that emphasize cooperative cultural and natural values. *Stardew Valley* (ConcernedApe) is a farming simulation game that allows players to create and maintain a farm while interacting with the local community and exploring the surrounding environment. The game emphasizes the importance of community by encouraging players to form relationships with the game's various characters, including their neighbors and fellow farmers. By doing so, they can unlock new areas to explore and learn more about the history and culture of the game's world. These character arcs create non-linear cycles of the story, allowing the player to explore the world through the relationships that they have formed.

*Stardew Valley* also places a strong emphasis on the natural world and its cycles. The player must plant and harvest crops, care for animals, and maintain their farm in order to thrive. The game also features a dynamic weather system and changing seasons, which affect the player's crops and overall progress. In this way, the game encourages players to slow down and appreciate the little things, such as natural beauty and the satisfaction of hard work. While the game does have an ending, it is not the most important aspect of the story. Instead, the story is centered around the player's ability to understand and work with people and the natural world, and their successes and struggles in these endeavors.

Games do not need to emphasize natural values to draw inspiration from the indigenous storytelling structure, however. In *Sky: Children of Light* (thatgamecompany), the game's social mechanics and constraints allow players to experience and create stories together. They begin at their home base in the center of the world and are free to travel outward and explore. Seasonal events cause the story to change and evolve over time, bringing the players' shared experiences into the world narrative, reflecting and mirroring it.

# Non-linear Poetry

Non-linear poetic structures allow poets to break free from traditional narrative frameworks to offer a more flexible and often interactive reading experience. These non-linear structures offer readers a multi-perspective reading experience, challenging traditional narrative and temporal orders. This invites the reader to participate in creating the poem's meaning and reflect on the process of reading itself. As you can imagine, this shared relationship between storyteller and reader works nicely with the agency afforded in games. Let's look at a few notable examples.

## Cento poems

A cento is a poem created entirely of lines taken from other poets' work. Each line in a cento is borrowed and stitched together from other poems, creating a new and individual narrative from existing ones. The beauty of a cento is that each line is filled with its own history and context. In the hands of a skilled poet, these disparate lines connect and form a whole that is greater than the sum of its parts. These lines are rearranged and recontextualized to create a new work with a unique voice and meaning. Like a collage, a cento poem can be non-linear and disorienting, as it often includes lines from many different sources. One example of a famous cento poem is "The Waste Land" by T.S. Eliot. This poem is composed entirely of lines and phrases from various literary and cultural sources such as Shakespeare, Dante, and Greek mythology, and the poem is arranged in a fragmented, non-linear structure. David Bowie was also known for crafting his song lyrics by creating collages of the newspaper headlines of any given week, stripping out the context of world events and abstracting and reinterpreting them.

The overarching narrative of *What Remains of Edith Finch* (Giant Sparrow) isn't strictly linear, much like a cento. In this game, the player chooses the order in which to explore the Finch house, and each room provides a fragment of the family's overall story. Instead of borrowing lines of poetry, the game borrows from various game genres and narrative techniques. Every piece of the narrative is presented with a different gameplay mechanic, drawing the player deeper into the rich tapestry of the family's history. Each narrative piece tells a family member's unique story by using a completely different style, from the comic book horror of Barbara's tale to Lewis's increasingly engrossing daydreams, which blend third-person narration with first-person gameplay. Each of these experiences began with a prototype created by a different game designer, all bringing their unique perspectives.

Forum or succession games like those played in the intricate, procedurally generated world of *Dwarf Fortress* (Tarn & Zack Adams/Kitfox) are also interesting to consider in relation to a cento poem. In a succession game, players take turns playing a single game, usually passing the control of the play session on from one to the other at the end of an in-game year. Each player thus adds to the ongoing narrative created by their predecessors, much like the lines of a cento poem are culled from existing works. Each line in the poem and each player in the succession game carry the narrative forward, building upon what has been established while introducing new elements and directions.

In a cento, the poet uses lines that hold significance in their original context and breathes new life into them, giving them a new meaning within the context of the new poem. Similarly, in succession games, players inherit the world from the previous player and bring their unique vision to it, shaping the game world and narrative in new ways while maintaining the continuity of the existing story. Like the cento, succession games can be unpredictable and full of surprises. Since each player can play the game in a completely different way, the narrative takes unexpected turns, akin to how a line from a different poem can change the tone or direction of a cento. There's a sense of collaboration and shared creativity. The final product is a combination of individual interpretations and expressions stitched together to form a cohesive whole. It's a group effort, and the final narrative becomes richer and more layered due to the multiple contributors.

## Lyric sequence

A lyric sequence is a collection of poems that share a common theme or subject but don't necessarily have a linear narrative. Rather than telling a singular story, the poems in a lyric sequence work together to explore a particular emotion or idea. Each poem stands on its own, but they are arranged in a deliberate order to create a larger, more complex work. The sequence can be cyclical or recursive, meaning that the poems may return to certain themes or motifs throughout.

In *Unpacking* (Witch Beam), the player unpacks the protagonist's boxes following a move to a new home. In each room, the objects removed from the boxes represent a different moment or experience in the protagonist's life. The player experiences these moments in a non-linear sequence, but they are linked by a shared emotional tone and the overarching narrative of the protagonist's life. Similarly, in lyric sequence poetry, individual poems or stanzas explore different moments or experiences but are connected by a shared emotional or thematic focus. This is because *Unpacking* and lyric sequence poetry both explore emotions and personal experiences through a series of interconnected, non-linear moments or vignettes. The objects in *Unpacking*, when viewed individually, may seem arbitrary at first. However, when they are placed in the emotional and environmental context of each phase of life, they gain greater depth and meaning. Like with lyric sequences, imagery, and symbolism are used to convey emotional and personal experiences.

## Multi-dimensional poems

*Star Gauge*, or *Xuanji Tu*, is an extraordinary example of non-linear poetry. Composed in the fourth century by Chinese poet Su Hui, the poem consists of a grid of 841 characters arranged in a symmetrical pattern that is designed to be read in multiple directions— down, up, diagonally, and even zigzagging. The number of possible readings is said to be in the thousands. Not only does this structure allow for an immense variety of interpretations, but it also gives readers a direct hand in unfolding the poem's narrative. The reader directs the content based on the direction in which they choose to read, letting their perspective and agency dictate the content and interpretation. One could argue that this poem has high "replayability" because it can be read again and again, with new interpretations and understandings emerging each time. The narrative journey is a complex web of potential paths and understandings, rather than a straight path.

Similarly, procedural narrative systems use content and rules to create the foundation for a story that is driven by player agency. In *Watch Dog: Legions* (Ubisoft), you can recruit and control any one of the millions of possible characters within the game, each with a unique backstory, skills, and characteristics. The story shifts and evolves based on which character you are playing, offering a multitude of narrative perspectives and outcomes. Just like the reader navigating the poem's grid, the player navigates the game's world, shaping a unique narrative path with the decisions they make and the characters they choose.

Complex procedural systems aren't necessary for building agency-driven stories, however. *Her Story* (Sam Barlow) is a detective game where players watch video clips and try to piece together the story of a woman being interviewed about her missing husband. The order in which players find and watch the clips isn't linear, and it's up to the player to piece together the narrative, much like navigating the various directions of the *Star Gauge*. Both the poem and the game rely on the participant to assemble the narrative from disparate non-linear fragments.

## *Villanelle*

Villanelles are poems that consist of 19 lines. They use a fixed rhyme scheme and repeat lines according to a prescribed pattern. A villanelle is usually divided into five tercets (three-line stanzas) and one concluding quatrain (four-line stanza). The same two rhyming sounds are used throughout the poem, and several of the lines are repeated in various places. The repetition creates a haunting, melancholic effect and reinforces the poem's theme or mood. Villanelles typically have a strong musical quality due to their repetition and rhyme scheme. One of the most famous examples of a villanelle is "Do Not Go Gentle into That Good Night" by Dylan Thomas.

*Kentucky Route Zero* (Cardboard Computer) uses language and visual imagery to create an immersive and atmospheric experience for the player with some striking similarities to a villanelle poem. It is divided into five acts, similar to the villanelle's tercets, with the equivalent of a concluding quatrain in the completion of the delivery that initiated the journey. The game features a surreal, dreamlike world that is brought to life through striking visuals and filled with repeating motifs. While there are not two repeating rhyming sounds in the game's dialogue, the ambient music of the soundtrack does use tonal sounds that repeat throughout the five acts. The dialogue between characters is often poetic and introspective, exploring themes of loss, memory, and identity reminiscent of poetry.

In addition, the game's non-linear narrative structure allows players to explore different paths and make choices that impact the story and characters in meaningful ways. This structure is similar to the way a poem can offer multiple interpretations and layers of meaning, depending on how it is read. The game's slow pace and focus on character development create a sense of contemplative reflection, inviting the player to engage with the story and characters on a deeper level.

# Immersive Theater

Immersive theater often employs a non-linear narrative structure that invites audience members to explore the story in their own way. This can be achieved through multiple paths, alternate endings, and different perspectives on the same story. Using a variety of techniques, including interactive elements, multisensory experiences, and intricate set design, immersive theater creates an environment where audience members feel like they are part of the action rather than just being passive observers. The environment engages the audience's senses—sight, sound, touch, taste, and smell—this can include the use of live music, odors, flavors, and physical sensations to enhance the story. It's fascinating how immersive theater rethinks spatial storytelling, especially in the hands of Punchdrunk, the pioneering British theater company.

Audience members at Punchdrunk productions don masks as they navigate the interactive productions. This anonymizes the audience, creating a background of non-player characters that observe the actors/players as they act out the story in parallel looping narratives. This is not a passive experience, however. Audience members are granted agency in how they interpret, follow, and explore the story. Punchdrunk employs interpretive dance to communicate narratives viscerally and non-verbally. There is very little spoken dialogue, relying more on body language, space, light, and sound to guide and manipulate audience members. A set is like an open-world game, giving them the freedom to explore and dig into lore that is delivered purely through environmental storytelling, lush imagery, and individual objects. As the audience explores this world and follows the characters, they make choices about how they spend their time—what characters, environments, and stories they want to immerse themselves in.

The *Dark Souls* (From Software) series has become well known for its distinct brand of environmental storytelling, relying on the player's ability to piece together fragments of lore found throughout the experience to build a rich narrative. Players need to piece together short snippets of dialogue, experiences with characters, and bits of lore peppered into object descriptions to form the whole narrative. In both Punchdrunk and From Software productions, the audience requires multiple sessions to piece together the full story, and they often debate its nuances with their peers.

 Throughout a Punchdrunk production, intimate encounters between an actor and an audience member, termed 1:1s, forge a moment of direct connection where the mask is removed. This is the moment when an anonymous audience member is pulled into the action, and they become, in essence, a player. These experiences are often intimate, with the actor taking the hand of an audience member and pulling them into a secret room. I have been to many Punchdrunk shows and have been fortunate enough to have had 1:1 experiences on multiple occasions. They vary wildly and are deeply connected to the character/player performing them—I've had tea with a witch, wiped the blood from the eyes of a villain, explored a labyrinth in the dark, had my hands bound by a servant, and shared secrets and sake with a bartender. Each of these experiences was an intimate, individualized scene between myself and the actor, drawing me deeper into the narrative in adrenaline-fueling interactions. The anticipation, tension, and unpredictability of these interactions share DNA with the unexpected romantic turns and outcomes of Japanese visual novel games such as *The House in Fata Morgana* (Novectacle), where player choice and investment in branching plotlines reveal deep secrets, intimate encounters, and dramatic performances.

Pairing film screening activities with immersive sets, Secret Cinema is a theater company that centers its performances on iconic films. Attendees are not mere spectators in these recreated film universes; they become participants, with some events taking on festival-like proportions, welcoming attendees into expansive, meticulously detailed sets. One significant facet of the Secret Cinema experience is the element of character creation and backstory. Before each event, attendees receive guidelines about their designated characters. These guidelines often include a dress code and brief backstory. This evokes memories of massive multiplayer online role-playing games (MMORPGs) like *Star Wars: The Old Republic* (BioWare). In MMORPGs, players adopt a role, don an outfit, and follow a particular path in a well-known galaxy teeming with stories and other characters. Similarly, in Secret Cinema, the attendees' costumes and backstories don't just serve an aesthetic or immersive purpose; they integrate attendees into the larger narrative, making them essential components of the story, much like every player character in an MMORPG.

By diving into various traditional narrative structures and connecting them to similar works in games, hopefully, you've been able to lay some foundational storytelling methods to build our design system of Context, Action, and Emotion. Now, let's look similarly at UX design.

# UX DESIGN IS DIFFERENT

User experience (UX) design, a term coined and popularized by Don Norman in the 1990s during his early days at Apple, is the process of designing digital products or services with a human-centric focus. The goal of UX design is to create products that are intuitive, easy to use, and meet the user's needs and expectations.

Traditional product design and web design both focus on creating a functional and efficient user experience. This often involves designing interfaces that are easy to navigate and that provide users with the information they need to complete a task or make a decision. **In games, however, user experience is driven by immersive and playful interaction**. The player is an active participant in the experience, making decisions and taking actions that shape the course of the game. Therefore, game UX design needs to account for the player's goals, motivations, and preferences in a way that is different from traditional product or web design. Good UX design can reduce frustration, improve engagement, and ultimately lead to a more successful game.

The concept of UX design in games can be traced back to the earliest video games. In the 1980s, game designer Richard Garriott introduced the concept of player-centric design, which emphasized the importance of designing games with the player's experience in mind. This was followed by the emergence of game design studios such as Sierra On-Line and LucasArts, which focused on creating immersive storytelling experiences for players. Their games were some of the first to integrate narratives that guide the player's actions and shape the overall experience. (That evolution is one of the many reasons this book exists!) This change required that game designers consider how the narrative is integrated into gameplay, along with its impact on the player's engagement and emotional connection to the game. In later chapters, there will be an extensive discussion of how interactive storytelling has evolved in video games. For now, it's something important to keep in the back of your mind if you are coming to video games from web or physical design disciplines.

Today, UX design is an established discipline and an essential part of game development, with many studios conducting user testing and employing dedicated designers to ensure a smooth and engaging gameplay experience. These designers actively advocate for the player, emphasizing principles and goals around coherence, guidance, and understanding.

## UI AND UX DISCIPLINES

User interface (UI) and user experience (UX) design are two separate disciplines of game design. Although these terms are often used interchangeably and heavily debated, they are distinct areas with their own goals and best practices. However, well-designed UI and UX play crucial roles in a game's success, and they work together to ensure that a game is both visually appealing and enjoyable to play. It is common for one person to perform both UI and UX functions. It's also common for UI and UX designers to closely collaborate in game studios, so it is important to understand and articulate the differences and similarities of these crafts.

**UI design** focuses on the visual element of game interactions, including the graphical elements, layouts, typography, and color schemes. It encompasses all the visual and interactive elements that players encounter, such as buttons, icons, menus, feedback, and text. The goal of UI design is to create an attractive and intuitive interface that allows players to seamlessly navigate and interact with the game.

**UX design** focuses on how a player experiences and understands the game. The discipline considers the game's overall flow, how players interact with it, and how they feel about those interactions. UX designers strive to create a seamless and satisfying experience for players and account for aspects such as difficulty, pacing, and player engagement. UX design also considers factors such as accessibility and user research to understand player needs and preferences.

**UX Research** focuses on understanding player behavior through a variety of research practices and means. Researchers design and execute playtest sessions, surveys, and interviews to gather information about how users interact with and feel about the game. We'll discuss specific playtest and research methodologies in Chapter 2.

# A BRIEF OVERVIEW OF UX DESIGN PRINCIPLES

Understanding the psychology of human behavior and how it relates to design is the foundation of good UX. Therefore, it is helpful to have a basic understanding of these foundational principles and ideas. The next section of this book provides an overview of some key concepts, but it is by no means exhaustive. We'll talk about these principles more deeply in future chapters, but for now, you should familiarize yourself with the general ideas.

## Gestalt Principles

The Gestalt principles are a set of psychology theories that describe how humans perceive and organize visual information. These principles were devised in the 1920s by German psychologists Max Wertheimer, Kurt Koffka, and Wolfgang Kohler. Understanding them can help us as designers make better decisions (Figure 1.5).

**FIGURE 1.5**  Gestalt principles.

- **Proximity:** People perceive objects that are close to each other as a group. This principle can be applied in games by placing related elements (such as buttons or icons) close to each other to make it clear that they are part of the same group or function. You often see proximity used in skill trees to denote skills that are similar in function and style.
- **Similarity:** People see objects that look similar or share a visual characteristic as being related. UX and UI designers make specific choices around using consistent colors, fonts, and other visual elements to make it clear that elements belong together and serve similar functions. This allows players to readily find the information they need. Similarity is frequently used in crafting or inventory interfaces and icons so players can easily locate the ingredients or objects necessary to craft or upgrade items.
- **Continuity:** When objects are arranged in a way that denotes a line or direction, they are perceived as a continuous single object. The principle of continuity posits that the human eye will follow a path or line, often preferring to see a continuous flow or direction rather than disrupted objects or lines. Continuity is often applied to create the appearance of paths on a map or to group a series of individual steps into a single flow of information.
- **Closure:** Humans tend to fill in missing parts of incomplete objects to create a sense of completeness. Even if an object is incomplete, our eyes tend to fill in the missing information and perceive it as a whole. UX designers often use elements such as buttons or icons that suggest a certain action or outcome, even if the exact details are not visible. Closure is also a helpful principle to leverage when designing tutorials that help guide the player in completing tasks.

The Heads-Up Display (HUD) in games is a primary example of good user interface design, often relying on Gestalt principles to ensure users can quickly understand and interpret on-screen information. Let's take a look at an industry-standard HUD interface as an example of these principles in action (Figure 1.6).

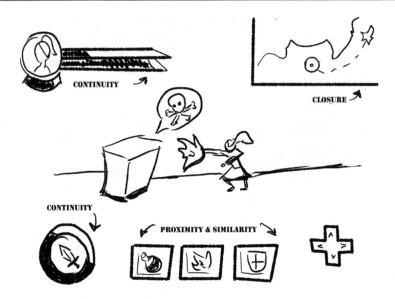

**FIGURE 1.6**   Gestalt principles in practice- The Head's Up (HUD) Display.

Health and mana/energy bars are often placed next to each other in **proximity** because they are both vital stats for a character. The mini-map and its associated icons (e.g., mission points and player icons) are also kept close together so they are seen as a unit.

Status icons, like those for being poisoned or stunned in a role-playing game (RPG), often have **similar** shapes, colors, or designs to indicate they are all status effects. Likewise, ammo counters for various weapons might use similar fonts or colors to indicate they're all related to weaponry. Skill or ability icons may also share similar border designs to show they belong to a player's skill set.

Health bars often deplete in a **continuous** manner, helping players quickly identify the direction and speed of health loss. The trajectory lines in games, like when aiming in a golf game or determining a path in a strategy game, show a continuous path for better clarity. Some games use smooth, continuous animations to shift from one HUD element to another, guiding the player's attention.

**Closure** means that while a mini-map might not show the details of every building, players can perceive the entire layout of a city or area. Health bars can sometimes be represented by chunks or sections, but players still read them as a singular bar representing health.

Designing with Gestalt principles in mind can lead to a more intuitive and efficient interface. These principles guide players' attention and help them process information quickly, which is especially crucial in fast-paced gaming scenarios.

# Don Norman's User-Centric Design Principles

In his various books and publications, Don Norman has identified several design principles that focus on creating products and services that are usable, understandable, and enjoyable for humans. These principles focus on creating intuitive products that are easy to use and understand. I highly recommend his book *The Design of Everyday Things* if you are looking for a place to get started.

- **Mental models:** Designs should mirror both the real world and the player's background knowledge. When a player learns from in-game or real-world experiences, they build new mental models. Therefore, understanding the player's background, their existing world knowledge, and how they learn is essential to creating intuitive and accessible experiences.
- **Visibility:** Players should be able to easily see and interpret the state of the systems they interact with. For instance, when the "walk" sign at an intersection changes color and iconography, it indicates that the road should be safe for you to cross. Visual cues are common in real-world systems, and they're also common in games. For example, when your character is close to death in *Uncharted* (Naughty Dog), the screen colors and sound become more muted to indicate you need to pay closer attention to the action.
- **Feedback:** Players should receive feedback when they take an action. This feedback can take many forms, such as a sound or a visual cue, and it should help the user understand the impact of their actions. When you flip a light switch, for instance, its position should provide visual information about the light's state. Likewise, when your character casts a spell in *League of Legends* (Riot), the visuals and sounds indicate the accuracy, strength, and status effects to reinforce the spell's effectiveness.
- **Affordance:** An object's design should suggest its use. When you wake up in the morning, for instance, the handle on your coffee or tea pot suggests, or affords, an opportunity for you to pour a hot beverage. In video games, an object's design can offer similar cues. In many of the *Zelda* (Nintendo) games, players are tasked with finding secrets by bombing walls. The bombable walls are sometimes distinguished from regular walls by having a slightly different, often crack-like appearance. (This was especially true in earlier games.) Since the presence of cracks on a wall intuitively indicates fragility or a weakened structure in the real world, this creates an intuitive affordance. In the game's context, a wall with visible cracks also suggests that it might be broken or destroyed. Affordances **facilitate** the action that results in the desired outcome for the player (Figure 1.7).

**FIGURE 1.7**    Affordances and signifiers.

- **Signifier:** A signifier is an indicator or perceptible signal that hints at how an affordance should be used. When you encounter a sign on a door that says "push," that sign is a signifier telling you how to use the door's affordance. Games use signifiers in the same way. When lightning would be an effective attack in *Pokémon* (Pokémon Company), for example, you choose your Pikachu to make the attack because the shape of his tail signifies a lightning bolt. Signifiers **indicate** the action that will get the desired result for the player. It should be noted, however, that when affordances and signifiers don't work together, this can cause even more frustration and confusion for the player (Figure 1.8).

**FIGURE 1.8**    Norman door.

- **Mapping:** The relationship between a system's controls and the results they produce should be intuitive. When you want to turn your amp up to 11, the knob controlling the volume should be mapped to a direction and action that indicate you are turning the volume "up." Game systems should be equally intuitive. When you press the right arrow on a classic Nintendo controller, for instance, Mario moves to the right on the screen.
- **Consistency:** A system's design should be consistent across all parts of the system, and even across different systems. Whether you use a vending machine in Japan, Sweden, or the United States, the visuals and interactions are consistent from country to country. Similarly, when you play the original *Tetris* (Alexey Pajitnov), controls and visual feedback are consistent with the later *Tetris Effect* (Enhance).
- **Constraints:** A system's design should include constraints that prevent the user from taking actions that would lead to errors or undesired outcomes. When you have a toddler in the house, for example, the safety caps on your medicine and bleach keep your child from accessing them. Likewise, when you sell items in *Dragon Age: Inquisition* (BioWare), the items you have equipped are not available for sale to prevent you from meeting your next enemy without weapons or armor.

# Jakob Nielsen's 10 Heuristic Principles of Usability

Jakob Nielsen is an expert in usability and an early champion of user testing. He has published a great deal about accessibility and digital interfaces, but my personal favorite is his book *Mobile Usability,* which he co-authored with Raluca Budiu. Nielsen is perhaps most well known for his *10 heuristic principles of usability.* These heuristics share several similarities with Don Norman's work (in fact, these two UX powerhouses own a firm together), but it is still worth exploring them in detail to highlight the differences.

Nielsen's principles relate to games in a wide variety of ways:

- **Visibility of System Status:** A design system should always use feedback to keep users informed. In other words, a game should keep players updated by providing appropriate feedback within a reasonable amount of time. Loading screens often display progress bars or animations to indicate the game is loading. When Solid Snake gets too close to an enemy while trying to be sneaky, a giant exclamation point appears over the enemy's head and players hear an alarming noise that sounds like discordant violins.
- **Match between the System and the Real World:** Games should use terms and concepts that are familiar to the player. The game should speak the player's language by integrating familiar words, phrases, and concepts rather than unfamiliar system-oriented terms. Games should also follow real-world conventions, making information appear in a natural and logical order. For instance, racing games use familiar concepts like red to indicate braking and green to indicate acceleration. Game controls often mimic real-world actions for this reason (e.g., pulling a controller's trigger to shoot).

- **User Control and Freedom:** Players often perform actions by mistake, and they should not be punished for this unless they are completing feats of skill associated with the game's challenges. Many games display "confirm" and "back" or "cancel" buttons when players make selections, especially with complex menus or when players make in-game purchases. If you give players challenges to overcome in the game, create safe spaces where they can learn and fail, giving them maximum agency before testing their prowess. As a genre, rogue-lites encapsulate this concept beautifully, as they provide the player with tools to overcome obstacles as they fail and learn.
- **Consistency and Standards:** Games should be consistent in both words and actions. Designers can do this by following platform and industry standards. For instance, the "X" or "A" button (depending on the platform) is frequently used for selecting or confirming, while the "O" or "B" button is used for going back or canceling.
- **Error Prevention:** Games should be designed to prevent players from making errors. This can include providing helpful warnings, confirmation dialogues, or disabling actions that could cause errors. It should go without saying that you should create a confirmation window before allowing players to make purchases (more on dark patterns later), but it's also incredibly important to thoroughly test games to prevent players from getting stuck in walls, losing progress, or getting trapped in dead-end content loops.
- **Recognition rather than Recall:** Games should minimize the impact on a player's memory load by making information and actions visible. For instance, players should not have to remember information from one part of the interface to another. Additionally, a game's icons should be visually represented with easy-to-understand iconography and metaphors (e.g., a sword icon for a melee attack). In games with complex controls, a brief tooltip or overlay can remind players of the function of specific buttons in certain contexts, particularly when the action is required.
- **Flexibility and Efficiency of Use:** Games should cater to inexperienced and experienced players and a variety of playstyles. Games often have different difficulty levels or control schemes to cater to both new players and veterans. In my opinion, every game should have a variety of difficulty options, and players should not be punished or shamed for taking the less difficult route (I'm looking at you, *Metal Gear* chicken hat).
- **Aesthetic and Minimalist Design:** Games should only show relevant information. The more information an interface contains, the more difficult it is for a player to quickly locate the details they're interested in. Every extra unit of information competes with relevant units of information, diminishing their relative visibility. As a result, the HUD in most games only shows crucial information like health, ammo, and objectives; non-essential details are hidden.
- **Help Users Recognize, Diagnose, and Recover from Errors:** The game should be designed to help players recover from errors. This can include providing clear error messages and instructions for how to recover. It also means

integrating saving and checkpoint systems that prevent players from getting stuck or losing progress.

- **Help and Documentation:** The game should include documentation and help features. Players should easily be able to find and use the help features, and the help should be understandable and comprehensive. We'll discuss onboarding and tutorial design in later chapters, but keep in mind that players often leave games for long periods of time before picking them back up again. Reboarding is often just as important as onboarding.

By following these heuristics, we designers can create interfaces that are easy to use, are easy to understand, and help players accomplish their goals efficiently and effectively.

# Celia Hodent's Stages of a Game Experience

Celia Hodent is a UX expert who has written extensively about the role of perception and memory in UX design. Her excellent book *The Gamer's Brain* explores how principles from neuroscience and UX design can be applied to video game design. Hodent argues that video games are uniquely suited to studying how the brain processes information because they engage multiple senses and require a high level of user involvement.

The book is organized around the five key stages of the game experience: attention, perception, decision-making, engagement, and memory. Hodent explains how the brain processes information for each stage and offers practical advice for designing games that take advantage of these processes. She also discusses the importance of user research and testing throughout the design process.

The five stages of the game experience can give designers a unique perspective and approach on creating intuitive player experiences. Let's dive in.

## *Attention*

Attention refers to the player's ability to focus on relevant information and filter out distractions. People have limited attention spans and can generally only focus on a few things at a time. Good UX design should prioritize the most important information by making that information easy for users to find and interact with. Understanding attention is important because it helps designers create interfaces that prioritize the most important information and reduce cognitive load. When designing for attention, there are four key aspects to consider:

- **Limited Capacity:** Players have a limited capacity for attention, and too much information or too many distractions can cause cognitive overload. To reduce cognitive load, designers should prioritize the most important information and minimize distractions. This especially becomes relevant in tutorials and onboarding players into new features or challenges.

- **Bottom-up Processing (Automaticity):** Bottom-up processing refers to how our brains automatically process sensory information. Our brains are wired to automatically process certain types of information, such as faces and movements. Things that we do, over time, become automatic or habitual in response. Designers can take advantage of this by using visual cues that attract attention, such as animation or contrasting colors. Creating consistent visual feedback can increase the player's understanding of the game and how their actions affect it. Bottom-up processing allows players to get into a flow state and be reactive to the events and action in a game.
- **Top-Down Processing:** Top-down processing refers to how our brains use our knowledge and expectations to interpret information. Top-down processing allows us to see an abstract part of an object and still interpret it as a whole or read heavily misspelled text (ehavily isspmelled ttex), but it also takes longer than bottom-up processing. Understanding how context and motivation influence this thinking is key to designing intuitive player experiences. The Stroop effect is a classic example of top-down processing—users are given a list of words printed in different color ink and prompted to name the color rather than the word. In cases where the associated color doesn't match the context of the word, our brains take a longer time to name that color. Top-down processing allows players to interpret abstract systems and make strategic choices.
- **Attentional Bias:** People tend to pay attention to information that is relevant to their goals or interests. Designers can use this to their advantage by designing interfaces that are personalized and tailored to players' interests. UX research is a key component to this design principle, as you need to truly understand your players in order to tailor to their interests.

## Perception

Perception refers to how our brains interpret and make sense of the information we receive from our senses. In UX design, understanding perception is important because it helps designers create interfaces that are intuitive and easy to use. When designing for perception, there are three key aspects to consider:

- **Gestalt Principles:** These principles (which were described in depth earlier in this chapter) describe how we perceive and organize visual information. UX designers can use these principles to create interfaces that are visually pleasing and easy to understand.
- **Mental Models:** I've mentioned mental models a few times already, so hopefully you are getting used to the concept! These are the internal models we create in our minds to help us understand how things work. Good UX design should align with players' mental models so they can quickly understand how to use an interface. Like attentional bias, UX research is a key component to understanding and leveraging existing mental models.
- **Emotion:** Our emotional state can influence how we perceive information. UX designers should be aware of this and design interfaces that evoke

positive emotions and avoid negative ones. It's also important to understand how the emotions of the game can reflect how we process information, both top-down and bottom-up (I'll touch more on emotion mapping and cognition in a later chapter).

## Decision-making

Decision-making refers to the process of evaluating options and choosing a course of action. People go through a process of evaluating options while making decisions. Good UX design should guide users through this process by presenting information in a clear and organized way and using visual cues to highlight important information. In UX design, understanding players' decision-making is important because it can help designers create interfaces that guide users toward desired behaviors. When designing for decision-making, there are two key aspects to consider:

- **Rational and Emotional Decision-Making:** People make decisions based on both rational and emotional factors. Good UX design should take both factor types into account and create interfaces and interactions that appeal to players' emotions and rational decision-making processes.
- **Cognitive Biases:** People have cognitive biases that can influence their decision-making, such as confirmation bias (the tendency to seek out information that confirms their beliefs) and sunk-cost fallacy (the tendency to continue investing in a project even when it's no longer rational to do so). Designers should be aware of these biases and design interfaces that minimize their impact. I'll be talking about biases throughout this book, so keep an eye out for them as we delve further into design principles and best practices.

## Memory

Memory refers to how we encode, store, and retrieve information over time. In UX design, understanding memory is important because it can help designers create interfaces that are easy to remember and use over time. When designing for memory, there are three key aspects to consider:

- **Working Memory:** This is the part of our memory that temporarily holds information while we're working on a task. It is what allows us to focus on the current jumping puzzle we are trying to successfully navigate (if you are as bad at these games as I am, sometimes this information makes it all the way into long-term memory) or the boss we are fighting. Good UX design should minimize the cognitive load on working memory so that users can focus on the task at hand.
- **Long-Term Memory:** This is the part of our memory that stores information over a longer period of time. This is where lore, the backstory of your favorite character, *Street Fighter* (Capcom) combos, and prior narrative choices end up. Good UX design provides signposts and sensory clues

to trigger long-term memory in the correct context as players navigate the game and its world.

- **Forgetting:** Our memories are fallible, and we can forget things over time. Good UX design should make it easy for players to retrieve information they may have forgotten, such as through reboarding sequences, journals, or dialogue history. It is important to remember that your players often walk away from your game for weeks, months, or even years. They should not have to rely on buggy and inaccurate fanwikis to bring themselves back to the game.

## Engagement

Engagement refers to the user's level of involvement with an experience. In UX design, engagement is important because higher engagement can increase user satisfaction, drive user behavior, and create a sense of community. Immersion is the extent to which a player feels fully engaged in an experience. In UX design, immersion is important because it can increase user satisfaction and make an experience more memorable.

Immersion is equally, if not more important, for narrative, as it keeps the willful suspension of disbelief going to keep players in a state of story flow. When designing for engagement and immersion, there arc five key aspects to consider:

- **Sensory Stimuli:** Players should be able to engage with an experience through multiple senses, such as sight, sound, and touch. This can help create a more immersive experience. Haptic feedback on controllers and handheld devices are great tools for increasing the state of immersion in games when designed thoughtfully.
- **Challenge:** Players should be challenged and feel a sense of achievement as they engage with an experience. This can help create a sense of flow (that juicy state that you get into when you are completely focused on a task and time goes away) and increase immersion. Balance, however, is key. If an experience becomes too difficult (or too easy) too suddenly, that is a quick route to breaking immersion (and occasionally, churning or rage quitting).
- **Autonomy:** We've talked a bit about player agency already, and this aspect is directly related to that principle. Players should feel autonomous and have control over their experience. They should feel like they have the ability to make choices and influence the game through their actions and interactions. This can increase engagement and make the experience feel more personalized.
- **Feedback:** Players should receive clear and timely feedback as they engage with an experience. This can help increase engagement and create a sense of progression. Helping them understand the goals and giving them feedback on their progress is key.
- **Social Interaction:** Humans are, by nature, social creatures. Players should be able to engage with others (this could be "real-world" individuals or "game world" characters) during an experience, whether through collaboration

or competition. This can help create a sense of community and increase engagement.

- **Motivation:** Understanding player motivations is key to keeping them engaged. Players should feel a sense of meaning and purpose as they engage with an experience. This can help create a sense of fulfillment and increase engagement. I'll talk more about extrinsic and intrinsic motivations later on in this book, but for now understand that you, as a designer, should never stop asking the question of "why" when it comes to your players.

Phew! That was a bit of a whirlwind wasn't it? This was probably a lot to learn (or review), but hopefully now we have a solid foundation to build upon. Understanding these core foundational principles of storytelling and user experience are essential ways to enrich your practice as a designer. It is always important to look outside the medium of games for inspiration and understanding as you expand your design tools. The rest of this book will have a slightly different tone as we delve more deeply into these areas and the design systems and functions they affect. As we move into future chapters, try to identify these foundational principles in practice.

# BIBLIOGRAPHY

Abernathy, Tom, and Richard Rouse. "Death to the Three Act Structure." *GDC Vault*, 2014, https://www.gdcvault.com/play/1020535/Death-to-the-Three-Act. Accessed 31 January 2023.

Bernstein, Jeremy. "Reimagining Story Structure: Moving Beyond Three Acts in Narrative Design." *GDC Vault*, 2013, https://www.gdcvault.com/play/1019675/Reimagining-Story-Structure-Moving-Beyond. Accessed 5 April 2023.

Campbell, Joseph. *The Hero with a Thousand Faces (Mythos Books)*. Princeton University Press, 1972.

Field, Syd. *Screenplay: The Foundations of Screenwriting*. Random House Publishing Group, 2005.

Freytag, Gustav. *Technique of the Drama: An Exposition of Dramatic Composition and Art*. University Press of the Pacific, 2004.

Garriott, Richard, and David Fisher. *Explore/Create: My Life in Pursuit of New Frontiers, Hidden Worlds, and the Creative Spark*. HarperCollins, 2018.

Han, Sui. 仇十洲璇璣圖 *Qiu shi zhou xuan ji tu. The Picture of the Tuning Sphere (璇璣圖), also known as one kind of figural poem, was created by Su Hui (蘇蕙) during the Sixteen Kingdoms Period* (304–439). 16th century, British Library, London, England.

Hodent, Celia. *The Gamer's Brain: How Neuroscience and UX Can Impact Video Game Design*. CRC Press, Taylor & Francis Group, 2017.

Jones, Dan SaSuWeh, and Rebecca T. Miller. "How American Indian Storytelling Differs From the Western Narrative Structure." *School Library Journal*, 15 December 2021, https://www.slj.com/story/american-indian-storytelling. Accessed 4 April 2023.

King, Brad, and John M. Borland. *Dungeons and Dreamers*. McGraw-Hill/Osborne, 2003.

Koffka, Kurt. *Principles of Gestalt Psychology*. Mimesis International, 2014.

Koster, Raph. *A Theory of Fun for Game Design*. O'Reilly, 2013.

Meier, Sid, and Jennifer Lee Noonan. *Sid Meier's Memoir! A Life in Computer Games*. WW Norton, 2020.

Murdock, Maureen. *The Heroine's Journey: Woman's Quest for Wholeness*. Shambhala, 1990.

Nielsen, Jakob. "10 Usability Heuristics for User Interface Design." *Nielsen Norman Group*, 1 January 1995, https://www.su.se/polopoly_fs/1.220913.1422015209!/menu/standard/file/10%20Heuristics%20for%20User%20Interface%20Design_%20Article%20by%20Jakob%20Nielsen.pdf. Accessed 7 March 2023.Schmidt, Victoria. *45 Master Characters*. F+W Media, 2001.

Norman, Don. *The Design of Everyday Things: Revised and Expanded Edition*. Basic Books, 2013.

Norman, Don, and Tamara Dunaeff. *Things That Make Us Smart: Defending Human Attributes In The Age Of The Machine*. Basic Books, 1993.

Shikibu, Murasaki. *The Tale of Genji*. Translated by Royall Tyler, Penguin Publishing Group, 2003.

Short, Tanya X., and Tarn Adams, editors. *Procedural Storytelling in Game Design*. Taylor & Francis, 2019.

Stokes, John, et al. "Haudenosaunee Thanksgiving Address —Greetings to the Natural World." *National Museum of the American Indian*, 1993, https://americanindian.si.edu/environment/pdf/01_02_Thanksgiving_Address.pdf. Accessed 4 April 2023.

Thomas, Dylan. *The Poems of Dylan Thomas*. edited by John Goodby, New Directions, 2017.

# Research and Development

# 2

---

## INTRODUCTION

---

Making games is never easy. Every new game is filled with new and exciting problems to solve. The best narrative and UX design systems are seamlessly integrated into the game's core loop (the actions a player will do over and over again) and meta layers (the additional content that supports and reinforces the core) in order to handle this complexity and variation. By embedding the narrative and user experience into the core loop and meta layers, we are constantly answering the player's questions—ideally by doing, rather than telling. The complexity of this ecosystem means that in game design, it is common to create additional problems every time you solve your initial problem. Well-designed iterative development processes and research methods can help you anticipate, analyze, and solve those problems early.

### What You Will Learn in This Chapter

- Best practices in iterative development
- Crafting hypotheses
- Research best practices
- Crafting initial vision statements and design pillars
- Rapid prototyping methods
- Overcoming assumptions and bias
- List of questions to ask at different stages of development
- Qualitative and Quantitative testing methods

DOI: 10.1201/9781003342977-4

# THE ITERATIVE GAME DEVELOPMENT PROCESS

Before we start digging into research and development processes and best practices, it is important to fully understand the difference between developing video games and creating other commercial products. I've found that many individuals new to games stumble when they try to understand and map the development process. While the processes of making games often borrow from other software development methodologies, they rarely transfer neatly. Additionally, they often vary from project to project. Why is this? From my perspective, there are two primary factors.

The first is that games, unlike traditional software, often try to solve many problems at once. **Games are complex motivation engines** that turn actions and feedback into expression and achievement. In a single game, there are many verbs that describe what the player does—players may create, destroy, explore, solve, build, navigate, combine, and more. When you compare these verbs to those that you would use to describe, say, a word processing application or photography app, they are not only more numerous but also significantly more varied. This variation means that creative problem-solving in game development requires both a holistic view of the overall experience and a deep and detailed understanding of each individual system.

The second reason that product development processes don't transfer well to video games is less concrete. Game designers are expected to create experiences that engage users in ways that traditional software does not. Games, more often than not, need to be "fun" (there is lots of debate in the games industry as to whether or not fun is an actual requirement, and we'll touch on this in later chapters). But what is fun? If you ask three people on the street, you are likely to get three different definitions. While there are ways to define the fun in a game to some extent (I'll speak more on this later in Chapter 5), this key factor of a game's success—which is complex and often elusive—often relies directly on the previous factor, the game's complex systems of motivations and actions.

If these two factors make it so difficult to create games, how can successful ones be released every year? The answer is one of the many reasons that user experience design and narrative design go together so beautifully: curiosity and creativity within an iterative and looping research and development process.

## The Importance of Strong Hypotheses

You may be surprised to see a reference to the scientific method— hypotheses — immediately after mentioning the words "fun," "curiosity," and "creativity." However, crafting well-designed and documented questions, assumptions, and desired outcomes is a key component of creative work that is as complex and interdependent as game development.

As I've said before, games are beautiful and complex motivational engines. Therefore, a core step in early game design and discovery is answering the question of what motivates and drives *your* players. As game designers, we are constantly asking questions, but asking "why" and "who" is key before starting to answer "what" and "how." Creating strong hypotheses is essential in product design as it helps guide the design process and ensures that the team solves the right problems.

The first step in designing a game is to clearly define the problem you are trying to solve by creating the game. Your team's initial design process should be problem-focused rather than solution-focused. The problem could be design-, story-, or market-related. For instance, you could have a specific story you want to tell or a set of activities you wish to explore. Focusing on the "why" and "who" of your game keeps you firmly in the problem space and quickly establishes constraints on the solutions as you answer them. For example, your team may craft an initial problem statement such as, "as people get older, they have less time to play games." This very quickly creates constraints on the "what" and "how" by understanding that the design problem must factor in smaller commitments of time and attention. In this sense, the scientific method applies nicely to the early prototyping phase of development because it creates a circular output and feedback loop that allows for early failures and the learning that occurs as a result. Documenting this problem space in an easy-to-understand and executable manner is key to creating a successful and productive early development phase.

Documenting involves conducting player research and gathering data to gain a deep understanding of the problem space. If we continue with our example problem statement, our next step would be gathering market insights around and doing some interviews with gamers who have recently become parents or have high-powered jobs that take up more time and energy. Once you gain this knowledge, you should be able to craft a specific and testable hypothesis, such as "As gamers age they have less time and energy to play games, but the desire to play them has not diminished." Using this hypothesis statement as the core of your design, you can craft your design pillars and prototype around verifying and testing it. And then you iterate. Seems simple enough, right?

Not really. We can easily get into sticky territory because it's so difficult to quantify how "fun" an experience is and because, in the end, we need to deliver a final profitable product within a specific budget and timeline. Luckily, the smart people at Stanford University's Hasso Plattner Institute of Design have developed a process that can help guide and mitigate some of the tensions that arise during the early phase of development. The process is designed to be human-centered and is based on the belief that the best solutions come from understanding the people (i.e., players) for whom you are designing.

# The Stanford Design Process

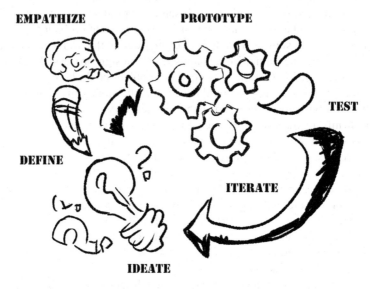

**FIGURE 2.1**   The Stanford Design Process.

The Stanford Design Process consists of five key stages: Empathize, Define, Ideate, Prototype, and Test. Designed to encourage creativity, collaboration, and user-centered design, it provides a structured approach to solving the kind of complex problems we often face in designing games (Figure 2.1).

The **Empathize** stage involves understanding the needs, motivations, and pain points of the people for whom you are designing. This stage involves conducting user research, but it also requires you to get into the mindset of your players. Understanding what motivates and drives them by asking when, where, how, and—most importantly—*why* they play games should guide the way you craft your problem space. When I talk about understanding the player, I don't just mean their motivations or playstyles. I also mean understanding their state of mind when they are playing. In the case of our example hypothesis, we would look into habit formation around short cycles, when and where our identified player group has spare time, and how much attention they can devote to a game during those times. We'd find out what motivates them and gives them energy when so much of their lives is draining it, and why they enjoyed playing games in the first place.

Too often in this industry, I hear designers say, "We don't need to talk to players—we make games for ourselves." These same individuals are the ones who are most shocked during early beta testing when a playtester struggles to understand a complicated controller scheme or fails to identify their next objective. Developers must always remember that as we design, we gain game literacy. We spend hundreds if not thousands of hours focusing our energy on the rules and experience. As a result, we often run the risk of overengineering systems or creating experiences that require high levels of expertise in early onboarding. By putting the player first at the start of the design process—by talking to them and empathizing with them—we set our games up for a greater chance of success.

The **Define** stage involves documenting the insights gathered during the Empathize stage and synthesizing them into a clear problem statement and hypothesis. This stage is critical for focusing the team's efforts and ensuring that everyone has a shared understanding of the problem they are trying to solve. During the Empathize stage, you should have gained an understanding of your players' needs. This might require some investigation on your part; rarely are players able to articulate what they need. As you define these needs and insights, avoid focusing on the solutions they proposed and instead hone in on the problems and desires they mentioned and the stories they told. You'll have to do some Holmesian sleuthing to discover common themes and needs in those stories, but having them in hand while you define the problem space will ensure that you put the needs of the player, and thus, your target market, first.

Once you've built the problem space, you can begin filling it with ideas. The Ideate stage involves generating many potential solutions that fit within the problem space. This stage is about being creative and encouraging the team to think beyond conventional solutions. Encourage your teams to generate a diverse range of ideas and be open to exploring new and unconventional approaches. However, it is important to always keep the problem space at the front and center of the ideation phase to prevent the team from jumping straight to known or existing solutions.

The **Prototype** stage involves building physical or virtual prototypes of the most promising solutions. These prototypes can be simple or complex, depending on the problem and the stage of development. The goal of prototyping is to test and validate the solution's feasibility and generate feedback from potential users.

The **Test** stage involves using the prototypes to conduct user research that validates or invalidates the solutions. Getting games into the hands of players is a vital step in verifying designs, validating hypotheses, and discovering new problems to solve. This stage is critical for refining and improving the solution and ensuring that it meets the needs of the people for whom it is designed.

Game development requires a deep understanding of the problem you are trying to solve, the space to create innovative solutions to that problem, and the expectation of experimenting and testing those solutions in looping cycles until you have a solid idea of what the core experience is like. Hypothesize, test, learn, and adjust until you and your team have created an experience that players will love to return to.

## Think Like a Scientist, Then Like a Child

Richard Feynman was a physicist who became well-known for his ability to explain and teach complex ideas in a simple way. If you read his lectures or memoirs, you'll see many examples where he leverages real-world knowledge and metaphors to teach these difficult concepts. Famously known for his emphasis on the difference between "knowing" and "truly understanding" something, Feynman believed that knowing something's name or being able to recite a concept or process was different from intimately understanding it. In a lecture he presented at the National Teachers Association in 1966, he talked about this difference:

When I was still pretty young—I don't know how old exactly—I had a ball in a wagon I was pulling, and I noticed something, so I ran up to my father to say that "When I pull the wagon, the ball runs to the back, and when I am running with the wagon and stop, the ball runs to the front. Why?"

How would you answer?

He said, "That, nobody knows." He said, "It's very general, though, it happens all the time to anything; anything that is moving tends to keep moving; anything standing still tries to maintain that condition. If you look close you will see the ball does not run to the back of the wagon where you start from standing still. It moves forward a bit too, but not as fast as the wagon. The back of the wagon catches up with the ball, which has trouble getting started moving. It's called inertia, that principle." I did run back to check, and sure enough, the ball didn't go backwards. He put the difference between what we know and what we call it very distinctly.

Too often, I see game teams leap from trying to understand the problem straight to solutions. They leap to the flashy name. True understanding, according to Feynman, is being able to explain a concept in simple terms, having the ability to derive it from basic principles, and using it to predict or explain phenomena. The Feynman technique is a method for learning or explaining a concept in a simple, straightforward way. It involves four key steps:

1. **Choose a Concept:** Pick the concept you want to understand or communicate more clearly.
2. **Teach it to Someone Else, as if They're a Child:** Doing this forces you to simplify the concept and break it down into its most basic elements. It pushes you to avoid jargon or complex language.
3. **Identify Gaps in Your Explanation and Fill Them:** If you struggle to explain something simply, that often indicates a gap in your own understanding. Return to your sources, fill those gaps, and then try to explain the concept again.
4. **Review and Simplify Further:** If your explanation is still complex, review it again. Use analogies, examples, and visual aids to make your explanation more intuitive and accessible.

If we apply the Feynman technique to ideation with a team, it looks something like this:

1. **Choose Your Problem Space:** Detail the vision for your problem. Make sure everyone agrees on and understands the space this blueprint creates.
2. **Have Your Team Pretend to Explain It to a Child:** Try to simplify the concept as much as possible. For example, if the feature is a character's magic power that manipulates time, explain it as "this character can make everything go very slow or very fast."
3. **Ask Questions to Identify Gaps:** Have someone on the team roleplay as a toddler for a bit. This person should first ask the questions that seem most obvious. The team should alternatively try to answer those questions as if they are speaking to a toddler. Then, they should ask questions that seem less obvious.

4. **Review and Simplify Further:** To each accompanying answer to the questions, ask an additional "why?" Keep doing this until you've come up with the simplest ways of describing the action. Work with your team to make the answer more intuitive and relatable until all the "whys" are answered.

Remember, the aim of the Feynman technique is not only to teach but also to learn. So, it is important to encourage your team to question, critique, and offer alternatives to strengthen the group's collective understanding.

Let's look at our example hypothesis, "As gamers age they have less time and energy to play games, but the desire to play them has not diminished." and try to apply the Feynman technique to it.

- The problem space:
  - "As gamers age they have less time and energy to play games, but the desire to play them has not diminished."
- The simplified explanation for a child:
  - "As people grow old they play less games."
- The questions:
  - Why do they play less games?
    - Because they don't have the time or energy
  - Why?
    - Because they have kids or jobs
  - Why don't they play games with their kids or at their jobs?
    - Because most games are difficult to pick up and teach a child or play on a break from work
  - Why?
    - Games are often complex or require special machines
  - What kind of machines?
    - Computers, phones, or consoles
  - Can I have a phone?
    - When you are older, maybe.
  - What does complex mean?
    - Games require a lot of knowledge or special skills
  - Why?
    - Because solving problems and learning new things is fun
  - Why?
    - Because humans are curious and smart
  - Why?
    - Go ask your father...

This exercise allows your team to get to the heart of why you are trying to address your problem, and can often have you exploring the space in ways you didn't expect. Once you've looked at your problem space from all angles, look at it again and see if it needs revision.

From this exercise, I can tell our problem statement needs a bit of simplification. Let's change it to: "Gamers often have less time and energy to play games as they age."

# Learning the Language of the Game Together

Once the problem space is clearly defined, ideation can begin. I love using word association games for brainstorming ideas because it allows me to bring the existing language of the problem statement into the lexicon of the game's design. By prepping the space with an existing language framework established by the pillars and vision statement for your problem, you can help your team create fantastic ideas that are grounded deeply in the game world and the player's foundational knowledge. (We'll talk more about foundational knowledge and mental models in Chapter 3.)

Many people believe that creativity is about generating new, unexpected, and wacky ideas. However, speculative fiction author Jeff VanderMeer disagrees. He talks extensively about creativity in his visual guide *Wonderbook* and describes it as synthesizing ideas to create something that is believable and unbelievable at the same time:

> Modern ideals of functionality and the trend toward seamless design in our technology have taken the very human striving for perfection and given us the illusion of having attained it (which, ironically, seems very dehumanizing). In this environment, some writers second-guess their instincts and devalue the sense of play that infuses creative endeavors: 'This antique Tiffany lamp must provide light right now, even before I screw in the lightbulb and plug it in, or it's worthless.' At best the imagination can be seen as heat lightning with no real weight or effect, instead of the source. At worst, it's dismissed as frivolous and a waste of time, with no real-world applications.

When we creatively solve problems, we must grant ourselves the luxury to explore solutions that may be less functional but more fun. And to do this, we must play in our process. Fun foments creativity. Word association games allow you to maintain a level of playfulness while keeping the team grounded in the realities of player understanding.

Let's look at our example hypothesis, "Gamers have less time and energy to play games as they age."

If I wanted to get a team to look at this problem statement in a different light, I would choose three key words from this statement and do a simple word association deep dive activity. This activity requires participants to go three to five layers deep in word association to explore options that might not come up at first glance. Let's give it a try. For the purpose of this example, I'll choose the words time, energy, and age:

- Time
  - Time > Free Time > Work > Break > Phone
  - Time > Clock > Pendulum > Curve > Arc > Story
  - Time > Time Travel > History > Mythology
- Energy
  - Energy > Light > Intensity > Frequency > Waves
  - Energy > Tired > Sleep > Bedtime rituals > Bedtime stories
  - Energy > Calories > Workout > Weight Loss
- Age
  - Age > Middle age > Middle ages > High fantasy

- Age > Life > Alive > Adrenaline > Rush
- Age > Family > Friends > Social

By taking the core concepts of our problem statement and exploring them in a creative way, we've come up with some fun areas to explore as we move into our vision phase.

## ASKING THE RIGHT QUESTIONS

It is essential to maintain an experimental and scientific mindset throughout development by encouraging curiosity and asking questions. Each stage of the iterative development process brings new problems to solve, and with them, new questions.

### QUESTIONS TO ASK DURING THE EMPATHY AND DISCOVERY STAGE

- What do we want the player to feel when they play this game?
- What do we want the player to learn?
- When do we want the player to feel and learn these things?
  - More on emotion mapping in Chapter 8.
- What are the primary motivations we want the player to have?
- What are the biggest problems we want to solve? Are these problems the same for us as they are for the player?
- How does this game fit into the player's everyday life?
- How can we observe players experiencing these aspects of our game as early as possible?

### QUESTIONS TO ASK DURING THE DEFINITION/IDEATION STAGE

- What did we learn in discovery? What are the key insights we need to address?
  - Do we need to adjust our key hypotheses? Do we need to add any?
- What are the biggest risks and unknowns we have in this design so far?
  - How can we discover as much about this as quickly as possible?
- What are the key values and pillars of the game based on what we discovered in the empathy stage of design?
  - How do our proposed design solutions reinforce those values and pillars?
  - How can we find out how these design solutions interact with one another as quickly as possible?
- What does the competitive landscape look like for the type of game we are making?
- Which market needs or opportunities can this game fill?
- Which player needs can this game address?

## QUESTIONS TO ASK DURING THE PRE-PRODUCTION STAGE

- What did we learn in definition/ideation? What are the key insights we need to address?
    - Do we need to adjust our key hypotheses? Do we need to add any?
- What are the biggest risks and unknowns in this design so far?
- How can we discover as much about this as quickly as possible?
- What are the main actions and verbs the player experiences?
- What systems support these actions?
- How do these systems work together? How do they connect?
- Is this core loop of systems and actions fun and engaging?
    - More on how to measure fun later in this chapter.
- How might we sell this core loop to players? To investors or publishers?
    - More on fantasy statements and documentation in Chapter 3.
- What world supports our marketing goals, key values, and core loop?
    - More on world-building in Chapter 3.
- What metaphors can we use for the systems and actions? Do these metaphors fit our game world?
    - More on game verbs in Chapter 4.
- What technology and tools will we need to support this experience?

## QUESTIONS TO ASK DURING THE PRODUCTION STAGE

- What did we learn in definition/ideation? What are the key insights we need to address?
    - Do we need to adjust our key hypotheses? Do we need to add any?
- What are the biggest risks and unknowns we have in this design so far?
    - How can we discover as much about this as quickly as possible?
- Is the game fun?
- How quickly can players with an aptitude for similar products learn the core loop of the game?
- How quickly can non-games learn the game's core loop?
- Where are players getting stuck?
- Where are the players delighted?
- What is surprising to players?
- What adjectives do players use to describe the game? Do these match our key values and pillars?
- How many stories can the players tell about this experience after they try it? How deep are those stories?

In addition to answering these questions, I recommend adding "why" to every single one as a supplement. Doing so will help with the next phases of development. Keep in mind, however, that the "why" may change as you learn about the players and the game you are creating.

# PRINCIPLES OF UX RESEARCH

UX research has roots dating back to the early twentieth century, amidst the hustle and bustle of the industrial revolution. It all started with time-and-motion studies that scrutinized factory workers' movements to boost efficiency and productivity. This was our earliest flirtation with ergonomics and human factors—the ancestral spirits of modern UX research.!

But enough history—let's talk about methodologies that will help you leverage UX research to optimize your design process. UX research is like a well-stocked toolbox; it's filled with an array of techniques that are suitable for different occasions. There's qualitative research (think interviews, focus groups, ethnographic studies) that digs into emotions, opinions, and motivations. Then there's quantitative research (A/B testing, analytics) for when you need hard data to back your insights. Let's go over some core principles to get started:

- **Player-Centric:** The player is usually your game's protagonist, and thus they should be at the center of your research. Since the player's needs, desires, and pain points should guide your design decisions, conduct research to understand your target audience's needs, goals, and behaviors.
- **Contextual:** The best UX research is done in the user's natural environment. This context provides invaluable insights into their behavior and interaction with your design.
- **Iterative:** UX research is a cyclical process. Design, test, gather feedback, refine, rinse, repeat. Each iteration of your game makes the design more user-friendly and efficient. Test the game with players throughout the development process to identify and fix issues early on.
- **Evidence-based:** Data is your ally. Whether it's qualitative insights or quantitative metrics, UX decisions should be rooted in solid, reliable evidence. Utilize methods such as surveys, interviews, and observation to gather data on user experience. Then, use the data you collect from user research to inform design decisions and make changes that improve the user experience.

## The Importance of Research

A strong scientific mindset goes hand in hand with creative problem-solving. Therefore, critically assessing research and inspiration is just as important for a game design team as creating strong hypotheses. The video game industry, in general, has a research problem. I like to call it the "first page of Google results" method of design. When a game developer is given an assignment to create an icon, character, feature design, or execute just about any creative task, they often look it up on the internet, click the first legitimate-looking link or image result they find, and use that shallow research as the primary base for their inspiration (this is only getting worse in the age of machine learning and large language models).

This results in repeating the same ideas ad nauseam throughout a medium that is only limited by our imagination, time, and tools. It also creates inauthentic experiences that feel shallow, inconsistent, and unsophisticated under scrutiny.

However, there is an easy remedy for this problem. Looking critically and deeply into research drawn from multiple sources fuels creative world-building and game-making. Fortunately, we live in an age where information is readily available, and there are many ways to increase your team's aptitude for delving deeper into inspirational source material. Let's look at a few.

## Market Research

You can make the best game in the world, but if it doesn't fit your target market or your players don't know it exists, none of your beautiful work will matter to anyone but you. Understanding trends and unmet market needs can give you an edge in getting the attention your game deserves and gaining access to players who will play and evangelize your game.

When you embark on the discovery phase of your game development process, understanding the competitive landscape is an essential part of ensuring that your game will get the attention and interest it deserves. Take a look at the landscape of existing games, and do research on upcoming titles. Stay informed with industry resources and on community forums. Gamers are, in general, a savvy market, and if there are games already out there that are fulfilling their needs it is likely that you will have a hard time making them interested in yours. Once you have a full view of the competitive landscape, it's a good idea to map where your game might fit within (or outside of) it. You can refine and define the elements that are valuable to your playerbase, along with what makes your game special, by crafting a **Unique Value Proposition** (UVP).

The UVP is the statement that details the value your game gives to its players as well as the unique position it has in the market. It's the primary reason your players will want to buy the game. It should be concise, straightforward, and compelling. To map out your UVP, create a venn diagram of what your playerbase needs and cares about (from the first two stages of the Stanford Design Process), your game's vision and pillars, and what the competitor's games do. The areas of overlap will help you map out and define the value according to players, the established value in the market, and what truly makes your game unique. If you do this exercise and find that there is nothing in the unique quadrant, it's a good idea to revisit your game design vision and pillars unless you have an established franchise or a massive marketing budget.

After you've crafted your UVP based on your market research, the next step is validation. Market testing allows you to preview how your brand, world, and game will resonate with your target player base, and your game's UVP should be the primary focus in testing.

Does this mean player feedback and market research should entirely dictate your world-building and design choices? Of course not. That is why we engage in…

# Narrative Research

In November 1992, a curious incident befell *The New York Times*. The grunge music scene was at the zenith of its popularity, and the *Times* was determined to keep its readership informed of the latest trends. Attempting to unmask the mysterious lingo of this musical subculture, they reached out to Caroline Records, an independent record label associated with several significant grunge bands.

Their call was answered by Megan Jasper (who later became the CEO of Sub Pop), a receptionist with a sharp wit and an aversion to pretension. She fabricated a lexicon of nonsensical "grunge speak" words and phrases, feeding them to an eager *Times* reporter who then published the terminology in a feature article titled "Lexicon of Grunge: Breaking the Code." The terms included "lamestain" (uncool person), "swingin' on the flippity-flop" (hanging out), "wack slacks" (old ripped jeans), and more. Jasper had made them all up.

This incident with the *Times* underscores the need for careful and thorough research. The saga of the fake grunge lexicon was a master class in the pitfalls of cultural appropriation by the media, teaching us that no level of earnestness can replace the authenticity born from living and breathing within a cultural scene. Authenticity is paramount. When crafting narrative for video games, the key is to ensure that it stems from a deep understanding of and respect for the characters' backgrounds, cultures, and lifestyles. It's the writer's responsibility to depict these characters not as caricatures but as authentic individuals, and the language used in the game should mirror their reality.

In its rapid expansion, the video game industry has become an avenue where cultures from around the globe interact. Kate Edwards, a pioneer in the field, has passionately championed the cause of **culturalization** in games. Culturalization is distinct from **localization**. While localization typically involves translating a game and adjusting some of the content (idioms, for example) for a particular region or audience, culturalization dives deeper. It's about ensuring that a game's content is both culturally relevant and appropriate. It also involves making sure the game resonates well with local audiences, thereby avoiding cultural misunderstandings or potential controversies. Even seemingly innocuous symbols or narratives can have profound cultural implications. Delving beyond the mere surface of translation and adjustment, culturalization seeks to weave the fabric of local cultures into a game's narrative, mechanics, and aesthetics.

The first rule of doing narrative research is to dig deep into your subject matter. It doesn't matter whether you are making a game about decorating, tanks, fashion, dragons, or candy. A common adage is "write what you know," and you can't create a believable world for players without fully understanding the subject matter. In my opinion, this statement doesn't mean that you should only write and design from your own experiences and perspective—it means that you should learn and grow your knowledge and perspective to understand what you are writing and designing and consult experts along the way to ensure you retain accuracy and authenticity.

This often includes answering questions and doing research on aspects of the game and its world that are never surfaced explicitly to the player. We'll discuss this in more detail in Chapter 3, but here are the five key activities that you should immerse yourself in when doing narrative research for your game:

- Be curious. Ask lots of questions and actively search for answers.
- Understand the game's core loop, major systems, and features.
- Create a rich repository of inspirational images and text pulled from multiple primary and secondary sources.
- Gain a deep understanding of the history or background of the elements that make up the game's primary iconography and actions.
- Live and breathe the lore once it is established.

Once you have a baseline understanding of the game's world, characters, and themes, it's time to verify them with reliable and vetted information. This is the time for you to be skeptical, critical, and exploratory. Go to museum websites (bonus points if you can visit the actual museum), borrow books from the library, watch films, and explore cities. Talk to people who have similar cultures, regions, and backgrounds to your characters. And lastly, get expert help from historians or cultural editors, if possible, to supplement your own research. This will save time, enrich your material, and bring fresh perspectives to your work.

Engaging experts who are intimately familiar with the culture you are representing can prevent misrepresentations and offer richer insights. A noteworthy example is the award winning *Never Alone: Kisima Ingitchuna* (Upper One Games/E-Line), a game developed in collaboration with the Cook Inlet Tribal Council and writer Ishmael Hope, a storyteller and poet of Tlingit and Iñupiaq heritage. The game beautifully integrates Iñupiat folklore by adapting an oral story passed down through families to create, as Alan Gershenfeld, co-founder and President of E-Line called it, "a living game for a living culture." It beautifully brings to life the story of an endless blizzard through the journey of a young girl named Nuna and an arctic fox, ensuring an authentic representation while educating players about a distinct culture.

In games that pull heavily from real-world events and eras, the depth of understanding and level of accuracy is even more crucial. These games don't just use history as a backdrop; they weave it into the very fabric of their narratives and mechanics, making it integral to the player's experience. This requires a more comprehensive and nuanced understanding of the historical periods and events the game portrays. The crux of culturalization and research is valuing and respecting the culture and history of the world the game is based in. *Assassin's Creed Mirage* (Ubisoft), set in ninth-century Baghdad, offers a commendable example. While developing the game, Ubisoft partnered with historians Dr. Glaire Anderson and Dr. Raphaël Weyland to educate and support the game team, giving in-house lectures and reviewing game documents. They had a cultural expert present at every voice over recording, ensuring accuracy and authenticity.

This not only empowered the game team to create an authentic experience in the game world, they also developed an extensive in-game historical guide. Not only is the game being used as a teaching guide in college history courses but it also inspired game reporter Rob Dwiar to start learning Arabic on Duolingo. Such efforts deepen the bond between game developers and their global audience, proving that games can be both entertaining and culturally enlightening.

A strong understanding of primary source material is even more important when your team intends to modernize or twist a well-known story or ground your game world in existing intellectual property. In Supergiant's award-winning game *Hades*, the player plays as a lesser-known demigod, Zagreus, the god of blood and son of Persephone. As Zagreus continuously attempts to escape the land of the dead and reunite with his mother, he meets many characters from Greek mythology and receives boons from the gods to help him on his quest.

Supergiant takes quite a bit of artistic license with the tone of the dialogue and character direction in this game. They find many playful ways to modernize aspects of the world to make it interesting and relatable while exploring humorous and surprising twists to character backgrounds and relationships. They would not have been nearly as successful in maintaining immersion and believability while doing so if they had not thoroughly understood the world of Greek mythology (Figure 2.2).

**FIGURE 2.2** Hades can bring modern themes into the narrative because of the strong understanding of the source mythology.

This understanding allowed them, as Creative Director Greg Kasavin aptly put, "to stick to the spirit of the source material, more than the letter." He not only studied classic works like those of Homer but also dove into more obscure materials. Because of this foundational knowledge of the source material's history and lore, the player experiences a world that blends seamlessly with the game mechanics. The underworld and its regions are the looping dungeons Zagreus tries to break through, and as he dies, he is sent right back to the foot of Hades's throne.

The boons from each god fit their personalities and flaws; Dionysus grants abilities that confuse enemies in a drunken stupor, Zeus electrifies weapons with bolts of lightning, and Aphrodite charms and enamors enemies. Each of the gods has a distinct voice and personality, and their petty squabbles often result in the player having the opportunity to make interesting design decisions as they progress further into the game.

These elegant connections of mechanics to well-known mythology help guide the player through the world, but it is the deeper exploration of these personalities and relationships that keep the player engaged as they spend the many hours of play required to beat the game. I'll speak more on using characters to keep players engaged long-term in Chapter 8, but the team's extensive research into the source material is a large part of what makes these interactions so engaging, fun, and surprising.

## Curate Critically

Once you have gathered a wide variety of research, references, and resources, it is time to prune and organize them. Curation is especially important when dealing with machine learning/AI tools or procedural systems since, once established, they lower the threshold for developers to jump from research to creation. While I'm all for getting results faster so teams can iterate and experiment, it is important to recognize that these tools only create output based on what we add as input. If your source materials are not carefully curated, this can create manifold problems such as projecting unconscious biases, inaccuracies, and banalities at scale.

As you evaluate the materials you've gathered, ask critical questions like:

- Have I drawn my resources from a monoculture or from a single perspective?
- What is my ratio of primary sources to secondary and tertiary sources?
- Where are the gaps in my research? Do I need to reach out to experts to fill those gaps?
- Do these materials fit with the core pillars and themes of my world? Do they fit with the core loop and actions?
- What doesn't fit well within this body of research? Should I remove it or supplement it?
- Do any conflicting themes arise from my research? Do they conflict in a way that fits my game and world?
- What is the proper balance between fun and accuracy?

Game designer Sid Meier is renowned for his meticulous historical research, and his works serve as a great example of how game designers can (and often should) use real-world history as a foundation for their lore while still maintaining playfulness and agency. One of Meier's famous tenets, highlighted in his talk "The Psychology of Game Design (Everything You Know Is Wrong)," is that fun comes first, even before historical accuracy. In other words, historical accuracy can inform game mechanics and world-building, adding depth and authenticity to the game, but the player's experience should always take precedence. This is especially evident in the *Civilization* (Firaxis) games, where historical context informs the technology tree, the different civilizations, and the world events. But if a *Civilization* player wants to focus on hitting cultural milestones while ignoring military conflict, the game allows for this. It might not be historically accurate, but it caters to different playstyles and strategies, enhancing the fun factor.

This is where careful balance comes in. As game designers, it's crucial to remember that while games can be used to educate and inform, the player's expectation is to be motivated and entertained. However, it is possible to circumvent these expectations. Brenda Romero did just that with her game *Train*. In this game, players are tasked with efficiently loading as many figurines as possible onto model trains. Only at the end do players discover that they've been simulating the act of sending people to Nazi concentration camps. The goal isn't fun. Instead, it's an emotional gut-punch, a moment of stark realization designed to provoke thought and discussion.

"The mechanic is the message," as Romero puts it, meaning game mechanics can be used to convey a message or theme, often more powerfully than any amount of dialogue or exposition. *Train* isn't about entertainment; it's about conveying the horror and senselessness of the Holocaust.

Another example more directly related to digital games is the open world adaptation of Thoreau's *Walden* (Tracy Fullerton/USC Game Innovation Lab). Over six hours, players experience a year in the woods, with 15 minutes representing each day. During that time they have to keep their inspiration (a resource in the game) high by exploring the woods and interacting with animals, while also working on their cabin and planting crops to stay alive (which lowers inspiration). If their inspiration gets too low, the colors and sound around them become muted. The game also features storylines that draw directly from Thoreau's experiences, creating a rich narrative that immerses the player in his life at Walden pond. While the game can't be called traditionally "fun," it is able to emulate the stillness and reflection from the source material, creating an enriching experience. Historical accuracy is less about enhancing immersion or gameplay enjoyment, and more about respect and authenticity. Games like these have the potential to serve as educational tools, shedding light on aspects of history that are often overlooked or misunderstood.

# BUILDING THE GAME'S BLUEPRINT

Early-stage creative direction is akin to building the blueprint for a house. A properly defined problem should be concise enough for the team to understand but detailed enough to create constraints to operate within. If your problem is too open-ended, the team will hamster-wheel its way through solutions, expending a lot of energy but not making any progress. If the problem is too complex and constraining, the team's creativity will be hampered and you may miss out on opportunities for innovation (Figure 2.3).

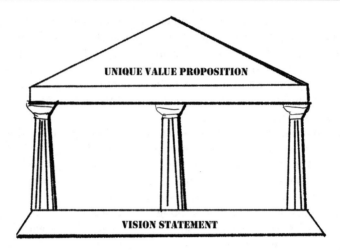

**FIGURE 2.3**    Creative house.

I like to limit my blueprint to one succinct vision statement accompanied by three pillars. You can think of these pillars as the blueprint for ideation. The vision statement acts as the foundation, the testing element that ensures that the proposed solutions stay true to the initial intention. It should tie directly to the UVP: The pillars act as the load-bearing walls that enclose the space for ideation. You can use this model to visually test your ideas as you come up with them, mapping them within the three-dimensional space of your problem statement to understand how well you are addressing it.

Let us look at our example hypothesis, "Gamers have less time and energy to play games as they age."

Let us assume that during our design process, we discovered the following information in our market research phase (for the case of this example, all of these findings are fictional):

- Gamers after the age of 35 lower their play time by at least 65% due to family or career obligations
- They play sessions that are less than 30 minutes during the week (usually before bed) and 2–4 hours on the weekends
- They prefer to play more short sessions than less long sessions, but occasionally will indulge for titles that they are especially excited about
- They are less likely to buy a new console or computer
- Gamers that are motivated by action, story, social, and competition motivations prioritize their play time over all other hobbies
- Romance games with action gameplay saw an increase in downloads by 60% over comparable titles in the over 35 demographic and there are only 3 titles on Steam and Console that fit the profile of being both "action" and "romance"
- A remake of a beloved vampire series has been announced to be released in two years and there is a lot of hype for it with our identified player base

- Over 35 gamers have strong market overlap with streaming services, with a recent increase in searches and views for mythology documentaries and magical realism titles

With this information in mind, along with what we discovered in our brainstorming exercises, here are examples of three different vision statements and pillars I could pitch as a creative director:

1. "Immersive fantasy while you work out."
   a. Pillar 1: Burn calories, gain XP
   b. Pillar 2: Big stories, small screens
   c. Pillar 3: A romance for the middle ages
2. "Intense action on your lunch break"
   a. Pillar 1: Mythic stakes—play as gods and monsters in team competition
   b. Pillar 2: High energy gamerounds and fast loading times that keep players coming back for multiple sessions per day
   c. Pillar 3: Losing is as fun and intense as winning
3. "Vampire hunter by night, vampire dater…by night"
   a. Pillar 1: Immersive sim meets dating sim
   b. Pillar 2: Make them laugh, make them blush
   c. Pillar 3: Bedtime stories for adults

Same hypothesis and problem statement, three very different creative game visions. Which is why prototyping and testing is so vital. Any of these ideas could sail or bomb depending on timing, design choices, and a myriad of other factors. It is best to explore them quickly, keeping what works and discarding what doesn't early in development to avoid costly errors later on. Which brings us to…

# RAPID PROTOTYPING

When we're eager to test a new mechanic, storyline, or aesthetic as we kickoff early production, we don't want to spend eons in development. Rapid prototyping (the rapid creation of core parts of the game) allows us to explore the riskiest parts of our games early in the design process so we can fail—and learn—quickly. Rapid prototypes should focus on the core gameplay mechanics rather than detailed graphics or sound. Paper prototypes and quick, easy tools like Figma and Twine are low-cost ways to test game mechanics, discover risks and big problems, and get early feedback from players. Build prototypes quickly and test them with players and peers to identify issues and gather feedback. Include multiple phases of iteration in your design process, and assume you'll make lots of mistakes and learn along the way. The more innovative your product, the more iterations you should plan for.

There are several different prototypes designers can use, and they vary in both style and complexity. First up, we have the modest, humble, but remarkably agile **paper prototype**, which is used at the start of the design process. This format is all about taking digital ideas and molding them into a tangible physical form. Paper prototypes can be created using literal pen and paper, Post-It notes, or even board game pieces. They work wonders for testing game mechanics, flow, and balance without wasting precious code.

Using a paper prototype is like creating initial sketches before painting a masterpiece. But how do you test a paper prototype? Imagine you're running a *Dungeons & Dragons* session. You've got your prototype laid out, and your testers are the players. Let them interact with your papered brainchild while providing essential context, observing how they respond to different mechanics, how they progress, and where they get stuck.

Next on the docket is the **digital prototype**. This might be a basic version of a level, a blocky version of a core game mechanic, series of interactive wireframes, or a rudimentary rendition of a character. The digital prototype is your rough draft, the first time your ideas come to life on the screen. Testing a digital prototype involves letting players loose in this digital playground. Track their behaviors and actions, using analytics if available. Are the players using your mechanics the way you intended? Or, more importantly, are they discovering uses you hadn't imagined? At this stage, you're like a naturalist who observes, studies, and learns from their subjects. Try to guide less and observe more.

Lastly, there is the **vertical slice**. A vertical slice is a highly polished thin segment of your game that looks and feels like it could be part of the finished product. It not only provides players a more polished experience, it also helps teams scope out the final product. The vertical slice is all about testing your entire game design ecosystem, from the art and sound to the mechanics and player progression. Testing a vertical slice involves more in-depth playtesting. You're examining player immersion, investment in the story or characters, and emotional responses. You can also use the vertical slice to conduct usability testing and determine whether your controls, UI, and tutorials are up to snuff. Keep a keen eye out for player frustration points or moments of delight; those are invaluable as they allow you to identify and solve problems early in development.

Prototyping can often lead to more innovative solutions, since it gives your team time to experiment and play. Ian Dallas discusses how his team used rapid prototyping in his GDC talk "Weaving 13 Prototypes into 1 Game: Lessons from *What Remains of Edith Finch*." During development, the team created 13 different prototypes of various gameplay mechanics and narrative structures, then combined the best elements from each prototype into the final game. This allowed them to create innovative mechanics while giving the game its unique, curated feel.

Just like we prototype gameplay mechanics in our early phases of development, we can—and should—prototype our narratives. **Twine** is like a labyrinth architect's dream tool. It's an open-source tool for telling interactive, non-linear stories and is perfect for crafting choose-your-own-adventure-style narratives. It allows you to visualize how different narrative branches interweave, create variable outcomes based on player choices, and prototype interactive dialogue. The real beauty of Twine lies in its simplicity. It doesn't require any coding knowledge, making it accessible to writers, designers, and anyone with a story to tell.

For high-level narrative prototyping, we have **story maps**. A story map breaks the narrative into bite-sized sections—maybe chapters or scenes—allowing you to see the entire plotline at a glance. Sometimes story maps look like user flows; other times, they are literal world maps with a story overlay. They're especially useful with branching narratives or when multiple subplots are at play. Story maps give you a bird's-eye view of your narrative landscape, helping to ensure that pacing is on point, emotional beats hit at the right time, and player choices are meaningful. (We'll talk more about mapping in Chapter 7 to explore this format more thoroughly.)

For testing your narrative with players, I recommend **cinematic storyboarding** (this can be especially powerful when paired with Twine or similar). Here, we borrow a page from the world of film, using visual representations to plan out game cinematics or important narrative moments. Each storyboard panel sketches a particular game moment, complete with notes about dialogue, sound effects, character movements, and camera angles. Cinematic storyboarding allows you to prototype the visual and auditory aspects of your game narrative, helping to ensure that they bolster the story rather than detract from it.

Narrative prototyping tools offer a low-cost, low-risk way to experiment with different narrative paths, test branching dialogues, or tweak the emotional pacing. They provide a tangible representation of your narrative, enabling you to spot plot holes, pacing issues, or incongruences early in the development process. And they foster better team communication, giving everyone—designers, artists, and programmers—a clear vision of the narrative goals and structure.

Remember, with each of these prototypes, neutrality is your best friend. Your role is not to lead but to observe, document, and learn from players. After all, when it comes to crafting the gaming world's next grand opus, your players are your most valuable resource.

## NARRATIVE ITERATION: THE VALUE OF THE WRITER'S ROOM

In television, the writer's room serves as a pivotal nexus where writers converge to collaborate, brainstorm, and craft a show's overarching narrative. With the gaming industry gradually leaning toward complex and narrative-driven titles, it's clear that the essence of storytelling has become integral to this medium. Recognizing this, one can see the potential advantages of integrating the concept of a TV writer's room into game narrative design, enhancing the creation of consistent, deep, and impactful storylines.

In television, assembling a diverse team of writers ensures varied perspectives and more intricate storylines. These talented individuals bring forth different life experiences and sensibilities, which, in turn, makes narratives more resonant and multifaceted. Moreover, having a dedicated space—whether physical or virtual—where these writers can freely discuss, critique, and evolve ideas without judgment is essential to fostering unbridled creativity. **Collaboration**, a cornerstone of the writer's room, is pivotal for refining ideas and ensuring **consistency**, leading to the production of **groundbreaking content**. Furthermore, by working closely together, the writers ensure that the evolving narrative aligns with the show's broader goals and vision, satisfying both the audience and stakeholders.

Game writing should operate in a similar way. A team of narrative designers and writers from diverse backgrounds can contribute a wide range of narrative arcs, side quests, and character developments. Such diversity enhances the overall gaming experience. Moreover, creating dedicated spaces or platforms for discussing the game's lore, mechanics, and intersections between story elements ensures the development of a rich gaming universe. Collaborative brainstorming ensures a vivid, consistent, and immersive game world. To achieve this, it's vital to maintain a shared understanding among team members. Just as TV series require consistency across episodes, games demand uniformity in gameplay mechanics, lore, character backstories, and even the repercussions of player choices. Only through close collaboration can a team ensure that all narrative elements seamlessly interlace with other game components, providing a harmonious gaming experience.

As Antony Johnston says in his GDC talk "How to Run (and Survive) a Writers' Room," it's profoundly important to ensure that every team member, regardless of rank or experience, has an equal voice in the room. Such an approach guarantees fresh perspectives and uninhibited creativity. Moreover, the world of game development is dynamic, and waiting for the "perfect" idea often becomes a hindrance. The mantra should lean toward rapid prototyping, brainstorming, and constant iteration. Maintaining open communication channels fosters trust and ensures that team members can pitch ideas or voice concerns without reservations. In other words, a respectful and supportive environment is the backbone of a productive writer's room—creating a safe environment where ideas can be tested, refined, or even discarded is pivotal for continuous innovation. Finally, daily sync-ups or check-ins keep everyone on the same page, ensuring everyone adapts to and aligns with any changes.

An unofficial list of tips for creating a successful writer's room:

- **Diverse Voices, Richer Stories:** Embrace diversity in your team. Different backgrounds bring unique ideas and narratives.
- **Your Space, Your Sanctuary:** Whether it's a cozy room or a virtual platform, ensure it's a space where everyone feels free to share without judgment. A little kindness goes a long way. Keep critiques constructive and remember that everyone's in this together. Not every idea will be a winner, and that's okay. Provide a space where people feel free to experiment.
- **Every Voice Matters:** Remember, rank doesn't dictate the value of an idea. Encourage everyone to speak up. Two heads are better than one. Collaboration is the heart of a writer's room. Bounce ideas off of each other, refine them, and watch them evolve into something great.
- **Keep Communication Open:** Foster an environment where team members feel they can approach with ideas or concerns anytime. A quick check-in can align the team, orient everyone to changes, and ensure everyone's on track.
- **Consistency is Key:** Make sure everyone is on the same page. Whether it's a TV episode or a game's lore, keeping things consistent makes for a smoother story. Regularly touch base with the broader goals. Ensure the narrative complements the overall project or game mechanics.
- **Don't Wait for Perfection:** Aim for progress, not perfection. Brainstorm, prototype, iterate, and keep the ideas flowing.

# USER TESTING

Before we dig deeper into specific types of user testing, let's make a quick stop at a peculiar moment in history. It involves a horse by the name of Clever Hans. Hans became a celebrity in the early 1900s due to his math prowess. He'd tap his hoof in response to mathematical questions, producing solutions that left onlookers flabbergasted.

The twist? Well, our equine Einstein wasn't a mathematician at all. Hans merely reacted to subtle, unconscious cues from his human handlers. He had become adept at reading their unintentional signals, which revealed the answers. Once the experimenter knew the answer to a math problem, Hans could find it, too. This phenomenon, now known as the **Clever Hans effect**, warns us of the pitfalls of inference based on subtle cues and expectations.

You're probably thinking, "What's this got to do with user testing in video games?"

Stick with me here. When conducting user tests, it's possible for designers, researchers, or testers to give away subtle cues or prompts that influence the test user's behavior. If we're not careful, we might end up with skewed results, believing our players are navigating the game like parkour masters when they're responding to our subtle cues, just like Hans. This could be the way your team frames a question, or even their unconscious body language as they ask it. Humans are even better at reading subtle social cues than horses, so it is important to be aware of both conscious and unconscious biases (more on this later).

If we unknowingly guide players toward certain solutions or actions, we might entirely miss how players could repurpose or misuse mechanics in ways we'd never anticipate. These unintended uses could reveal powerful insights about our design or help us unearth hard-to-spot bugs.

The lesson here? When we're testing, it's important to create conditions that are as neutral as possible, with testers giving minimal guidance or influence. Our players should organically interact with, explore, and experience the systems we've crafted, much like a player getting lost in the vast expanses of a newly discovered RPG game world. Otherwise, we may be setting ourselves up for a Hans-style revelation further down the line when our cues are gone and our users are left tapping their hooves, unsure of where to go next.

Playtesting involves observing users as they play the game and gathering data on their behaviors, emotions, and opinions. It should occur throughout development, but should start early with your prototyping phase to identify issues with the game's usability and inform design decisions. This often saves the team time in the long run.

There are many effective ways to recruit players for playtesting. The first step is to define your target audience—in other words, determine the type of player you want to test your prototype with; also determine where to find that player. Once you have done this, you can enact the following strategies:

- **Use social media and communities** such as Reddit or Discord to find and recruit players who are interested in testing games.
- **Attend gaming events** and receive feedback in real time from engaged gamers.
- **Offer incentives** such as early access to the game to encourage players to test your prototype.

When recruiting players to test prototypes, it's important to find players who represent the game's target audience. This means recruiting players who have experience with similar games and who fit the demographic profile you've established. However, it is important to recruit a diverse pool of participants in playtesting, including players with different skill levels, backgrounds, and preferences. This not only brings different perspectives for your testing, but it allows you to gain additional insights on your potential audience. Additionally, it's important to provide players with clear instructions (while remembering Clever Hans) on how to play the prototype and what feedback you're looking for. This will ensure that you receive actionable feedback that will help you improve the game.

I could write an entire book about best practices in playtesting, but for the sake of brevity, here are some common best practices to consider before you start testing:

- Clearly define your research goals and objectives.
- Create realistic scenarios for testing.
- Ensure that your research is conducted in an ethical and unbiased manner.
- Carefully analyze and interpret the data to avoid drawing false conclusions.
- Iterate and refine your research process based on findings.

If you want to learn more, I highly recommend digging into Celia Hodent's *The Gamer's Brain* and Tracy Fullerton's *Game Design Workshop*, both exhaustive and excellent resources on the subjects of game research, prototyping, and testing. In the meantime, let's dig into some of the tools and methods used to test games both internally and externally.

# Qualitative Tools and Methods

Qualitative research will help you unearth the "why" behind player behaviors, feelings, and preferences. So be curious, be open, be empathetic, and let players guide you through their journey.

## Interviews and focus groups

Interviews and focus groups (whether conducted remotely or in person) allow for a deeper dive into player motivations and behaviors. Both techniques allow you to ask open-ended questions, follow up on interesting points, and probe into why players play the way they do. The difference is scale.

Researchers can conduct remote interviews and user testing sessions through in person or video interviews. Video conferencing tools can be especially useful for remote teams or when testing with geographically dispersed participants. When using remote research tools, it's important to ensure that participants have a stable internet connection and a quiet environment for testing.

Interviews—the classic one-on-one chat—are useful for gaining a deeper understanding of an individual player's motivations and experiences. They provide an opportunity to gather detailed insights from specific players. You could ask about their experiences with your game, what they enjoyed, what frustrated them, their favorite moments, or any other topics that align with your research goals. The key is to make the interview feel like a conversation.

Encourage participants to share anecdotes, examples, and stories—it's these gems that truly illuminate the player experience. They can provide qualitative data and insights that surveys may not be able to capture. However, interviews can be time-consuming and findings from a single interview may not be representative of the larger player population, so it's important to pair the data you gather with other qualitative sources to validate and verify.

If interviews are solo quests, focus groups are party missions. Focus groups involve bringing together a small group of players who have played the game to have a conversation about it. They are useful for gathering feedback from multiple players and observing how these players interact with a game. The dynamic nature of focus groups can lead to diverse viewpoints, group discussions, and unexpected insights. They can also provide valuable information about player behavior and preferences while identifying potential usability issues. It's important to ensure that the discussion stays on topic and all participants get a chance to speak. Although focus groups allow you to connect with more players than an interview does, they can also be time-consuming and findings may not be representative of the larger player population. As with interview data, it is important to validate your findings with quantitative methods and observation sessions.

### Playtesting and observation

Usability testing is a method for evaluating the player's user experience and the ease of your game's use. It can identify areas of a game that are confusing or frustrating for players, and it can also suggest design improvements. Observation studies, or playtests, are a great way to understand players. These studies involve watching people play your game (or similar games) and taking note of when they seem to be having fun, when they're frustrated, when they're engaged, and when they're bored.

This method works best when observing players in their natural gaming environment. It could include visiting a player's home or watching them play at a gaming cafe. By observing players in their usual context, you can gain insights into their behaviors, habits, rituals, and social interactions that might be missed in a more controlled environment.

When conducting usability testing, researchers can employ user testing tools to record and analyze a user's interactions with a product. These tools can help identify usability issues and areas for improvement. Depending on your research goals, you could ask players to think aloud as they play, pause the game to probe certain experiences, or conduct a post-playtest interview to gather reflective insights.

Diary studies have participants document their gaming experiences over an extended period, usually in the form of a diary or journal. They might note what they played, how long they played, how they felt during and after playing, and any other observations. Diary studies can offer a longitudinal view of the player experience, capturing shifts in emotions, engagement, and preferences over time.

## Quantitative Tools and Methods

Where qualitative methods are all about depth, the strength of quantitative methods lies in their breadth. We're talking numbers, statistics, charts—the kind of data that can make patterns and trends pop. Quantitative data is invaluable in answering questions like "how many," "how often," or "how much" in your game research. Let's dive into some key methods.

## Survey tools

Surveys are a good tool for quickly and cost-effectively gathering quantitative data and insights from a large group of players. They can collect information about player demographics, gameplay preferences, satisfaction levels, or any other quantifiable aspect. The beauty of surveys lies in their scalability. With online distribution, you can gather data from hundreds or even thousands of players, providing a broad view of the player landscape.

UX researchers can use them to gather feedback on specific aspects of a game, such as gameplay mechanics, user interface, or story. However, they might not provide in-depth insights into the player's experience or the reasons behind their responses. When using survey tools, it's important to craft the questions carefully to avoid bias. It's also important to ensure that the survey is short enough to encourage participation.

## Analytics tools

Analytics involves tracking and analyzing in-game data. When combining modern game engines and modern analytics tools, you can collect data on virtually any aspect of gameplay—session length, progression speed, item usage, failure points, and so much more. Analytics can offer a treasure trove of insights into player behavior, often in real time. The trick is to know which data to track and how to interpret it in a meaningful way.

Analytics tools track user behavior and collect data on user interactions with a product. These tools can provide valuable insights and help identify areas for improvement. When using analytics tools, it's important to carefully track and analyze the data to avoid drawing false conclusions. It's also important to interpret the data in the context of the overall user experience.

Analytics tools can provide quantitative data on how players interact with a game— length of play, completion rates, and monetization. Analytics can also identify areas of a game that are under-performing or need improvement. However, many of these tools may not provide insights into the player's motivations or experiences. If your game has an achievement or quest progression system, tracking the completion data can give you insights into what experiences your players engage with the most. When you combine this information with your qualitative research results, you can get a full picture of the overall player experience.

## A/B testing

A/B testing, also known as split testing, is a research methodology used to evaluate two versions of a design or experience to determine which one performs better. For instance, you could use this method to compare different versions of a level, a mechanic, a UI element, or even the narrative. By exposing different player groups to each version and comparing the results, you can make data-informed decisions about which version to implement.

A/B testing involves randomly assigning participants to one of two groups: the control group, which receives the current or standard version of the design or experience, and the experimental group, which receives a modified or alternate version (note that this means that the player experience will be different for these two groups, affecting overall consistency). It's important to keep track of what you are testing, as every A/B test in your game can interfere with the data in already existing tests.

The groups' performances are then compared based on a predefined metric such as conversion rate, click-through rate, or completion rate. Benchmarking involves comparing these metrics against industry standards or previous versions of the game. This can help you gauge where your game stands in terms of performance, and it can also identify areas that need improvement. Benchmarking can quantify the impact of any changes you make during the development process. If you are going to do A/B testing on your game, make sure you have at least one person on your team that has a deep understanding of data analytics and research methods.

A/B testing can be useful for optimizing game mechanics, user interface, or monetization strategies. However, it requires a large sample size to be statistically significant and may not provide insights into why one version is more effective than the other, so pairing with playtest interviews or recordings is ideal.

## Heatmaps

Heatmaps are a visual representation of how players interact with a game. They can help identify areas of a game that are not getting enough player attention, as well as areas where players are spending a lot of time. However, heatmaps do not provide insights into the player's motivations or experiences. Eye-tracking is a similar method that requires specialized equipment. It provides quantitative data on where players look while gaming. This data can be particularly useful when refining UI and HUD designs because it allows you to place key information in the areas where players naturally look.

Each UX research tool has its own strengths and weaknesses, and it's important to choose the right tool for the research question at hand. By combining multiple research methods, such as surveys, interviews, and usability testing, game developers can gain a more comprehensive understanding of their players and make informed design decisions to improve the player experience.

# Cognitive Bias, Ethics, and Playtesting

Remember Clever Hans? To avoid having your research and methods tainted by similar errors, it is important to have a thorough understanding of bias. *Thinking, Fast and Slow* by Daniel Kahneman describes several cognitive biases that can affect human decision-making. The book introduces two systems of thought—System 1, the quick, intuitive, and often biased approach, and System 2, the slower, more deliberate, and logical one.

Let's explore a few of the cognitive biases Kahneman discusses and consider how they might weave their way into user testing and research.

- **Confirmation Bias:** This is the tendency to seek out, interpret, and remember information that confirms our existing beliefs while conveniently ignoring or downplaying anything that contradicts them. During player testing, researchers may pay more attention to data that validates their design decisions and overlook feedback that challenges those decisions. This can lead to skewed interpretations and missed opportunities for improvement.

- **Anchoring Bias:** Anchoring is the phenomenon where we rely too heavily on the first piece of information (the "anchor") that we encounter when making decisions. In player testing, initial impressions or the first feedback about a design can disproportionately influence subsequent interpretations and judgments, both from researchers and testers.

- **Availability Heuristic:** We tend to overestimate the likelihood of events that are easily recalled or imagined. In the context of user research, experiences or feedback that are more memorable or dramatic might disproportionately influence the interpretation of user data or reports, leading to designs that cater to rare or outlier use cases.

- **Framing Effect:** The way information is presented (framed) significantly affects how we perceive and react to it. In player testing, the framing of tasks, questions, or feedback requests can drastically impact the player's response—and, therefore, the insights derived from the testing session.

- **Hindsight Bias:** This is the tendency to believe, after an event has occurred, that we knew it was going to happen all along. In player research, it could lead to downplaying surprising results or minimizing the failure to predict user behavior, thus preventing the researcher from learning from these unexpected outcomes.

- **Overconfidence Bias:** This bias occurs when we are more confident in our judgments and knowledge than we should be. (In other words, we believe we know more than we actually do.) It can lead to underestimating the time, resources, and challenges associated with implementing changes based on user feedback.

Being aware of these biases is the first step in mitigating their impact. It's critical to remember that the people participating in your tests can be biased, but so can you as the researcher. By being mindful of these cognitive biases, you can strive to conduct more effective and objective user testing, ensuring your results are as reliable and informative as possible. Remember, the goal of user testing isn't to confirm that you're right—it's to discover how to make your designs better.

Remember, there's a human being at the heart of every data point, feedback comment, and gameplay session. In addition to being aware of biases in the user testing process, it's essential to act ethically. Ethics in user testing is not just nice to have—it's an essential component of any good research practice. Here are some key principles to consider:

- **Informed Consent:** Participants must understand what they're signing up for—what the test involves, how long it will take, what data will be collected, how it will be used, and any potential risks.

- **Privacy and Confidentiality:** All data must be anonymized, securely stored, and only used for the purposes specified in the consent form. Any data that could identify an individual, like names or addresses, should be handled with particular care.

- **Voluntary Participation:** Participation in user testing should always be voluntary. This means participants can choose not to participate or withdraw at any point without facing negative consequences.
- **Beneficence:** Researchers should strive to minimize harm and maximize benefits for participants. This includes physical harm, psychological distress, and misuse of participant data.
- **Non-Deception:** While there might be cases where some level of deception is necessary for the study design, these should be the exception, not the norm. If researchers use deception, a thorough debriefing should occur after the testing session to clarify the study's true nature.

Following these ethical guidelines fosters trust between researchers and participants, making for more reliable and valid data. But more than that, the guidelines reflect the researcher's respect and empathy for users, acknowledging users as partners in the quest to create better, more engaging experiences.

It takes a lot of time and energy to develop and (hopefully) ship a game. Understanding principles and best practices around research and development can help you and your team understand player needs and address them with your game. By creating a cycle of learning, testing, and iterating, you can discover and resolve the design problems that will inevitably crop up throughout your process. In the next chapter, we will discuss how you can take learnings in your research and development process forward into creating and conveying the world of your game.

# BIBLIOGRAPHY

Bentley, Michael. Feynman's Lecture to U.S. Science Teachers on "What Is Science" and Today's Mistrust of Science. Association of Teacher Educators At: Caribe Royale Conference Center, Orlando, FL, 2017.

Castello, Jay. "How Hades brings Greek Mythology into the Modern Day." *Eurogamer*, 27 February 2019, https://www.eurogamer.net/how-hades-brings-greek-mythology-into-the-modern-day. Accessed 28 December 2023.

Dallas, Ian. "Weaving 13 Prototypes into 1 Game: Lessons from 'Edith Finch'." *GDC Vault*, 2018, https://www.gdcvault.com/play/1025016/Weaving-13-Prototypes-into-1. Accessed 28 December 2023.

Dwiar, Rob. "Assassin's Creed Mirage's use of language made me add Arabic to my Duolingo." *TechRadar*, 20 December 2023, https://www.techradar.com/gaming/assassins-creed-mirages-use-of-language-made-me-add-arabic-to-my-duolingo. Accessed 28 December 2023.

Hamilton, Rowan. "Tools Tutorial Day: Playtesting 'Overwatch.'" *GDC Vault*, 2018, https://www.gdcvault.com/play/1025012/Tools-Tutorial-Day-Playtesting-Overwatch. Accessed 28 December 2023.

Hodent, Celia. *The Gamer's Brain: How Neuroscience and UX Can Impact Video Game Design.* CRC Press, Taylor & Francis Group, 2017.

Jackson, Sharna. "Saltsea Chronicles – Translating Ideas to Reality: The Writers' Room." *Die Gute Fabrik*, 16 August 2023, https://gutefabrik.com/saltsea-chronicles-translating-dreams-to-reality/. Accessed 24 August 2023.

Johnston, Antony. "How to Run (and Survive) a Writers' Room." *YouTube*, 25 May 2022, https://www.youtube.com/watch?v=VflCBFogAB0. Accessed 24 August 2023.

Kamen, Matt. "How 'Never Alone' turns cultural heritage into video game history." *Wired UK*, 23 November 2014, https://www.wired.co.uk/article/never-alone-interview. Accessed 28 December 2023.

Marin, Rick. "Grunge: A Success Story." *The New York Times*, 15 November 1992, https://www.nytimes.com/1992/11/15/style/grunge-a-success-story.html. Accessed 4 July 2023.

McKay, Gabriel. "Assassin's Creed Mirage: Edinburgh Uni professor helps with research." *The Herald*, 5 July 2023, https://www.heraldscotland.com/business_hq/23633438.assassins-creed-mirage-edinburgh-uni-professor-helps-research/. Accessed 28 December 2023.

Meier, Sid. "The Psychology of Game Design (Everything You Know Is Wrong)." *GDC Vault*, 2010, https://www.gdcvault.com/play/1012186/The-Psychology-of-Game-Design. Accessed 4 July 2023.

Nightingale, Dana. "UX Summit: 'DEATHLOOP's' User Research and User Experience Death Loop." *GDC Vault*, 2022, https://www.gdcvault.com/search.php.Accessed 28 December 2023.

Norman, Don. *The Design of Everyday Things: Revised and Expanded Edition*. Basic Books, 2013.

Norman, Don, and Tamara Dunaeff. *Things That Make Us Smart: Defending Human Attributes In The Age Of The Machine*. Basic Books, 1993.

Peterson, Britt. "Can a Video Game Capture the Magic of Walden? Henry David Thoreau's famed retreat gets pixelated." *Smithsonian*, 30 October 2023, https://www.smithsonianmag.com/arts-culture/can-video-game-capture-magic-walden-180962125/. Accessed 28 December 2023

Pogrebin, Robin. "In 'Walden' Video Game, the Challenge Is Stillness (Published 2017)." *The New York Times*, 24 February 2017, https://www.nytimes.com/2017/02/24/arts/henry-david-thoreau-video-game.html. Accessed 28 December 2023.

Romero, Brenda. "Brenda Romero: Gaming for understanding." *TED*, 2013, https://www.ted.com/talks/brenda_romero_gaming_for_understanding. Accessed 4 July 2023.

Rousseau, Jeffrey. "Making Assassin's Creed Mirage culturally and linguistically relevant." *GamesIndustry.biz*, 11 October 2023, https://www.gamesindustry.biz/making-assassins-creed-mirage-culturally-and-linguistically-relevant. Accessed 28 December 2023

Shanks, Michael. "An Introduction to Design Thinking PROCESS GUIDE." *web.stanford.edu*, https://web.stanford.edu/~mshanks/MichaelShanks/files/509554.pdf. Accessed 4 July 2023.

VanderMeer, Jeff. *Wonderbook: The Illustrated Guide to Creating Imaginative Fiction*. Harry N. Abrams, 2013.

# World-Building

# 3

## INTRODUCTION

World-building is the act of creating the blueprint of how your world works and who lives in it. By creating a believable and consistent world, game designers can transport players to another time and place, allowing them to forget about the real world and fully engage with the game. Narrative designers use conceits and world-building to set players' expectations for the main actions within the game and its world. We then create compelling content to motivate the player to continue playing.

A well-crafted game world can immerse players in a rich, detailed environment that feels like a real place with its own history, rules, and characters. By contrast, a poorly constructed game world can feel shallow, confusing, or unconvincing and can undermine the player's suspension of disbelief. In this chapter, we'll discuss how you can build a strong world that helps guide your players in the experience, allowing them to absorb the rules of the game without dumping an overwhelming amount of exposition and instruction onto them.

### What You Will Learn in This Chapter

- Understanding mental models
- Discovering your conceit
- Building a strong world
- Building your innovation iceberg
- Documentation and lore best practices

## MENTAL MODELS

Understanding how players form mental models is key to building believable and immersive worlds. We touched on **mental models** in Chapter 1. The psychology of mental models is rooted in the way that our brains process information. Our brains are wired to seek patterns and connections in the information we receive, and mental models are a way of organizing and summarizing that information. As we move through the

DOI: 10.1201/9781003342977-5

world and learn from experience, we take in a ton of information through our senses and process it in our brains. We navigate crowds, interpret facial expressions and body language, react to stoplights and road signs, and exchange money for goods. People use mental models—representations of the world—to make sense of information, predict outcomes, and understand complex systems. We construct our mental models based on our past experiences, knowledge, and beliefs.

The process of creating a mental model begins with **perception**. The information we perceive is then compared to our existing mental models, and if it is consistent with what we already know, it is integrated into those existing mental models. If the information is inconsistent, it is either discarded or used to update our mental models. Once we create a new model, we use it to guide our behavior and inform our decisions. Many people stop at stop signs, pet dogs, and walk on sidewalks because of the mental models they have formed through daily life and experience.

This is particularly useful for understanding complex systems and situations since it allows us to simplify and reduce the amount of information we need to process when making connections between seemingly disparate pieces of information. This understanding, in turn, allows us to predict the outcomes of our actions, which can be useful in **decision-making**—especially the kind of quick, intuitive decision-making that a player regularly engages in while playing games.

When we use mental models, we create connections between new information and our existing knowledge, which makes it easier for us to remember that information. This helps us to categorize and retrieve information from memory more easily. However, it is important to note that because mental models are influenced by individual experience and world knowledge, they are often cultural and personal. This makes them susceptible to bias, unconscious or otherwise. This also makes it extremely important to understand your players when creating your game world since players may have vastly different world experiences.

Mental models form the basis of our foundational knowledge. But it's important to differentiate between knowledge we store as data in our heads and that which we act upon. Don Norman's principles, particularly those described in his seminal book *The Design of Everyday Things*, aim to minimize the gap between these two types of knowledge in design. He argues that good design should minimize the need for declarative (factual) knowledge and leverage procedural (skills) knowledge as much as possible through intuitive and familiar interfaces.

"Knowledge of" and "knowledge how" refer to two different types of cognitive understanding that people use in their interactions with the world. "Knowledge of" (**declarative knowledge**) refers to factual knowledge: things you know and can describe or declare. This includes facts, data, and information, such as knowing the capital of a country, understanding the rules of a game, or remembering a person's name. Declarative knowledge is often easier to articulate and communicate than procedural knowledge.

"Knowledge how" (**procedural knowledge**) refers to the practical knowledge or skills needed to do something. It's less about stating facts and more about performing actions. Examples include "knowing how" to ride a bike, play a musical instrument, or operate a complex machine. This type of knowledge is harder to articulate but is often easier to demonstrate.

Understanding mental models and how they are formed helps you as a designer to better understand your player. This understanding also helps you design reinforcement loops that allow players to create new mental models as they learn the game. We'll talk about this more in Chapters 4 and 5, but for now, understand that you have the power to change your player's perception of your game and the world around them if you can help them integrate it into their existing mental models.

# DISCOVERING YOUR CONCEIT

Before diving into your game world and narrative, it is a good idea to establish a **conceit**. The conceit of your game is the core principle that governs world logic and drives the action. It is the Unique Value Proposition (UVP) filtered through the lens of the player experience and narrative—a short and sweet version of the player fantasy, if you will. It can be thought of as the "hook" that draws players in and sets the game apart from others in its genre. The conceit contains the central rules of your game world—essentially, a loose agreement between the player and designer—and it should answer key questions about player motivation, leveraging world knowledge while laying the foundations of relatability. Conceits are often reflected in the game's mechanics, aesthetics, and narrative and can be a powerful tool for game designers looking to create a memorable and engaging experience.

The conceit outlines the formal rules that drive game design and creative development. It should be concise and simple but should also act as a blueprint for future development. The rules contained in the conceit are the ones you do not want to break while making the game and its world. Shigeru Miyamoto, the creator of many iconic Nintendo games, has emphasized the importance of strong game conceits in creating successful games, and this emphasis has led to the creation of many beloved IPs. Let's take a look at a few examples from some of my favorite games:

In *Portal* (Valve), the player is given a gun that creates portals between two points in space, establishing the primary conceit. This elegant design mechanic is used to create a series of increasingly complex puzzles that require the player to think creatively and manipulate the environment to progress.

The conceit of *Katamari Damacy* (Namco Bandai) is that the player is in the driver's seat of a small, sticky ball that rolls around a variety of environments, gradually picking up objects and growing larger. This simple mechanic is used to create a unique and whimsical experience that combines chaos and humor to make it a truly memorable experience.

In *Papers, Please* (Lucas Pope), the player experiences the conceit as an immigration officer at a border checkpoint with constantly changing criteria. This evolving mechanic is used to create a thought-provoking experience that challenges players to balance the demands of their job with their own sense of morality.

When building the world of your game, your conceit forms the principle rule that the rest of the world reinforces and branches from. Without a strong conceit to reinforce the gameplay experience, your world can quickly crumble into a confusing, disengaging heap of lore.

# BUILDING YOUR WORLD

Once you establish a solid conceit, you can start to build out your world more formally. World-building is an essential tool for game designers who want to create immersive and engaging experiences that keep players coming back for more. It does not matter whether your game is short or long, big budget or small, for phones or consoles; no matter the size or shape of your game, you need to invest time in building that game's world. A coherently built world can carry a lot of narrative weight that would normally be represented through text or dialogue.

The best game worlds give the player essential context on:

- What they are doing
- Why they are doing it
- What they get from playing
- What happens if they are not successful
- What their short-term goals are
- What their long-term goals are

Another benefit of world-building in games is that it can provide a sense of agency and control for players. By giving players choices that matter and allowing them to shape the world, game designers can create a sense of ownership that makes the player feel invested in the experience. This can be especially powerful in open-world games or games with branching narratives where players feel like they are making a real impact on the world and the story.

World-building scales according to the shape and size of the game you are creating, but it never fails to surprise me how often teams skip this vital step. And to some extent, I can understand why. When you are building a world for the game to live in, a large portion of the information and background you create is player facing, and that's a good thing! A richly built world allows for subtext and emergence. Telltale signs of thin world-building can include your team having difficulty making design or art decisions, incoherent characters and stories, or derivative ideas. Make sure you are giving it the time and attention it deserves.

## The Immersion Pyramid

N.K. Jemisin is an award-winning science fiction and fantasy author known for her intricate world-building and complex storytelling. Jemisin's approach to world-building is evident in her bestselling *Broken Earth* trilogy, which is set in a world where natural disasters are controlled by a group of powerful beings called Orogenes. This deep world-building has allowed Jemisin to create original, innovative, and believable worlds. As she has aptly stated in her lectures, "Fear of world-building is why we see so many similar worlds done to death: Iron Age barbarians, Star Trek-ian space navies, medieval northern Europe ad infinitum. Easier to copy than create (Figure 3.1)."

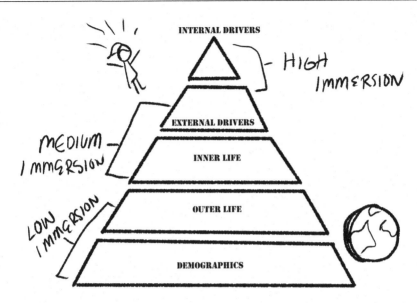

**FIGURE 3.1**    NK Jemisen's Immersion pyramid.

When designing your world, it is important to understand the level of immersion you offer to the player so you can make appropriate choices around characters, camera angles (first, second, or third-person perspective), actions, and story. The immersion pyramid is a tool that Jemisin uses to distinguish the different levels of immersive depth in world-building and the implications of each level. It's important to grasp that Jemisin's pyramid frames immersion in speculative fiction (and beyond) as a multilayered process. At its base, it contains the broadest and most superficial type of immersion; toward the apex, the immersion deepens, becoming more specific and profound.

At the broad base of the pyramid lies low immersion. In low-immersion environments, there is often a strong narrator to explain the history and action. Prologues are common, as are large character casts with complicated histories and relationships. System-driven games such as the *Civilization* (Firaxis) series are considered low immersion despite their deep grounding in history. This is reflected in the point of view, which often comes from a zoomed-out third-person perspective.

The pyramid's middle layer represents moderate immersion, an experience that relies on the story (or even interrupts it) to explain the world and what is happening in it. These worlds often rely on multiple but limited points of view to elaborate on the action. The player's experience is often cinematic but zoomed-out in second-person perspective; they view the action while also participating in it. *The Last of Us* (Naughty Dog) is an example of a game with moderate immersion. It grounds the player in the background of the world, using the events of Joel's past as a prologue to the events that take place primarily in the game world. *The Last of Us* also alternates between Joel's point of view and other characters' points of view to grant greater context and background, but sacrificing player agency and thus, immersion.

High-immersion worlds are at the apex of the pyramid. When games are set in these worlds, the player is dropped in with little to no explanation or onboarding. The strangeness of the world and its rules are conveyed through context and action, not necessarily through the narrative. Instead, the narrative deliberately details the stories of characters who react to the world—not the events that drive the world itself. If there is a strong narrator in a high-immersion game, it is likely an unreliable narrator. These games usually use the first-person or tight second-person point of view to emphasize agency and action rather than the surrounding environment. In a game context, the player reacts to the world rather than trying to understand it. *BioShock (2K)* is a good example of a highly immersive world because it provides the player with little context beyond what they can actively investigate and experience. *BioShock* is set in an underwater city called Rapture, which was built by a visionary named Andrew Ryan. The player knows very little about the protagonist and the world's history when they begin the game. As they explore the world, the game's story touches on themes of power, control, and morality, and it is presented primarily through audio diaries, environmental storytelling, and subtle clues scattered throughout the game. The player is left to piece together the story and make their own moral choices, creating a sense of agency and immersion.

## LEARNING FROM FILM TO CREATE MORE INCLUSIVE EXPERIENCES

Games are a relatively new medium in the grand scheme of things, so you could argue that game developers should be granted some leniency around some of the less…ahem…inclusive experiences. I would argue that with a rich history of blunders in the mediums that have gone before us, we have very little excuse to repeat these mistakes. Just as we can look to film for inspiration on timing and framing, we can also look to criticism of film to help us create more inclusive games.

Renowned feminist film theorist Laura Mulvey is known for introducing the concept of the "**male gaze**." The concept of the male gaze describes the dominant perspective in traditional cinema; from this perspective, that of a heterosexual male, women are often objectified as passive objects of desire. One classic film example comes from Alfred Hitchcock's *Vertigo*, where the protagonist's obsession with a woman epitomizes the male gaze since he sees her only as an object, not as a complex human being. Mulvey suggests that the male gaze perpetuates traditional gender dynamics and power imbalances while reinforcing gender stereotypes. To challenge this norm, she calls for alternative ways of visual storytelling that disrupt and subvert these traditional gender dynamics.

We do not need to look very hard to find similar examples in early video games, which used the damsel-in-distress and other well-worn tropes to objectify females for the player's pleasure. Anita Sarkeesian, founder of the *Feminist*

*Frequency* website, worked to put a spotlight on these tropes with a poignant video series that I believe is a must-watch for any aspiring narrative designer. Understanding these tropes and how they have been represented in past games can help us avoid the same mistakes in the future.

Recent games have started to challenge this paradigm. *Gone Home* (Fullbright) tells the story of a young woman who returns home and uncovers her family's secrets. The absence of traditional gameplay and the focus on personal narrative directly challenge the typical male gaze by allowing players to engage with a more intimate and introspective experience. This first-person game gives the player a female perspective in a female world. This is in fierce defiance of the male gaze and is underlined by the game's music (a wonderful mix of Riot Grrrl influences) and themes.

In *Dragon Age: Inquisition* (Bioware), the homosexual romance between Dorian and the player character allows for a deeper exploration of Dorian's character, relationships, and personal struggles. Furthermore, the game's cinematics provide opportunities to showcase the emotional connection and vulnerability between the characters, highlighting the complexity of their relationship beyond the lens of the male gaze. In one playful scene, the game even takes ownership of that gaze. By centering the gaze around a traditionally underrepresented romance perspective, the game subverts the heterosexual norm, providing a more inclusive representation of diverse sexual orientations.

Like those in *Dragon Age: Inquisition*, game cinematics can subvert the male gaze by providing more nuanced and inclusive representations of characters and focusing on their agency, personal growth, and emotional journeys. Games that broaden the range of narratives and perspectives contribute to a more diverse and representative gaming landscape.

Filmmaker Hamid Naficy delves into the idea of **"exilic cinema"** and the importance of timing in representing displacement and diasporic experiences. Exilic cinema explores the experiences of individuals who live in exile or displacement. Filmmakers representing these narratives often employ nonlinear storytelling and fragmented temporalities to depict the characters' fragmented identities and dislocation. An example is Wong Kar-wai's 2000 film *In the Mood for Love*; its nonlinear structure reflects the characters' longing and the temporal disjuncture they experience.

By manipulating the timing of events when telling stories of displaced individuals, filmmakers offer a distinct perspective on the human condition, highlighting the complexities and struggles these individuals face. Indie adventure game *A Space for the Unbound* (Mojiken Studio) is set in 1990s rural Indonesia and tells the story of Atma and Raya, two high school students who navigate the challenges of growing up, dealing with personal struggles, and exploring their dreams and aspirations. The game represents a specific time and place that might resonate with players who have experienced their own sense of displacement, longing, or nostalgia. Through its visuals, storytelling, and gameplay mechanics, *A Space for the Unbound* captures the essence of a particular cultural context while evoking the universal longing for connection and understanding.

Similar to exilic cinema's nonlinear storytelling, *A Space for the Unbound* employs a fragmented narrative structure. Players experience various vignettes and memories that gradually create a broader picture of the characters' lives and struggles. This approach mirrors Naficy's emphasis on fragmented temporalities, capturing the disjointed experiences and complex identities of those living in exile or facing upheaval.

# The Iceberg Theory

Ernest Hemingway was known for his unique and minimalist writing style, which he referred to as the "**iceberg theory**" or the "theory of omission." This theory suggests that the writer should only present a story's surface elements. leaving the underlying meaning and emotions hidden below the surface, like an iceberg. This creates a sense of depth and complexity as the reader is left to interpret hidden meanings. To achieve this effect, Hemingway uses short, simple sentences and precise language that conveys the essence of the story without explicitly stating it. He avoids flowery language and excessive description, preferring to leave much to the reader's imagination.

As we discussed in Chapter 1 when delving into top-down and bottom-up processing, we humans are exceptional at interpreting and understanding abstract concepts. Our brains love to fill in the blanks. **Apophenia** is a term used to describe the human tendency to perceive meaningful patterns or connections in random or meaningless data. It refers to the way the brain seeks out and makes sense of information, even when that information is not actually connected or meaningful.

We display apophenia in our natural inclination to find meaning and connections when we read or hear a story. Our brains automatically start looking for patterns and connections between the characters, plot points, and themes. This can sometimes lead us to make connections that are not actually there or to see meaning that was not intended by the author.

In part, humans are prone to apophenia because our brains are wired to make sense of the world around us. We evolved to detect patterns and connections in our environment, which helped our ancestors survive and navigate their surroundings. As a result, even without clear or meaningful information, our brains often try to find patterns or connections that aren't there. It is because of our ability to make these connections that we can build stories out of Hemingway's minimal sentences, allowing our minds to create connections that weave a rich tapestry of underlying story and subtext (Figure 3.2).

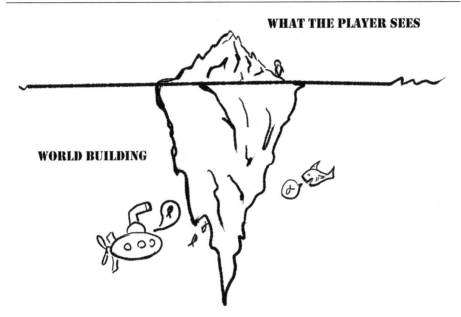

**WHAT THE PLAYER SEES**

**WORLD BUILDING**

**FIGURE 3.2**  Iceberg.

A well-built game world uses a similar methodology in which the player is presented with a world and story that are not explicitly explained. Instead, the game allows the player to discover and interpret them on their own. *Elden Ring* (From Software) is known for using minimalist storytelling to create a sense of mystery, drama, and intrigue. The game presents the player with a dark and foreboding world filled with hidden lore and secrets the player must piece together through exploration and observation of a world that has a big mysterious tree at the center. The game's story is not explicitly explained through cutscenes or dialogue, but rather through the environment and the items and characters the player encounters. This approach creates a sense of immersion and engagement as the player is left to interpret the story and world for themselves.

World-building is very different from the practice of lore-building. In world-building, you answer key questions about the game's foundational values, resources, and cultures whereas lore is the backstory that forms the historical reference for the game narrative. While these may not seem all that different at first glance, I have seen many game directors and creative leads make the mistake of creating epic and detailed lore documents during their pre-production cycles, only to have the vast majority of the work thrown out the window due to lack of alignment with product scope, design, and market goals. World-building is different. It is your foundation. When done well, it explains and holds up the core pillars of your game by explaining what makes the world unique and what makes it run.

# The Innovation Iceberg

Companies like Google often use a simple rule when determining the level of innovation to pursue within their product development. They focus 70% of their resourcing and efforts on foundational work that supports the core areas of the business, 20% on optimization and changes to that core experience, and 10% on blue sky innovation. We can learn from this method when building our game world iceberg.

The 70/20/10 rule was first introduced by Eric Schmidt, Google's former CEO, in his book *How Google Works*. Schmidt and his co-author, Jonathan Rosenberg, explain that the company's culture of innovation and experimentation has been a key factor in its success. They note that most of the company's energies are focused on its core business activities, which provide a steady revenue stream and support for other initiatives. The 20% allocation is devoted to adjacent or related projects that have the potential to expand the company's reach or create new revenue streams. The final 10% is reserved for entirely new and experimental projects that may not have an immediate payoff but have the potential to drive significant innovation and growth in the future.

The 70/20/10 rule has been credited with helping Google to develop some of its most successful products and initiatives, including Gmail, Google News, and Google Glass. The rule has also been adopted by other companies as a framework for promoting innovation and risk-taking in their own organizations. The LEGO Group uses a similar framework, mapping their innovation on a matrix table and adjusting their ratio depending on their priorities and appetite for risk each year. This means the majority of the company's resources are devoted to developing and refining new sets, themes, and building techniques.

If we view a player's cognitive energy using the same lens through which LEGO and Google view their business energy, we can apply a similar model to the world-building iceberg. Remember when we dove into memory in Chapter 1? Learning the rules of a new game requires a lot of energy toward repetitively doing a task and committing it to our long-term or short-term memory. If the player also has to spend a lot of mental energy trying to navigate and understand your game world, or interpret a large amount of history and exposition, they are going to have less mental energy to take on the challenges of the game. Therefore, it is essential to have a balance between foundation and innovation in your world-building (Figure 3.3).

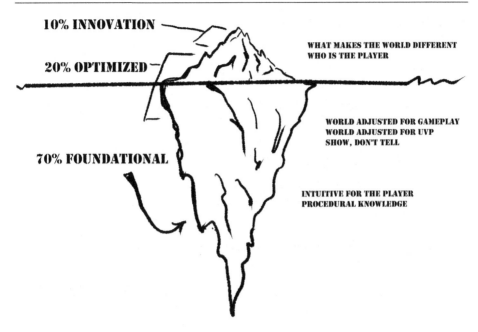

**FIGURE 3.3**  Innovation iceberg.

## *The foundational 70%*

Let's start with our base, the foundational 70%. You may recall that in Chapter 1, we discussed the concept of "bottom-up" processing. The reason we are able to effectively react to an animal jumping in front of our cars when driving, learn a new language when immersed in a different country, or pull items out of our fridge to make a meal is due to our ability to process the sensory information in the world around us. This relates to the mental models we discussed at the beginning of this chapter. If we build the majority of our iceberg using existing mental models, we can leverage the everyday knowledge that we as human beings acquire as we grow and learn the culture and environments around us. This world knowledge forms a baseline that allows us to make decisions quickly and accurately. The foundational 70% is where we put the "value" in UVP by creating a space for the player to learn, explore, and play in an intuitive and safe way. According to Norman, "knowledge how" is internal knowledge that is stored within an individual's brain. Therefore, it can only be accessed by the person who stores it. Your computer password is a good example of this, as it is personal to you and requires rote practice and memorization to commit to your long-term memory. Because "knowledge how" is opaque and often complicated, it can be unreliable. Therefore, relying on "knowledge of" for your foundational layer can help ensure coherence and minimize frustration.

As Norman elegantly states, "Simplified models are the key to successful application."

When I'm designing a game, I try to deeply understand the world knowledge of my intended player base. This allows me to build my iceberg with a built-in framework that the player can easily understand and access, thus reducing the mental energy required to learn about the rules of the world. This frees up space to let the player learn and master the game's unique rules. I like to think of it as a series of questions I'm indirectly answering for the player.

**List of world-building foundation questions**
**What is daily life like in this world?**

- What is the currency? How do people get the currency?
- What are the precious resources? Are they traded? How are they acquired?
- Where and how does trading or purchasing of goods occur?
- How do individuals get around from location to location? What technology do they use to do so? How far can they go in a day? How do the inhabitants navigate?
- What do the inhabitants eat? What is considered comfort food? What is a delicacy? What is revolting?
- What are relationships like? What kinds of relationships are there? How do people form relationships?
- How do the inhabitants socialize? How does courtship or friendship occur and evolve?
- What are the main categories of jobs or labor?
- How do the inhabitants clothe or decorate themselves? What materials do they use?
- What is the distribution of resources across populations? How are they distributed? How is that distribution conveyed?

**What is the history and culture of this world?**

- How do individuals and/or groups celebrate? How do they mourn?
- How do they start conflicts? How do they resolve them?
- What are the taboos? What happens to people who violate them?
- What are the primary values the people hold? Are there other people with competing values? How is that addressed?
- What personality traits are considered highly valuable in this world?
- What are some key events that shaped the world as it is today? Who were the key individuals or groups shaping it?
- What is funny in this world? What is tragic? How do the inhabitants express comedy and tragedy?
- How competitive is the culture? What drives competition?

**What does this world look like?**

- What are the climate regions? How many are there?
- What is the geological environment like? How are the continents structured? How varied is the landscape?
- What are the plants like? How do the inhabitants interact with them?
- How safe is the environment? What hazards are there? What are the safe areas like?
- What are the key building materials? What is considered strong or weak?

- How densely populated is this world? How is it populated (small towns, big cities, et cetera)?
- What do family spaces look like and how are they inhabited? What do professional spaces look like?

Since we're using these questions to build the iceberg's foundational layer, it is important that the majority of answers include 70% relatable core experience. That's because this information is likely to become the most visible through the player's interaction with and actions within the gameplay experience. Those of you who are frequent travelers may notice that many of these questions are similar to the ones you ask yourself before visiting a new place, and that is not a coincidence. Thinking of yourself as a tour guide for the player is an easy way to empathize with them when you're world-building. Putting yourself in this mindset enables you to create a player journey that is both engaging and intuitive.

Just like travelers can have a better experience by knowing how to get rupees in New Delhi or understanding how to hail a taxi in New York City, the player's journey will be better if designers make information accessible in the world-building process. Accessible information creates context for the player's actions and interactions within your game, and this context is based on the mental models they have established through their previous world knowledge. When in doubt, choose simplicity—rather than trying to reinvent the wheel, use a narrative that fits the actions and motivations of the world you are trying to create.

## *The optimized 20%*

Once you have answered the primary questions that shape the game world and its structure, you can do what I like to call a "creative design optimization pass." Take a look at your answers to the foundational questions, identify 20% of your world and story that ties closely to the actions of the game world, and do some brainstorming. Ask yourself how you can make your game world different—how you can make it unique while still keeping the foundational elements intact. As you do this, you'll still leverage known solutions. You'll just reconfigure them in ways that enhance the world, making them unique and identifiable.

This stage of world-building is a good time to revisit the early research and development processes and results we discussed in Chapter 2. If your team asked the right questions early on, you should have a good idea of what the player values and which innovations are key for your game. Revisit your UVP—does the world support it? How can it be better supported? Your iceberg's 20% and 10% innovation layers should reinforce those design tenets in different ways.

When creating the 20% optimization layer, you and your team should assess the core aspects you created in your 70% foundational layer against what you discovered during your early research and development phases. Essentially, this is the time to make sure your world supports your game design and product goals. You'll also make adjustments and optimizations to ensure that your game design and goals are in harmony with one another.

Because "unique" is at the forefront of your UVP, that means that you often will be introducing new concepts to your player base in the top 30% of your iceberg. You will have to make these new concepts readily available to your players so that they can become declarative ("knowledge in the head"). This can include things like maps, books, signs, and symbols. We'll talk about this more in Chapters 4 and 5. For now, remember that as you build your world, you'll need to teach this kind of information to the player through the systems and interactions in your game. Additionally, you can provide contextual help and support, such as tooltips or guides, that assist players in understanding and using the system. This will help players quickly and efficiently access the information they need.

**List of world-building optimization questions**

- What problems does this game try to solve? How does the player solve these problems in the game world?
- How do we want the player to feel? How does the game world create and reinforce these desired feelings?
- What are the player's main motivations? How can we ensure that the world's culture and environment support these motivations? We'll cover motivations in depth in Chapter 5.
- What actions and verbs does the player use in the game's core loop? Why is the player performing them? Does the game world support and reinforce these actions and verbs? We'll discuss game verbs and the core loop in Chapter 4.
- What do we want the players to learn while they play the game? What is the message they should walk away with after finishing the game? How do the values of the game world support these lessons?
- How does this game fit into the player's daily life? Does the size and scope of the world support that? Will players be able to immerse themselves in the world in their designed play session?
- How quickly can players learn the core actions? How challenging is the game in the beginning versus at the end? How does the world help the player learn the game and overcome its challenges?
- Does this world support the key values and design pillars we identified in our research and development?

Note that these questions are less about what we, as designers, know about the world and more about what we think we know or want to know about the player. In their innovation models, Google and LEGO use **adjacency** to create better experiences from product lines or services that already exist. To effectively explore these new experiences, these companies use detailed information about what does and doesn't work for their customers. Similarly, by understanding what we want the player to get out of the gameplay experience, designers can optimize what they have already established in the world-building process to reflect players' needs and desires.

Diving back into our travel metaphor, these questions reflect what happens when you start to better understand what you want out of your vacation and begin to make decisions accordingly. If you want a relaxing vacation, you might focus on hotels or locations that have minimal friction in the everyday experience, and you might choose a temperate or warm climate with friendly people. If you are looking for adventure, you might research the best areas for hiking or physical activity. Central Park in New York City offers a different experience than Manhattan, Brooklyn, or Queens. Which location will best fit the activities you have planned? By reassessing the game world through the lens of the experience you want the player to have, you can ensure that the world offers affordances for that experience.

## The innovative 10%

Just like Google and LEGO must consistently innovate to stay relevant, we as designers need to innovate our worlds to appeal to players and create memorable experiences. The final 10% of our iceberg, therefore, should focus on blue sky concepts that reinforce the unique aspects of the game. The industry is rife with games that use the same primary sources for their foundational worlds (I am Tolkein fan, but am quite tired seeing his influence in almost every fantasy game in existence). By starting with the key areas that make your world unique, and by directly tying them to the game motivations and actions, you can help future-proof the development of the product as it goes through the many hands and minds of the developers working on it while also ensuring that your player can enjoy the novel experiences you have created.

### List of world-building innovation questions

- Who is the player in this world?
- How is the conceit reflected in the game world? What reinforces the conceit?
- How does our unique value proposition manifest in the game world?
- What makes this game world different or special?
- How does the world convey the core game solution to the design problem?
- What delights the player about the world?
- What surprises the player about the world?
- What do we want the player to remember about the game years after playing?

If we return to the travel metaphor one more time, your iceberg's innovative layer is the experience you plan your entire trip around, the bucket list item that initially puts the destination in your mind. For instance, it might be seeing a musical on Broadway, learning to make tagine in a Moroccan home, seeing the sun rise over the Taj Mahal, or climbing Mount Everest. This single experience (and how it occurs) creates a frame of reference for the trip experience in its entirety. Although the trip's overall success or failure doesn't depend exclusively upon the bucket list item, that experience will greatly influence how you feel about your travels years later.

Just like innovative products and services can transform a company, innovative narrative decisions can have a ripple effect throughout the entire world and game. Because of this, it is incredibly important that you effectively communicate these concepts to your team and make room in your design phase to adjust accordingly.

## Innovation iceberg examples

Let's take a look at a couple of examples by analyzing some games that emulate this model.  The indie game *Stray* (Annapurna Interactive) takes place in a world where, presumably, humans no longer exist. Even so, the societal, political, cultural, and economic structures all draw inspiration primarily from Western capitalism. The core themes of human greed and hubris—and the resulting conflicts—reinforce these structures. These tenets form the world's foundational layer.

In the optimization layer, the world starts digging into how the human elements detailed in the foundation have changed or shifted in a society primarily populated by non-humans (in this case, robots). For example, the robots exchange oil instead of currency, and their music sounds like simple electronic chip tunes. These twists add depth to the world, making the concept of a post-human civilization inhabited by mechanical beings believable. Even though the robots have based their society on the one that was most familiar to them (and to many players), they have adjusted its rules and expectations to suit their reality. By recognizing the inherent conflict that can arise from robots trying to behave like humans, the game team is able to explore deeper themes and add a rich variety to a story that draws from the many familiar themes within its foundation.

The innovation layer, however, is where this game really shines. In *Stray,* the player embodies a stray cat. This is not an anthropomorphized cat that can move and act like a biped—it's just a simple cat that looks, moves, and behaves like one in the real world. (Albeit one with a backpack that contains a robot helper, which happens to be a great example of a helpful tutorial narrator—more on this in later chapters.) This simple innovation not only provides a baseline for the game's primary differentiating and positioning statements but also adds a whole new layer of verbs and associated actions (purr, scratch, and pounce) for the game team to draw from. It is a brilliant example of a creative constraint imposed by a world-building decision. Think of all the wonderful (and I'm sure, at times, frustrating) creative problems that the team had to solve throughout development due to this choice. The game's camera setups, level design, interaction design, and emotional journey all would have been impacted. But it is this choice—having the player's identity be that of an adventurous feline—that makes the game innovative, charming, and memorable (Figure 3.4).

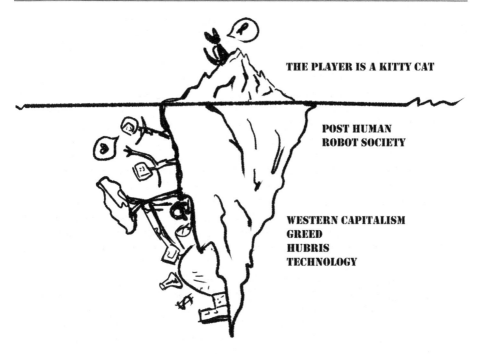

**FIGURE 3.4** *Stray* iceberg.

The foundational world for the eighth *Yakuza* game, *Yakuza: Like a Dragon* (Ryu Ga Gotoku Studio) is very similar to its predecessors. Set primarily in modern Yokohama (*Dragon's* timeline spans between 2001 and 2019), the world draws from real-world locations and experiences for those familiar with Japanese cities and culture. The primary currency is the yen, and the player can spend that money watching movies, singing karaoke, playing pachinko, or engaging in other various mini games peppered throughout the city. Anyone who has been to Tokyo will likely be able to understand and navigate the world with relative ease.

The optimization layer is represented directly in the title. As it suggests, the main character of this game, Ichiban, is involved in the yakuza crime syndicates. Therefore, much of the world that Ichiban inhabits involves lying, cheating, stealing, and violence. This doesn't make the title all that different from the previous *Yakuza* games, but it does add variety to the choices that the player can make, as they can choose whether they wish to engage in the criminal element of the game. Because the innovation layer adds an interesting twist to a well-established series-Ichiban wants to be a hero. He wants to be a hero so badly that he transforms the world around him to behave like a traditional, turn-based (real time) Japanese role-playing game (RPG). He and his companions learn new skills, equip items, and get into turn-based combat with various enemies throughout the game. Once again, here is where the innovation layer can get really interesting—it can allow designers to explore different genres and playstyles. By taking what typically would be an anti-hero main character and making him an eager and geeky hero wannabe, the world is transformed through his attempts at altruism and optimism.

This juxtaposition of a gritty criminal world overlaid with a goofy do-good premise not only creates a memorable game with novel mechanics for the series, it creates a more nuanced, interesting, and surprisingly funny game world.

## LUDONARRATIVE DISSONANCE

**Ludonarrative dissonance** is a term introduced by game designer Clint Hocking to describe a conflict between a game's mechanics (the "ludo" part of the term) and its narrative (the, ahem, "narrative" part of the term). It refers to a situation where the actions required by the game mechanics are at odds with the story or characters being portrayed in the game's narrative.

For example, a game might have a story that portrays the player character as a morally upstanding hero, yet the gameplay requires the player to engage in violent or unethical actions to progress. This creates a disconnect between what the game is asking the player to do and the message that the game is trying to convey through its narrative.

Ludonarrative dissonance can lead to a lack of player engagement and a feeling of disconnection from the game's narrative. It can also detract from the overall experience of the game by making it feel disjointed or inconsistent.

To avoid ludonarrative dissonance, we game designers must carefully consider the relationship between the game's mechanics and narrative and strive to create a cohesive and consistent experience for the player. This can be done by designing gameplay mechanics that align with the game's narrative and characters, or by creating a narrative that accommodates the mechanics and the player's actions within the game world.

# GAME METAPHORS

A metaphor is a word or image that represents a concept other than the thing itself. When someone says, "I am an open book," they are referring to the fact that they are forthright, honest, or have nothing to hide. If someone is a "night owl" they are not avian in nature, but are usually the opposite of an "early bird." Game metaphors work in this same way; they are ideas, themes, or images that stand in for a game concept without literally stating the concept itself. They turn spreadsheets into engaging concepts. When Link finds a heart in *Zelda*, it represents healing. When I click a sword icon in an action RPG, it usually means that I will attack the nearest person or object. Game metaphors are an essential tool when designing affordances in features and systems. When you design your narrative and player experience, it is essential to take care with the basic metaphors associated with the actions and interactions of that design.

Steve Swink, an independent game designer and author of *Game Feel*, describes metaphor as "the ingredient that lends emotional meaning to motion and that provides familiarity to mitigate learning frustration." The choices designers make in our foundational themes and concepts let us connect to the player's built-in imaginative assumptions and mental models, and a well-executed metaphor helps gameplay tether elegantly to its narrative context.

### LEARNING GO

Learning the board game *Go* has been a humbling experience for me as a game designer. This simple-looking yet staggeringly complex game is always an absolute brain burner, yet I can't help but come back to it. This wasn't always the case, however. When my partner gave me a board and stones as a gift, I came very close to chucking the whole mess out the window while trying to learn it. It wasn't until I watched a video by professional *Go* player Stephanie Yin explaining the game metaphors that the rules began to click for me.

Imagine the *Go* board as a vast, unexplored land divided into territories by an intricate grid. You, an aspiring commander, are tasked with conquering this land using your loyal soldiers, the black or white stones. Your rival commander wields an army of the opposite color. Your mission is to claim the most land by the end of the battle.

In the beginning, the land is an empty canvas filled with air. As commanders, both you and your rival have equal opportunity to shape the outcome of this campaign. Your soldiers march onto the battlefield one by one, each move signaling a claim on a point of the land. These points are your territories, the spaces your soldiers stand ready to defend.

However, beware! The enemy can easily surround and capture a soldier who is stranded alone. (This is a metaphor for atari, one of the game's rules.) The enemy soldiers stand on all sides, leaving no route for escape. To prevent this, you must learn to keep your soldiers connected, forming shapes that are difficult for the enemy to surround.

As the battle progresses, so too does your understanding of the game. You start to see the patterns, the ebbs and flows of the battlefield, the dance of advance and retreat, attack and defense. You learn to perceive the *Go* board not merely as a collection of individual points but as a complex tapestry of interconnected territories.

All this metaphor and story behind a simple game of counters and squares! And yet I don't know if I would have ever understood the nuance and beauty of the game's mechanics without that story.

## Choosing Metaphors

Good metaphors leverage world knowledge while reinforcing the world of the game. They should act as a bridge between the design and the player, igniting their imagination while also acting as a guide. There are three primary factors I like to consider when guiding teams on their metaphor choices

- Feature complexity, frequency, and investment
- Player motivation and background
- World depth and design

You will use many metaphors throughout your game, so it is important to start with the primary features and concepts associated with your core loop to establish consistency. When choosing metaphors, it is important to consider the complexity of the feature or concept (this concept could be resources, skills, systems, et cetera). The more complex the concept, the more time the player is likely to spend with it. The more time they spend with it, the more cognitive energy they expend to learn it. Therefore, the complexity of the metaphors you choose should be directly related to the complexity and time spent on the feature.

Incorporating intuitive, action-oriented metaphors in your game can leverage the player's existing procedural knowledge. For instance, a player may not know the specifics of how to fly a plane in a flight simulator game, but they understand that the game's joystick stands in for the flight controls—it's a metaphor. Additionally, the player likely has a basic procedural understanding that pushing the joystick forward will make the plane descend, and pulling it back will make the plane ascend. This understanding can be used to design intuitive contextual (or metaphoric) controls that mimic real-world actions.

Motivation is another important factor to consider when choosing your metaphors. If you are designing a game for a more casual and broad audience—say, a merge game meant to be played during someone's downtime—you will likely be more successful if you choose broad and approachable themes that fit the mental models of a broader audience like cooking or gardening. On the other hand, if you are designing a game for people who have a very specific interest—say, an intense real-time strategy game with high-stakes decisions made in the moment-to-moment gameplay—you will likely be more successful choosing themes that are complex and highly focused in a specific genre, such as generational spaceship management or Napoleonic tactics. While there are overlaps in the demographics for these games (there are plenty of casual game players who also play intense strategy games), the key difference is the **motivation** behind why that player is playing your game.

Understanding what players already know can help you design intuitive metaphors that players are likely to understand. For example, using common symbols or concepts in your game's UI can leverage the player's existing knowledge. If a player knows that a heart usually represents life or health in a game context ("knowledge of"), you can use a heart symbol to represent the player's health in your game. This avoids the need for lengthy explanations or instructions.

Considering player motivation is equally important (if not more important) when designing a specific concept or feature. By tying the metaphor directly to the motivation, you help the player understand what is expected of them in play. We'll take a more in-depth look at motivations in later chapters, but the key thing to remember is that you should always ask questions on behalf of the player during your design process, and you should use the answers you discover to inform the context you create for them. Your metaphor should help answer the why, what, and how of the game by connecting the feature to established mental models. This is where the metaphor can truly act as an affordance between the feature and the player.

The last major factor to consider when choosing metaphors is the depth and design of your game world. Earlier in this chapter we built our iceberg around existing mental models using the 70/20/10 rule of innovation. When you start diving into the details of your game, you can enrich the player's understanding and experience of the iceberg by reinforcing your world through your metaphor choices. Instead of a generic health potion, why not choose a plant that teaches the player about the biome they are in? Instead of a ticket that gives the player an entry pass into another feature, why not a key to hidden pirate treasure? By making creative and deliberate decisions, you can add depth, variation, and interest to your game, and your players will thank you for it.

Well-constructed metaphors should be able to signpost the goals and pillars of the design element. They should connect the main verbs associated with those actions and problems in an elegant framework that enables intuitive decision-making, heightening immersion and flow states. When crafting your metaphors, it's important to ask yourself the following questions:

- **Is it simple enough?** Simple metaphors that relate directly to the desired action are best so you avoid mixing metaphors or themes. Sometimes the most obvious metaphor is the correct one.
- **Is it general enough?** Choose foundational knowledge as inspiration first. Too much specificity can create confusion or require a niche level of knowledge. Unless you are getting into complex crafting systems or building from a deep existing lore base, it's best to keep things less specific and more general.
- **Is it relevant to the player?** It is important that the metaphor is relevant to your target audience. Understanding your players' culture and experience of everyday life is key to ensuring that you create relevant metaphors.
- **Is it consistent with the action?** The metaphor should be able to convey what the player is expected to accomplish and how to go about doing it.
- **Does the metaphor reinforce the game world?** Metaphors are a strong way of reinforcing coherence. Understand your game world and create metaphors that fit within it.

Good metaphors will enhance the game experience. On the other hand, bad metaphors will interfere with product coherence. They will also confuse the player and break immersion. Since 1982, San Jose State University has been running the Bulwer-Lytton Fiction Contest for bad writing, asking entrants to come up with the worst possible opening line to a novel. Let's look at some of my favorite past winners to get an idea of what I mean by a "bad" metaphor. See if you can spot which questions the writers will-fully ignored in these delightfully bad sentences:

"'Hoist the mainsail ye accursed swine' shouted the Captain over the roar of the waves as the ship was tossed like a cork dropped from a wine bottle into a jacuzzi when the faucet is wide open and the jets are running full blast and one has just settled into the water with a glass of red wine to ease the aches and pains after a day of hard labor raking leaves from the front yard."

*—Joe Tussey, Daniels, WV*

"She walked into my office on legs as long as one of those long-legged birds that you see in Florida—the pink ones, not the white ones—except that she was standing on both of them, not just one of them, like those birds, the pink ones, and she wasn't wearing pink, but I knew right away that she was trouble, which those birds usually aren't."

*—Eric Rice, Sun Prairie, WI*

"Cheryl's mind turned like the vanes of a wind-powered turbine, chopping her sparrowlike thoughts into bloody pieces that fell onto a growing pile of forgotten memories."

*—Sue Fondrie, Oshkosh, WI*

Choosing the right metaphors in your game can help players better understand what is expected of them, motivating them to complete the actions and solve the problems your team has designed for them. If you strip the verbs and metaphors from your game design, you are often left with a checklist-like series of rote tasks, or even something as banal as a simple spreadsheet. By reinforcing the player fantasy with coherent choices around these verbs and metaphors, you are enriching it and driving it.

## Tracking Metaphors

When we choose our metaphors, we want to map them to that 70/20/10 iceberg to deeply integrate them into the game's world and action. For this reason, I like to track my game metaphors in a spreadsheet. This avoids duplication, helps visualize working or conflicting relationships, and acts as a final gut check to ensure that we use consistent iconography and metaphors. The spreadsheet is also a helpful tool for early user testing. Speaking of documentation, let's talk about…

### Introducing the player and your game team to the world

If you've ever been swamped by an avalanche of lore as soon as you boot up a video game, you know it is akin to being given a history book and being asked to memorize it. Hardly the fun or immersive experience you signed up for, right? Let us delve into why what I like to call the "**breadcrumb approach**" makes for a far better player experience.

An **exposition dump** is when a game crams all its backstory, world-building, and plot threads into one giant info dump, usually at the beginning of the game. While it may seem like a good way to familiarize the player with the game's world and plot, it often results in a tedious, hard-to-digest wall of text (or dialogue) that kills immersion rather than enhancing it. It's like watching a movie where the first 20 minutes are nothing but narrated exposition. It feels lazy, detached, and impersonal.

The breadcrumb approach is fundamentally different. This method immerses players gradually, feeding them little nuggets of lore as they venture further into the game. The game's universe unfurls slowly, giving players time to connect the dots, discover secrets, and naturally absorb the world's intricacies.

In the breadcrumb approach, environmental storytelling is key. For example, the worn neon signs and dilapidated buildings in *Fallout: New Vegas* (Obsidian) tell a story of a world that has seen better days, with a history of conflict and destruction. The scattered audio logs and graffiti in *BioShock* drip-feed us insights into the utopia-gone-wrong of Rapture. This approach turns every corner of the world into a potential treasure trove of knowledge, making exploration rewarding and intriguing.

This approach also relies on indirect lore to "show, don't tell." Instead of spoon-feeding the player every detail about the world, you allow them to piece things together through conversations with non-playable characters (NPCs), visual cues in the environment, item descriptions, and more. This method lets players learn about the world at their own pace and in their own way.

*Final Fantasy 16* (Square Enix) takes this one step further with the Active Time Lore system, which allows players to get additional information about the story in the context where it is introduced. At any given point in the game, whether they are in a cutscene or combat, players can pull up Active Time Lore to get descriptions of the characters they are engaged with or the location they are in. This method helps players navigate a complicated story and world, and it refreshes them on events if they have taken a break from the game.

Designing a game this way requires effort and nuance. Every piece of lore needs to be woven seamlessly into the fabric of the game world, making it feel like a natural part of the experience. When done right, however, the payoff is immense. Players are more engaged, they feel a greater sense of discovery, and the world feels more alive and immersive.

In essence, it's about making the lore part of the player's journey rather than a prerequisite to it. It's about turning a history lesson into a treasure hunt. And most players would rather go on a treasure hunt than sit through a lecture.

There are certainly moments when it's important to provide the player with background information so they can understand the context or stakes of their adventure. However, this doesn't have to involve throwing a chunky manual of text at them. There are many inventive, engaging, interactive, and fun ways that developers can introduce players to lore and backstory.

*Mass Effect* is a prime example of this done right. BioWare knew that not everyone hopping into *Mass Effect 2* or *3* would have played the previous game(s), so they wanted a way to effectively get new players up to speed and make key choices that could affect their story. Enter the interactive comic book sequence.

In *Mass Effect 2* and *3*, players who are new to the series or want to make different choices from a previous playthrough can use an interactive comic called *Mass Effect: Genesis*. This comic cleverly summarizes key events and choices from the previous games. The player watches the comic and makes decisions at key points, effectively shaping their own backstory and setting the stage for the adventure to come. It's a genius way to onboard new players while also offering returning players a chance to tweak their narrative.

Similarly, *Dream Daddy* (Game Grumps), a dating simulator where you play as a single dad looking for love, takes a unique approach to onboarding. The player character's backstory is revealed through an interaction with his daughter as they go through old family photographs together. It's a poignant, interactive sequence that lets players make choices about the character's past and relationship with his daughter. It not only establishes the backstory but also sets the tone for the heartfelt and personal narrative that follows.

These examples highlight that, when done creatively, introducing lore and backstory can be a compelling and engaging part of the game experience, rather than a chore to be done before the "real fun" starts.

Interactive and short experiences like these serve a dual purpose: they familiarize players with the world and its history, and they immerse players in the narrative from the get-go. By making the player an active participant in their own backstory, you ensure they're invested in the world and its characters from the very first moment. And by keeping these experiences brief and interactive, you ensure they're fun and engaging, rather than becoming a slog to get through.

In essence, the key is to make the player feel like they're shaping their own adventure, even in the moments when you're feeding them the necessary information. Make it interactive, make it personal, and above all, make it memorable.

# Design Constraints and Perspectives

Jesse Schell, a game designer and professor at Carnegie Mellon University, has developed a set of principles for designing games, including the use of **constraints** and **lenses**. In his book *The Art of Game Design: A Book of Lenses*, Schell describes how constraints can help guide and shape the design process while lenses can be used to evaluate and refine design decisions.

Schell defines a constraint as a "limitation or restriction imposed on the design process." Constraints can focus and direct creativity. Designers should carefully consider the constraints they impose and use them to guide the design process toward a specific goal or outcome. Constraints often relate to the pillars we talked about in Chapter 2—they can be the limited number of verbs available, the level of agency the player has, or the intended length of a play session. They can be as specific as the number of clicks it takes a player to complete an action, or as broad as the primary genre that the game is drawing inspiration from.

Schell's lenses, on the other hand, are a set of design perspectives that can be used to evaluate and refine game design decisions. Each lens represents a different way of looking at a game design problem and can be used to identify potential issues or areas for improvement. For example, the lens of the player can be used to evaluate how a player might perceive and interact with a game, while the lens of technology can be used to assess a design's technical feasibility and what platforms might be best to publish on. As you look through each of these lenses, you see the game's design from a different perspective, and ask different questions.

Schell's principles of constraints and lenses provide designers with a flexible and adaptable framework for game design. By using constraints to guide the design process and lenses to evaluate and refine design decisions, designers can create games that are more focused, engaging, and enjoyable for players.

**CREATIVITY TIPS: FIGHTING DESIGNER'S BLOCK**

Creativity is a muscle, and like the muscles in our bodies, it can get overused, exhausted, or injured. Fortunately, similar to our physical muscles, there are exercises and activities we can do to build up and replenish our creative muscles. Everyone has different methods that work for them, but here are a few tips that have worked for me over the years.

- Build time into your calendar and schedule to walk away from your desk.
  - There is a reason that so many of us come up with solutions to tough problems while we're in the shower, while we're taking a walk, or when we wake up in the morning. These are the times when we allow our brains to do some backup subconscious processing. Games are complex design systems, and sometimes we need to give our brains time to absorb that complexity.
  - Chaining yourself to your computer and forcing yourself to generate output doesn't just wear you out faster. It also results in lazy ideas and decisions. If you find yourself doing this, you should go for a walk. Seriously. Preferably outside.
  - By building this time directly into your team brainstorming or individual calendar, you are leveraging your brain's subconscious superpowers to come up with innovative solutions.
- Create a library of vision boards and ideas.
  - When you find yourself bouncing off the problem you are trying to solve, spend some time pulling together imagery or words associated with a different problem. It will help you refocus your efforts later, and it gives you an idea backlog to draw from for future problem-solving.
  - Word association games are another fun way of generating ideas and can help you focus or reframe a problem. I mentioned word association games in Chapter 2, but I think it's worth repeating here in the context of getting unstuck.
  - I also keep a "graveyard" of the worst ideas I've ever come up with. This allows me to get them out of my head instead of letting them rattle around, and it also provides good comedy fodder.
- Go down an encyclopedic rabbit hole.
  - Start with a subject area related to the problem that you are trying to solve and follow the breadcrumbs to a subject that is two or three references away. See where you end up and see if it relates to your current work.
  - I also like to keep a library of relevant texts at hand from various disciplines. These don't have to be textbooks or source material—I often have a stack that includes comics, art books, short stories—anything that relates to the game I am working on at the time, even

in abstraction. This allows me to grab a book, open a random page, and see if I can find something useful.
- This works for websites as well—Wikipedia and blogs with "random page" buttons are wonderful for this, although I suggest avoiding pages that have endless scrolling since this can often cause information overload.
- Keep physical materials at hand.
  - When we engage our bodies, we engage our brains. Computers are great, but to come up with creative solutions, we need to engage with materials and activities that are outside our routine.
  - It does not matter whether it is Post-its, a whiteboard, LEGO bricks, drawing supplies, Rubik's Cubes, knitting needles, or musical instruments. Find what works for you.
  - Keep a journal at your bedside so you can write down the ideas that come into your head in the middle of the night. Even if the ideas are complete nonsense, you will find you can sleep easier once they are out of your head, and you never know how they might come in handy.
- Eat a piece of fruit or other natural sugar source.
  - We are horrible at making decisions and solving complex problems when we are hungry. In his book *Thinking, Fast and Slow*, psychologist Daniel Kahneman refers to a study in which the researchers find that judges are much more likely to grant parole immediately after taking a break and eating a meal, such as lunch. In fact, the probability of parole being granted is around 65% immediately after a meal break compared to only around 10% just before a meal break. The researchers conclude that the judges' decision-making was influenced by their level of glucose, which provides the brain with more energy and increases its ability to make complex decisions. When you begin to experience design block or decision fatigue, do yourself a favor and grab a banana or similar snack.

# Documentation

Creating a variety of tools and documents that cater to different audiences within your game team is an essential part of keeping the game world coherent and engaging as development kicks off into production. Narrative documents are the design records created to help guide development and keep a historical record of characters and lore. They are an essential part of the design process, but are only worthwhile if they are read. I often see designers create rich lore documents that become the equivalent of a bound tome on a library shelf: occasionally taken out and dusted off but rarely used. Let's take a look at some common types of documentation for game worlds, along with their strengths and weaknesses.

## Story bibles

Story bibles are living documents detailing all the information about the game world and story. Over the years I've created many of these, and they can vary from game to game, but there are a few key components that I like to consistently include:

- **Introduction:** A two- to three-paragraph synopsis for the TLDR folks on the team. This generally introduces the game's conceit, the primary pillars of the game world, and key story moments. Essentially an elevator pitch.
- **Story Map:** We'll discuss these in a later chapter, but for now, understand that there are a variety of ways to visually map the narrative experience for your players, and including this in your bible can help the team understand the key story points.
- **World Map:** A visual representation of the game world. Does not have to be a 1:1 scale representation.
- **Lore Repository:** World-building iceberg and backstory. Details are important as this is often used for transmedia efforts.
- **Annotated World Map:** A visual representation of the game world that includes information about key questlines, characters, and associated game mechanics. Should represent the intended scale.
- **Location Descriptions:** Includes the primary purpose and values of each location. Start with high-level information and flesh it out as the team explores and builds the look and feel of the world.
- **Glossary:** List of key metaphors and terms.
- **Some or All of the Documents Listed Below:** You should either link directly to them or include them in your story bible.

This document can and should change throughout development, so it is important to use a format and organizational architecture that is easy to search, edit, and update. This also means that they can get very, very long. Dividing them up into several documents can help mitigate this.

## Story synopsis deck

This is the introduction section of your story bible that is put into presentation form. Similar to a pitch deck, but for story. Visuals are key—we want to show the story, not tell it. Keep it under 25 slides.

## Wikis

A wiki can be used for (or as a supplement to) your story bible if your team uses it regularly for design documentation. Make it searchable, easy to edit and version, and talk to someone on the UX team about information architecture to get help on structure. Even doing that, you will likely hate updating the wiki. But it will be worth it to have your team searching internal resources instead of looking on fanwikis (this happens *all the time*).

## Character bios

You will want to have detailed bio sheets for each of the characters in your game. These should include:

- A short synopsis including key character traits
- Key art with poses and facial expressions
- Backstory, including…
  - Fears and motivations
  - Wants and needs
  - Flaws and faults
  - Values and purpose
- Relationship map
- Casting notes for voiceover
- Key quest lines or story points, if applicable
- Costuming guidelines
- Sample dialogue
- Details around how they can and should be used in the context and action of the game's core loop and features, including associated stat tables and skills where applicable

We'll talk more about designing characters in a later chapter.

## Comics

In the GDC Talk "'Nuff Said: Comics as Design Documentation," Matthew Derby, a game designer and writer, argues that comics can be a valuable tool for documenting game design. He suggests that comics can be used to communicate design ideas more effectively than traditional design documents, which can be dry and difficult to understand. I've used comics in my process and can wholeheartedly agree. By using comics to convey design ideas, designers can more effectively communicate the narrative and emotional aspects of a game's design. Additionally, comics are a flexible medium that can be adapted to a variety of design needs, from character development to world-building.

Derby provides several examples of how comics can be used in game design, such as creating character bios, storyboards, and design documents. He emphasizes the importance of using visual storytelling to convey complex design ideas, and he argues that comics can help bridge the gap between designers and other team members, such as artists and writers. I like to create a new issue each year if possible to show major changes or updates to the story or showcase new tales. "Story room" sessions where I channel my inner Levar Burton and share these comics have become a staple at the studios I've worked at.

## Scripts

If your game has a linear story or you plan on hiring voiceover artists for your dialogue, then you will likely want to create a script. Some studios use cinematic format, and some break them down by character. Use whatever integrates best with your existing tools. Including notes around atmosphere, emotion, camera positioning, and sound can help guide the various actors and designers working on the game as they portray the game's story through their performances and work. Backstory is less important for great performances than current context and motivation cues.

## Strings spreadsheets

If your game does not have robust content management systems or narrative tooling, you are likely going to be using spreadsheets as the repositories for the text in the game. Talking to a spreadsheet-savvy teammate if you are new to managing strings this way can save you a lot of time and energy.

It is important to include character limits in these spreadsheets to ensure that the text displays in a readable font size without extending beyond the bounds of the UI. Always include a column for tracking character count and consult your localization and UI/UX teams on limits. Lazy developers may try to convince you that hard coding strings is much faster than creating CMS tools or spreadsheet imports. Don't hardcode strings. It results in bugs, inconsistencies, and a myriad of other issues. Just don't do it, okay? Use the spreadsheet.

## Content management systems and narrative tools

If you can invest time in your development schedule and/or budget for robust tooling for your string management and narrative design, you will find that editing, testing, and localizing your text will be much easier throughout development. I could write an entire book on narrative tool and CMS design, but here are a few things to consider when creating or evaluating them for your game:

1. **Versioning:** Being able to show the iterations of strings and narrative over time can help you avoid replicating work and add valuable context to developers who are testing.
2. **Character Limits:** Implementing character limits directly into the tools you use to create the strings can save a lot of time.
3. **Languages and Localization:** Being able to easily track and manage the strings in the languages your game supports in one system will save you time and money. Make sure to consider that longer languages such as German, require you to limit your character counts by as much as 30% for UI elements like buttons if you do not have a robust responsive UI system built into your game engine.
4. **Context:** It is essential for the game's developers, voiceover artists, testers, and localizers to be able to have additional context for each string in the game. This should be any relevant links to wireframes, screenshots, explanations of idioms or slang, character insights, narrative context, or design documentation.
5. **Testing Tools:** If you are using any variables or triggers in your narrative systems it is essential to be able to easily and readily test and edit these quickly and safely. While many narrative designers can code, having them directly edit or input that code introduces a lot of risk and overhead.

6. **Visual Branching Tools:** Using visual tools to map out and preview branching narrative will allow you to easily debug your branching and can help you visually track the complexity of your systems. There are lots of great and free tools available such as Inkle, Twine, or Yarnspinner that your team can use.

7. **Export Formats:** Being able to export your strings in a variety of formats can save you a lot of time and help avoid human error in your localization, build, or voiceover workflows.

## Different audiences, different documentation

It is important to gain an understanding of what documents work best for you and your team. Below I've created a table based on my experience, but since every team and game is different I recommend coming at this with an experimental mindset and seeing what works best for your situation.

A few other important considerations when creating your documents:

| FORMAT | BEST AUDIENCE |
| --- | --- |
| Story Synopsis Deck | Executives and directors, marketing and communications. Good for onboarding new hires also. |
| Story Bible | Narrative designers, writers, concept artists |
| Story Bible Wiki | Game team, community, QA |
| World Bible Wiki | Game team, community QA |
| Story Synopsis Comic(s) or | Game team, marketing and communication, community |
| Cinematic storyboards | Game team, marketing and communication, community |
| Individual Character Bios | Artists, writers, designers |
| Character Toolkit | Artists, designers |
| Game Script | Creative directors, writers, designers, artists |
| Strings Spreadsheet | Writers, designers, localizers/globalization, QA |
| Content Management System (CMS) and Narrative Tools | Writers, narrative designers, localizers/globalization, marketing, QA |
| Metaphor spreadsheet | Writers, designers |
| Anything else your game team needs | There will always be something. Seriously, I've never worked on a single game that didn't have something come up that was custom. |

## Make them searchable and translation tool friendly

a. If your team is planning on using AI tools anytime in the future, you will be happy that you used a format compatible with those tools. It is a giant pain to transfer documentation, so talk to your tech director or lead dev before you get started.

b. Sometimes, someone just needs to know the name of a specific mushroom or skill, and they don't want to read your entire tome on the origins of said mushroom or skill to find it.

c. Not everyone speaks your language, and writers (myself included) tend to get verbose and idiomatic, which isn't friendly to non-native speakers.

d. Establish naming conventions early for files and stay consistent. Work with the game team and localization to determine what will work best for them.

### Link them to each other and give the whole team view access

a. Don't be precious about who can see it, but be very precious about who can edit it.

b. When you get that new intern and they are eagerly perusing game documents, you will thank me for this later. It allows people to browse and dive as deep as they want without having to bug you for access. It also empowers the team members excited about the story to become evangelists and experts.

### Know that they will change, constantly

a. Make sure everything can be edited and maintained easily.

b. Keep up a strict archive regimen as things get changed or retconned

c. Keep track of versioning so that when the director who asked you to change a thing two years ago asks why it was changed, you can show them.

World-building is an essential part of the game narrative process. And by leveraging what we understand about procedural and declarative knowledge when building our world's icebergs, we can create amazing environments and stories that are intuitive and memorable. In the next chapter we'll talk about how to translate this world into game verbs and core loops that engage the player in what they came for... play!

# BIBLIOGRAPHY

Baker, Carlos. *Hemingway: The Writer As Artist*. Princeton University Press, 1972.

Derby, Matthew. "Nuff Said: Comics as Design Documentation." *GDC Vault*, 2014, https://www.gdcvault.com/play/1020456/-Nuff-Said-Comics-as. Accessed 28 Dec 2023.

Fullerton, Tracy. *Game Design Workshop: A Playcentric Approach to Creating Innovative Games*. CRC Press, 2018.

Hamid, Naficy. *An Accented Cinema: Exilic and Diasporic Filmmaking*. Princeton University Press, 2001.

Hocking, Clint. "Ludonarrative dissonance in Bioshock: the problem of what the game is about." *Well Played 1.0: Video Games, Value and Meaning*, edited by Drew Davidson, ETC Press, 2009. Accessed 7 February 2023.

Jemisin, NK. "Growing Your Iceberg." *N.K. Jemisin*, https://nkjemisin.com/wp-content/uploads/2015/08/WDWebinar.pdf. Accessed 12 March 2023.

Kahneman, Daniel. *Thinking, Fast and Slow*. Farrar, Straus and Giroux, 2013.

Locke, Charley. "N.K. Jemisin Has a Plan for Diversity in Science Fiction." *WIRED*, 10 August 2016, https://www.wired.com/2016/08/n-k-jemisin-plan-diversity-science-fiction/. Accessed 12 March 2023.

Norman, Don. *The Design of Everyday Things*. Basic Books, 2014.

Robertson, David, and Bill Breen. *Brick by Brick: How LEGO Rewrote the Rules of Innovation and Conquered the Global Toy Industry*. Crown, 2014.

Rowan Tulloch, Catherine Hoad & Helen Young (2019) Riot grrrl gaming: gender, sexuality, race, and the politics of choice in *Gone Home*, Continuum, 33:3, 337–350, DOI:10.1080/10304 312.2019.1567685

Schell, Jesse. *The Art of Game Design*. Taylor & Francis, 2008.

Schmidt, Eric, and Jonathan Rosenberg. *How Google Works*. John Murray Press, 2014.

Swink, Steve. *Game Feel: A Game Designer's Guide to Virtual Sensation*. Taylor & Francis, 2009.

*"The Bulwer Lytton Fiction Contest."* The Bulwer Lytton Fiction Contest: Home, San Jose State University, 1982, https://www.bulwer-lytton.com/. Accessed 25 July 2023.

# PART 2

# Action

# Let the Player Play

# 4

---

## INTRODUCTION

---

Creating intuitive gameplay allows your players to immerse themselves in the experience while they experiment with the game's systems and actions. Games are complex systems, which means that learning them often takes time. Understanding how to teach your players the rules of the game without interrupting their fun is an essential part of making sure they have a good experience. In this chapter, we'll discuss ways to avoid making your player into a passive observer so you can let them do what they came to do: play.

### What You Will Learn in This Chapter

- Creating core gameplay loops
- Game verbs
- Creating intuitive experiences
- Difficulty and accessibility
- Compartmentalization

---

## FINDING THE CORE GAMEPLAY LOOP

---

You may recall from a previous chapter that a **core gameplay loop** refers to the repeating cycle of actions a player takes as they play. This is the set of actions or verbs that players repeat over and over again during their time with the game. Think "run, jump, shoot" in a platformer or "gather, build, defend" in a survival game. Gameplay loops indicate moment-to-moment actions, creating micro activities and goals that help the player progress through the game and its world.

DOI: 10.1201/9781003342977-7

Designers should avoid thinking about moment-to-moment gameplay in isolation, however. In the web series *Extra Credits*, James Portnow discusses how important it is to have a holistic understanding of the core loop's integration into intermediate and macro goals. In the episode "The Real Core Loop—What Every Game Has In Common," he breaks down what he sees as the key steps shared by all gameplay loops, regardless of genre:

- Define your objective
- Gather information
- Form a hypothesis on how to achieve your goal
- Test your hypothesis
- Observe results

Those of you who have read Chapter 2 might find this eerily familiar. That is because good core loops allow the player to embody their inner scientist in a way that feels intuitive. They get to be a leveled-up Sherlock Holmes. And when the game development process mirrors this, we reinforce this. A player's journey begins with a simple but profound step: understanding their objective. This objective is not just a beacon illuminating their path; it's the core intrigue that propels them forward in the story. In *Hades* (Supergiant), this objective is for the main character, Zagreus, to escape the underworld. The goal is crystal clear. This is signposted to the player through dialogue, action, and the loop of death and revival that occurs throughout the game.

As Zagreus moves through the labyrinthine underworld, the player actively gathers information about the world and the characters within it. The landscape of *Hades* reinforces the death and revival loop through the narrative choice of setting it in the underworld. Every boon the player obtains, every snippet of dialogue they hear, and every room they explore helps them piece together a strategic puzzle that guides them on how to proceed. This repetitive loop leads to **mastery** of the game's mechanics.

With their objective clear and their information in hand, the player begins to form a hypothesis on how to escape the underworld. This hypothesis might involve choosing certain power-ups or weapons over others, determining which gods to seek favor from, or deciding the most effective way to navigate the treacherous terrain.

Once the player forms their plan, it's time to put it to the test. With every swing of Zagreus' weapon and every step through the underworld's echoing halls, the player tests their assumptions and hones their strategies. Perhaps their strategy works, bringing them closer to the surface, or maybe it falls short, sending Zagreus back to the House of Hades to try again. Either way, the game responds with feedback, turning the player's performance into a learning opportunity.

## Applying UX Principles to the Core Loop

This reinforcing loop allows players to safely experiment when designers effectively use UX principles to support their learning. In Chapter 1, we explored Neilsen's 10 heuristic principles for usability, and if we examine this loop through the lens of those heuristics, we can tie them to the design choices the team at Supergiant has made to support player learning and understanding:

- **Visibility of System Status**: In *Hades*, the HUD is clear and easy to understand. The health, boons, and other status indicators are always visible, allowing the player to easily view their current state as they navigate the underworld. The environments—the different stages of the underworld— also change to reflect and reinforce player progress. This information influences the player's decision-making process in the hypothesis formation stage.
- **Match between System and the Real World**: *Hades* uses familiar symbols and metaphors to present information, making the gameplay understandable and relatable. Real-world foods such as gyros and pomegranates offer power boosts, and the metaphor of mythological resurrection directly mirrors the actions of the core mastery loop while reinforcing the end game goal.
- **User Control and Freedom**: The game offers Zagreus—and, by extension, the player—the freedom to choose his path, power-ups, and strategies. This player agency is crucial when forming and testing hypotheses, allowing the player to experiment and fail or succeed accordingly.
- **Consistency and Standards**: *Hades* adheres to game conventions in its design, such as using red to signify danger and green for health. Furthermore, by tying the different skills to well-known figures in mythology, the designers have created a standardization system that is intuitive while employing enough narrative flavor to be engaging and fun to learn. Dionysus grants boons that intoxicate enemies, while Zeus's favor will imbue lightning into Zagreus's attacks. These metaphorical representations of what amounts to statistical adjustments create a consistent and coherent context for players.
- **Error Prevention**: Failures in *Hades* are opportunities for learning rather than mere setbacks, allowing the player to reassess their hypothesis and revise their strategy. Every time Zagreus is sent back to the halls of the underworld, he gains valuable information and progresses toward avoiding the same errors in his next escape attempt.
- **Recognition Rather than Recall**: *Hades* places all options and relevant information in front of the player rather than making them remember it all. Icons for power-ups, dialogues with gods, and other features facilitate the hypothesis formation and testing phases.
- **Flexibility and Efficiency of Use:** Catering to both novice and experienced players, the game allows for varied play styles and strategies. Different routes, weapons, and power-ups provide flexibility in hypothesis testing. I personally appreciate the mode that makes the game easier with each death, as it has allowed me to progress and learn in the game at my own pace.
- **Aesthetic and Minimalist Design:** *Hades* has a visually stunning yet uncluttered design. The game provides a lot of information without overwhelming the player, supporting the process of information gathering. The art style (aesthetic) is consistent throughout and carries a lot of the narrative weight

with its environmental storytelling and character representation. The visual weight of the various visual elements reflects their importance to the player during gameplay.

- **Help Users Recognize, Diagnose, and Recover from Errors**: When the player's hypothesis doesn't work out, and Zagreus is sent back to the House of Hades, the game provides feedback on what went wrong, helping the player diagnose their error, recover, and formulate a new strategy. The character of Hypnos, for example, often has pithy or clever dialogue related to the latest battle.

- **Help and Documentation:** Throughout the game's repeating loops, the player receives feedback in the form of character dialogue that comments on their progress, often giving helpful hints. The game also provides a helpful Codex of the Underworld that gets populated with information as the player progresses.

Well-crafted core gameplay loops, combined with UX best practices, can create a beautiful mastery loop for your players. As they engage with the game's repeated actions, they are able to gain mastery and overcome greater challenges. The player should be able to discern the success and failure states in the core loop, along with the spectrum of possibilities available to them within those states. As the game progresses, the action should repeat with increasing difficulty, allowing the player to practice the skill.

To accomplish this, designers introduce the concept of the core actions by showing those actions within the context of the game world and then motivating them to engage on their own by placing an objective or goal in their path. In the first level of *Super Mario Brothers* (Nintendo), Mario is placed in an environment that has a big gold box with a question mark on it in the air. This enticing object is what motivates the player to jump, teaching them one of the key actions in the core loop (Figure 4.1).

**FIGURE 4.1**    The gold box in Super Mario Brothers helps provide feedback for engaging in core verbs.

It is essential to playtest this early experience. Your core loop is what the player will experience throughout the entire game, and if they do not understand the "what," "how," and "why" of the actions available to them, they will become incredibly frustrated. If your player can't articulate this immediate objective and what is expected of them within the first five minutes (in mobile and free-to-play games, this timing is closer to 30 seconds), then you need to revisit that introductory experience.

I'm not suggesting that the player needs to understand the ultimate end goal for the entire game experience, but they should be able to understand the actions they need to take within the game's introductory phase. The key here is ensuring that the player knows what is expected of them. Mario doesn't need to know where Princess Peach will be at the end of the game, he only needs to know that he needs to rescue her. Once those expectations are established, you can introduce the action in a low-stakes environment, allowing the player to fail, succeed, observe, and learn. Feedback is essential in this phase. Good feedback helps players gauge their progress, understand their mistakes, and adjust their strategy accordingly. It's the element that guides a player's path toward improvement.

In addition, you should periodically introduce high-difficulty activities around the action, allowing the player to test their mastery. Mario encounters many challenges on his journey to rescue Princess Peach. He navigates rotating walls of fire, destroys hordes of enemies, and battles Bowser. These tests of mastery will keep the player engaged while giving them consistent feedback.

# From Core Loop to Mastery Loop

Mastery, at its core, is all about learning, and learning often involves cycles of practice, evaluation, and improvement. Well-designed game experiences are structured to guide players through this process by using pacing and checkpoints. **Pacing** is essential in forming the backbone of a game's learning curve. The timing with which the game introduces players to new concepts needs to match the player's skill growth, resulting in an optimal state of engagement. This is crucial for setting the difficulty curve because it ensures that players are neither overwhelmed with difficulty too early nor bored from too little challenge. **Checkpoints** serve as moments of rest and reflection. They're the "save points" in the learning process that prevent a player from losing progress. A well-placed checkpoint not only reduces frustration but also reinforces the sense of progress and achievement.

In *Beat Saber* (Beat Games), players slash blocks to the rhythm of a pulsating soundtrack, a concept that's simple in theory but can be demanding in practice. The game slowly escalates the challenge, starting with slower songs and fewer blocks. It gradually increases the tempo, complexity (the sequence and placement), and number of blocks. The precise pacing allows players to master simple mechanics before they are thrown into an entrancing, rhythm-fueled flurry. Much like the crescendo in a piece of music, the thrill is in the flow state achieved, the natural feeling of rhythm akin to dancing. Feedback comes in the form of score multipliers and clear indications of whether a swipe was a success or a failure, which is magnified by the physical inputs. *Beat Saber*'s checkpoints are the song completions themselves. Mastery comes through repetition, and each new song provides a fresh challenge.

*Dark Souls* (From Software) provides an entirely different experience. Its pacing involves fluctuating periods of intense combat and quieter exploration, gradually leading players toward more challenging areas. In *Dark Souls*, the game design embodies a philosophy of "tough but fair." It tests players' patience and skills with unforgiving combat, yet its pacing is meticulously designed. Instead of constant brutal combat, the game presents periods of exploration and quieter moments between battles, giving the player time to catch their breath and learn from previous encounters. Each area of the game is a standalone gauntlet that demands mastery in order to progress. *Dark Souls* takes players by the hand, guides them to a cliff, and then dares them to fly. Feedback is often harsh but instructive—players learn from each defeat. Each bonfire in *Dark Souls* is a haven, a place to rest and level up, and, more importantly, to establish a new starting point. These bonfires underscore the game's central theme of perseverance in the face of adversity, reinforcing the learning process by encouraging players to push on and master what lies ahead.

But as much as I appreciate *Dark Souls* as a designer, I have a confession to make – I've never played it for more than a few hours. It's just too punishing for my skill level, and I don't find the core loop engaging enough to overcome the challenges that often make me feel stuck and frustrated with little to no agency. For this reason, I was delighted when I picked up *Elden Ring*, a successor to the series by the same developer. While *Elden Ring* retains the core gameplay experience of its spiritual predecessors, it sets this experience in an open world. This seemingly small change opens the game up to a whole new host of players, giving choices on how they want to engage with the game's challenges, and the agency to explore other regions when they feel stuck. I'll discuss difficulty and accessibility in detail in a later section but I think it is worth noting that *Elden Ring* sold 20 million copies in its first year of release, whereas *Dark Souls 3* took four years to sell 10 million copies. And while the open world was not the only element that contributed to this success, it most certainly was a primary driver.

In terms of pacing, *Chicory: A Colorful Tale* (Finji) is brilliantly designed. The game puts players in the shoes of an anthropomorphic dog with the responsibility of wielding a magical brush that is used to color in a monochrome world. While the initial tasks are simple—filling in color here and there—the challenges gradually increase. This encourages players to grow, learn, and ultimately master the art of wielding the magical paintbrush. In a world devoid of color, it's the player's growing mastery that brings vibrancy back—a compelling narrative hook that makes the gameplay experience all the more rewarding. The pacing is such that players have enough time to understand and master one aspect of the game before another is introduced, facilitating a steady learning curve. As the player colors objects, characters react and new paths can open up. Seeing the world change due to your actions provides instant and satisfying feedback, and it shows the player how their growing mastery over the paintbrush can influence the world.

Checkpoints in *Chicory* come in the form of picnic spots. At these spots, players can save their game, get hints, and converse with a friendly character to get feedback on their journey. These rest stops are sprinkled across the world map, giving players regular intervals to consolidate their learning, experiment with their painting techniques, and reflect on their journey.

## Bloom's Taxonomy for Learning

**Bloom's taxonomy** is a hierarchical framework that classifies various stages of learning. Much like a well-designed mastery loop, each stage of the taxonomy is designed to engage the learner and promote active participation. Part of the appeal of video games is that they have the potential to elegantly encompass all six levels of Bloom's taxonomy. Players memorize, understand, apply, analyze, evaluate, and create—all within the confines of the game's world. They are not just passive content consumers but active participants in a learning process, and they undergo this process not because they have to, but because they want to. Let's look at these stages of learning through the lens of *Minecraft* (Mojang), a game that emulates this potential extremely well (Figure 4.2).

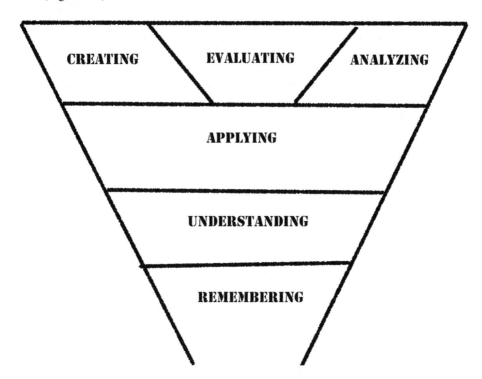

**FIGURE 4.2** Blooms taxonomy.

The lowest rung on Bloom's ladder is **memory**, also known as remembering. At this stage, learners interact with the knowledge they've acquired and understood, just as users interact with an application. This process often involves some form of memorization, similar to "bookmarking" or pulling up facts in a learning context. This stage of the taxonomy mirrors the initial steps of game onboarding, where players are introduced to basic controls and game mechanics. In *Minecraft*, this would be equivalent to learning the basic controls—moving, jumping, and interacting with blocks (procedural knowledge). Just as the players must memorize the inputs, interactions, and their respective actions, so too must a learner recall facts or concepts from their studies.

The **understanding** stage is where learners move beyond simple recall to grasp a concept's "how" and "why." Within the game world, players begin to learn the consequences of their actions by understanding cause and effect. For instance, in *Minecraft*, players quickly recognize that chopping down trees provides wood, an essential resource for survival and construction (declarative knowledge). Mirroring the mechanic of resource acquisition and crafting with the real-world metaphor of logging and building wooden structures facilitates understanding for the player.

At the **applying** stage, learners translate knowledge and comprehension into action, leading to creative experimentation. In games, this happens when the player begins to interact more actively with the game world, using the knowledge they've acquired and understood. In the *Minecraft* context, players may apply their understanding of the game's physics and resource mechanics to build complex structures or survive against hordes of creepers. This is much like applying a mathematical formula to solve a real-world problem.

As we move up to **analyzing**, learners break a complex whole into its constituent parts and understand the relationship between those parts. In a game, this happens when players begin to break down complicated structures or strategies to improve their gameplay. In *Minecraft*, players might analyze the effectiveness of different strategies as they fight creepers or the resource cost of different items to optimize their crafting and building.

**Evaluating**, the second-highest level of Bloom's taxonomy, involves learners making judgments about the value of material or methods. In a classroom, this might look like critiquing an argument's logic or assessing the effectiveness of an experimental design.

Likewise, a *Minecraft* player could evaluate a mob farm's efficiency or analyze the aesthetics of another player's structure.

Finally, we reach the pinnacle of the taxonomy: **creating**. At this point, learners produce new ideas, products, or perspectives. In an educational context, it might mean writing a dissertation, composing a piece of music, or designing an experiment. In gaming, this could involve players creating new strategies and character builds, or even modifying the game environment itself. In *Minecraft*, this could take the form of designing and building a magnificent castle or an automated farming system. YouTube is filled with videos showcasing the marvelous creations players have made; a functional computer, Greek temple, replica of the Titanic, even Middle Earth. Games like *Minecraft* offer the perfect digital playground for the creating stage, allowing players to shape the game world and create complex structures, limited only by their imaginations.

# Game Verbs

Taking your core loop mechanics and turning them into a series of **verbs** can build an intuitive bridge between declarative and procedural knowledge.

In Kaitlin Tremblay's GDC Talk "Storytelling with Verbs," she underscores the importance of defining game verbs early on to guide storytelling and UX decisions throughout the early stages of development. And it's not hard to see why. Knowing which actions your players will take most often can give you a scaffold around which you can build your narrative and user experience. These verbs can enhance player immersion and provide a rich context for the game world. They can also convey the characters' emotional states, creating deeper connections between players and characters, ultimately driving player engagement and retention.

## Mapping verbs to the player experience

When designing the player experience and game narrative, understanding and prioritizing the game verbs is a helpful early exercise that can ensure you create intuitive interactions. I like to visually map my game verbs in a variety of ways (Figure 4.3).

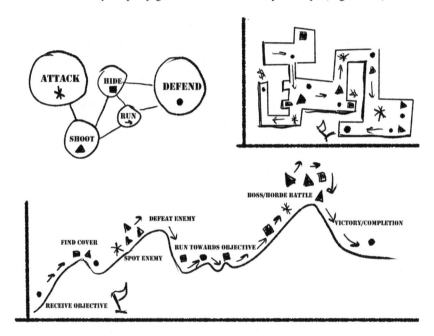

**FIGURE 4.3**   Verb mapping.

The first is to rank the game verbs and visually map their relationships. When ranking, I use a few different parameters to determine the prevalence and priority of the game actions:

- **Coreness**: A highly technical term, I know. But the first parameter you should examine is whether the game verb is a part of the core loop. The closer a verb is to the loop, the more important it is to tie it into the game world and avoid friction in the user experience.
- **Intensity:** How much cognitive load does this action require? What is the desired emotional state for the player when they are engaging with the verbs?

Does the action support this emotion? Does the player need to engage in multiple actions or inputs simultaneously? The answers to these questions will help you measure the intensity of the experience and ensure that you are not creating ludonarrative dissonance or additional cognitive load that can break immersion.

- **Longevity:** Understanding whether the verb and action are used throughout the entire player journey or simply during a beat in the experience will help you make informed design decisions about the timing of story beats, introduction of new concepts, and how deep the player needs to go to access information.
- **Frequency:** The frequency with which a verb appears, particularly when combined with longevity, should inform its inclusion in the "core-ness" as well as the ease of its use.

If your team has trouble connecting game verbs to the core story and experience, I recommend running a game verbs brainstorming session around the actions before diving into the details. Word association around player verbs is a great way to get started. It helps prevent ludonarrative dissonance, ensures that the team is aligned, and is a good way to include everyone in the narrative process.

Take a look at your verbs and ask yourself why the player is taking these actions. From there, create a list of goals for the player. Divide your goals into both short- and long-term. Once you have your lists of verbs and goals, take time to think about what could prevent players from achieving the goals by highlighting actions and verbs that counteract or conflict with the core goals and actions. Use this list of conflicts and obstacles as the foundation for the challenges you create throughout the game. They will be helpful for your rewards and progression systems later on.

I also like to map game verbs by creating a timeline of use alongside the player's journey. Mapping verbs can help you accomplish several things at once:

- Determining when and how to introduce new concepts to the game
- Prioritizing the primary verbs in your player journey and mapping actions that deepen them by creating obstacles or enriching the experience
- Mapping the narrative design and plot points to their associated actions

To create a player journey map, we begin by charting the course—by understanding who our players are, what motivates them, and where they experience pain points. To gather this data, we turn to the UX research methods we discussed in Chapter 2: interviews, surveys, usability tests, and so on.

The journey map is especially powerful when you combine it with an emotion map, which we'll discuss in a later chapter. There are a variety of formats and structures you can use, but I like to tie mine to the narrative structure I am using. Jenova Chen, in his 2013 GDC talk "Designing Journey," describes tying their team's player journey to a three-act structure, an approach inspired by stage and screen storytelling techniques, and the hero's journey, courtesy of our friendly neighborhood mythologist, Joseph Campbell. Each act introduces a new game mechanic that aligns perfectly with the story's rhythm (If you need a refresher course, both of these structures are discussed in Chapter 1 of this book).

Act I sets up the narrative. In *Journey* (thatgamecompany), the first act presents a desolate world and a mysterious mountain, filling the player with a sense of awe and curiosity. These feelings drive players to explore the game world, understand its cryptic ruins, and determine their own role in this world. In the beginning, players are presented with a blank canvas, a vast desert—and a single, simple game mechanic. Players can move around the world and explore. They can walk, and, oh boy, they can slide. Just like our budding hero, they're thrown into this unknown world with just a bare-bones grasp of what they can do.

During these initial stages, players are alone in a vast, sprawling desert with just the dunes for company. The environment mirrors the hero's initial solitude, their life before the adventure begins. It's a kind of preparatory isolation, an overture before the dance commences. As players trudge along, they soon discover they can jump and even fly for a short while by interacting with floating pieces of cloth. The unlocking of these verbs creates a gentle, wondrous moment of revelation, a perfect symphony of curiosity and discovery. This echoes Campbell's "Call to Adventure" and "Supernatural Aid" beats in which the hero receives a call to leave their known world and is provided with a tool or guide.

Then, as players venture further into the unknown, they spot another figure in the distance. This new anonymous companion also brings new verbs, recharging the jump ability, calling out for the player to provide emotional support, or leading them to hidden areas. This maps onto the "Supernatural Aid" stage of the hero's journey, where the hero encounters someone or something that provides guidance. This mechanic of mutual aid and companionship is deepened in the later stages of the game, where environments become more challenging.

Act II develops the conflict. Whenever the player enters a new area, they're offered both a new mechanic and a subtle change in the game's tone. The addition of the flying mechanic coincides with entering a mysterious, almost magical underground city, marking a shift from the initial awe and isolation to intrigue and exploration. It's here, in the midst of danger and fear, that the power of companionship is underscored. Together, the player and their companion will navigate an ominous tower, providing solace and assistance to each other amidst the looming threat. They're not competing. They're not fighting. They're just . . . journeying. Together.

The game transitions from exploration to imminent threat when players enter a dark, foreboding tower. Here, players must hide from monstrous flying creatures—an entirely new mechanic that introduces an element of fear and suspense, mirroring the "Road of Trials" stage of the hero's journey, in which the hero faces their greatest fear. This is where the threats become tangible. The winds howl, and creatures lurk in the darkness. The player's journey becomes arduous, stirring up feelings of fear and anxiety. The treacherous journey to the mountain peak, the epicenter of the conflict, begins.

Act III brings resolution when players reach the mountain peak. As the player climbs the snowy mountain, they are stripped of their flying ability, forcing them to trudge slowly up the peak. This mirrors the "Apotheosis" stage of the hero's journey, in which the hero endures a great sacrifice or hardship and achieves their goal. The player is bathed in light, regains their lost ability, and takes flight. It's an ethereal, poignant experience, a cathartic release of all the fear and anxiety that builds in Act II. Here, another player's companionship becomes less about practical assistance and more about emotional support. It's an embodiment of the "The Ultimate Boon" and "Magic Flight" stages of the hero's journey—where the hero faces their greatest challenge but also experiences their greatest triumph. In *Journey*, this triumph is shared.

In the end, the player's calls become not just a means of communication but also an expression of shared experience and emotion. The player isn't just signaling their location; they're expressing joy, surprise, fear, triumph. In a world without words, these calls become a language of emotion.

So how does this tie back to player journey mapping? Imagine the story, combined with our timeline of game verbs, as a compass that indicates the experience we are taking our player on. By visually mapping this, we can identify areas that might be missing key elements, or places we need to amplify or heighten the action of the player experience to match the same energy we have in our story. The team at thatgamecompany even used their player journey map to inform the design of the environment, matching the peaks and valleys of the landscape to the emotional highs and lows of the overall story.

## STARTING IN MEDIA RES TO GET YOUR PLAYER INTO THE ACTION

*In media res* is a Latin phrase that translates to "in the middle of things." It's also the name of a common literary technique in which a story starts midstream. This construction is also often used in games. Sometimes, the best way to kickstart the player's journey is to drop them into the center of a tale that has already begun.

Films, television shows, and literature commonly begin in media res. For instance, Homer's epic poem *The Odyssey* starts when the Trojan War has already been over for ten years. And in the hit television show *Breaking Bad*, the viewer is introduced to the lead character, Walter White, as he drives through the desert in an RV stuffed with dead bodies and meth-making equipment.

One of my favorite examples of a game that begins in media res is *Uncharted 2* (Naughty Dog). It opens with Nathan Drake waking up, bleeding profusely, in a wrecked train car hanging precipitously off a cliff. By dropping the player at the center of the action in the middle of the story, the game engages players more deeply, moving from passive observation to active speculation.

In *Persona 5* (Atlus), the player is introduced to the setting and characters through the game's final scene, which then loops back on itself to start again at the beginning in a kishotenketsu (mentioned in Chapter 1) form. Each accompanying loop in the narrative centers around changing the internal mindset of a different character by entering and battling through their mind in addition to fighting their existential demons and monsters. Between these activities, the player lives a fairly regular high school existence: doing homework, going on dates, eating in restaurants, and so on. Each unexpected turn arises with a new character who must be helped and whose mind palace must be explored. This loop repeats as the player explores new mind palaces, slowly revealing the plot as they complete each iteration. At the finale, the player is returned to the opening scene from the beginning of the game, bringing closure to the prior events.

# CREATING INTUITIVE EXPERIENCES

Once you have drafted the player journey map, you can use it as a blueprint for introducing new verbs, systems, or controls. If your players have trouble immersing themselves in the game experience, they will have trouble engaging with the story. Therefore, it is equally important to **eliminate friction** when it comes to your core game verbs. Imagine, if you will, being presented with a controller or keyboard for the first time and starting a game with no instructions or tutorials to guide you. Yet, within minutes you're comfortably navigating the world, knowing instinctively which button to press, which path to take. This is intuitive design at its best, creating a frictionless, seamless experience that allows players to concentrate on the unfolding narrative and gameplay rather than the mechanics of interaction. Intuitive UX is about more than just designing a game that is easy to play. It's also about creating a game that feels natural to play. It's about building an experience that gently guides the player down a path of discovery, using a **balance** of **challenge** and **reward**, complexity and simplicity, to create an experience that feels at once new and familiar.

In essence, intuitive UX is about disappearing, about making the controls and interfaces fade into the background so that the game itself can take center stage. It's about removing barriers and creating a conduit for the player to become truly immersed in the world the game presents. That is the ultimate goal of UX design in video games: to become invisible in service of the player's experience. We spoke about UX foundations in Chapter 1. By mindfully applying those foundations to our player journey and core loop, we can create a more intuitive experience for the player and get out of their way.

**Feedback** gives players a clear understanding of their actions' outcomes. Good feedback helps players gauge their progress, understand their mistakes, and adjust their strategy accordingly. It's the element that guides a player's path toward improvement. We've discussed Don Norman's user-centric design principle of feedback in interactive systems in Chapter 1, but I think it is especially relevant when it comes to creating intuitive experiences.

**Visibility** ensures that a user's actions and their outcomes are clearly perceptible. Immediate feedback, following closely on the heels of an action, helps users associate their actions with the system's responses. When players try to guess a word in *Wordle* (Josh Wardle/New York Times), the game instantly color-codes each letter—green for correctly placed, yellow for present but misplaced, and gray for absent. This instant and unambiguous feedback nudges the player toward that elusive five-letter word one color-coded tile at a time. It's elegant in its simplicity and remarkably effective in keeping players engaged.

While feedback needs to be noticeable, it shouldn't disrupt the user's workflow or tasks—this is the principle of non-disruption. *Bastion* (Supergiant) is a game lauded for its dynamic narration, which provides immediate narrative feedback that's deeply woven into the gameplay. The narrator's gravelly voice recounts the player's every move, victory, and blunder, all in real time; the player's actions shape the story, and the story, in turn, informs their actions. This virtuosic intertwining of the interactive and the narrative breathes life into the ruins of Caelondia.

*Outer Wilds* (Mobius Digital, Annapurna) uses a more subtle approach. The feedback is woven into the narrative and environment. Discoveries, be they alien ruins or cryptic messages, often serve as feedback mechanisms that reflect the player's progress in unraveling the mysteries of the universe. The real-time celestial mechanics provide a feedback loop on a grand scale. The game's innovative 22-minute time loop acts as a recurring checkpoint, providing a sense of progression with every loop. In *Outer Wilds*, the player starts each time loop afresh from the same point, but with newly gained knowledge. It's the game's clever way of employing repetition without redundancy.

There are many ways that video games provide feedback to players, but I like to divide this feedback into two distinct categories: **contextual** and **informative.** Contextual feedback is relevant to a player's actions and their situational context, whereas informative feedback communicates the result of those actions, providing guidance for future decisions and corrective measures in the case of errors. In *Papers, Please* (Lucas Pope), the game's interface sounds are more than just window dressing; they serve as integral contextual feedback mechanisms. The thud of the stamp, the rustle of paper, the harsh buzz of a discrepancy—all serve to create a sense of immediacy and **tangibility**. The evolution of the core loop creates informative feedback by showing the player the consequences of the choices they make as they try to balance increasingly complex and opaque rules against a pressure to earn enough money to survive. It's a game that transforms bureaucracy into a poignant narrative experience.

# Interface Organization

Compartmentalization and mapping of interfaces are crucial in crafting intuitive experiences in game design. In both compartmentalization and mapping, the goal is the same: to ensure that the player can quickly and easily access the information they need with as little friction as possible. The layout should feel natural and intuitive, taking into consideration both the game's unique requirements and the general principles of human-computer interaction.

**Compartmentalization** refers to the ability of the game experience to hold information for the player and provide it when necessary. This allows the player to focus on their immediate actions and goals within the game. Compartmentalization, in the context of interface organization, refers to the segregation of different game interface elements into self-contained units. The key to success is arranging these units in a way that makes logical sense to the player. This type of compartmentalization functions like a city map where each district serves a different purpose, yet they are all interconnected and form a cohesive whole. In a video game interface, compartmentalization allows us to break complex systems into manageable chunks. Instead of presenting the player with all the information at once—a cognitive deluge that would quickly become overwhelming—we can use compartmentalization to sort information into distinct, manageable sections.

In the *Final Fantasy* (Square Enix) series, battle options are neatly grouped together in one place, inventory in another, and character stats in yet another. Even within these compartments, further organization exists: potions are separated from weapons, magic spells from physical abilities. This approach allows players to quickly navigate to the information they need without having to sift through a jumble of unrelated data.

**Mapping** refers to the logical visual and organizational layout of these compartments, which can greatly influence a player's experience and intuition. We present the interface in a manner that feels intuitive to navigate, based on established patterns of human perception and cognition. *The Witcher 3: Wild Hunt* (CD Projekt Red) is a wonderful example of effective mapping; the game's radial menu presents the player with quick access to various potions, tools, and signs. It's a compact, organized way to represent multiple options without having the player navigate through a traditional linear menu. It leverages the gestalt principles of **proximity** and **similarity** in an elegant and consistent way. It's as if you're reaching into Geralt's own mind, echoing the immediacy of the in-game decision-making.

## Consistency and Error Prevention

Design consistency allows players to predict and respond to challenges, making difficulty an engaging pursuit rather than a source of frustration. I love adventure games and RPGs where rich, complicated narratives transport me into worlds with clever characters and deep systems. Unfortunately, the lack of design consistency and visibility in how those systems operate often results in me throwing my controller at my television. We as designers too often expect players to read our minds and discover how delightfully clever we are through their efforts.

Modern video games often strike a delicate balance between challenge and accessibility, familiarity and novelty. A well-designed game, developer Ben Lewis Evans argues in the GDC talk "To Err is to Play," delves deep into understanding human behavior and cognitive processes. Leveraging an understanding of player behavior and cognitive biases allows us as designers to build the experience around these existing behaviors, making the game feel more intuitive. Recognizing that to err is, indeed, to play, designers are empowered to craft experiences that resonate, entertain, and endure.

The complex systems and inputs of games require a lot of mental energy, and sometimes players momentarily forget their game objectives. One effective way to counter these **inattention errors** is by offering guiding tools that move with players, whether in the form of quest markers, in-context actions, pinned activities, or journals. Metroidvania games embed these tools directly into the game verbs, often reinforcing game mechanics before presenting new challenges, ensuring players are always prepared.

Another vital principle for minimizing friction is **input consistency**. When players hit a button or use a menu consistently throughout a game, they expect that behavior to stay the same throughout their experience. Players should never have to second-guess their actions, and a predictable control scheme forms the backbone of this. Nintendo, for instance, stands out not just for its unique control schemes, but also for its longstanding consistency. This consistency is further enriched by an unwavering use of iconography and color cues, which guides gameplay in an intuitive manner. If you do decide to break the consistency of your inputs (and this can be a valid design choice, we'll discuss this more in later examples), make sure you fully understand the implications of doing so.

## INPUTS: WHERE THE FINGERS MEET THE ACTIONS

The history of video game controllers has been one of evolution and innovation. A good controller doesn't merely allow you to play a game—it disappears in your hands, leaving you in a state of flow and pure engagement with the virtual world. Therefore, it is important to keep certain best practices in mind when mapping your game verbs and actions to their accompanying control schemes.

Designing haptic controls (controls with physical feedback properties) involves thinking about how a player's actions, via the controller or other haptic devices, translate into in-game actions. This is a multidisciplinary approach that considers the principles of game design, user interface design, and even the physiology of human perception. It takes an understanding of all the principles we've outlined in the past few chapters, plus a few more.

**Ergonomics:** The human hand has certain natural movements and grips, so controls that align with these movements tend to feel more natural. The first home console, the Magnavox Odyssey, released in the early 1970s, introduced simple controllers with knobs for controlling on-screen movement.

The size of the controller is also important to keep in mind, as it affects the angle and reach of the player's fingers during play. This may seem like common sense, but there have been numerous controllers over the history of game development that have violated core principles in ergonomics by being either too big or too heavy for players' hands. The first Microsoft Xbox controller was often criticized for its bulky design, but the subsequent controller made significant improvements.

For games intended to be played during long sessions, it's crucial to ensure that the controls are comfortable over time. This includes both the physical design and the way actions are mapped to the controls. For instance, actions that will be performed frequently should be easy to perform without causing strain or discomfort. The NES controller brought us the D-pad, a design still used today, but its rectangular design did not meet the principle of longevity for extended play sessions—the controller quickly grew uncomfortable in players' hands. The DualShock controller, however, has followed the principle of longevity with an ergonomic design suitable for long play sessions. Input frequency can be just as important as shape and placement-I have a distinct memory of getting a massive blister on my thumb in college from playing hours of *Tekken Tag Tournament* (Namco).

Phone and AR/VR headset manufacturers should take note of ergonomics, as their hardware varies widely in terms of size, weight, and support, which often restricts the amount of comfortable session length for players. I enjoy the immersion of VR experiences, but as long as the hardware involves a heavy, sweaty face box, my sessions with these devices will always be limited by the comfort of my face and neck.

**Intuitiveness:** The controller's shape and fit should help facilitate actions that feel smooth and intuitive for the player. For instance, the "pinch to zoom" gesture on a touchscreen maps well onto the real-world action it represents. *Pong* (Atari) uses a straightforward dial controller to move a paddle up and down. This minimalistic control scheme is easy to learn and understand, demonstrating the principle of intuitiveness (as well as simplicity, which we'll discuss next). *Katamari*

*Damacy* (Namco Bandai) uses the Playstation DualShock controller's twin joysticks in a way that is both innovative and intuitive. The sticks are used in combination to roll a ball around, a control scheme that perfectly mirrors the game's mechanic. It's a great example of mapping control design to in-game actions.

**Simplicity Versus Complexity:** The level of complexity in the controls should match the game's target demographic and the complexity of the game itself. A game designed for casual gamers or children might benefit from a simpler control scheme, while a simulation game might have a more complex scheme to give the player more control. The iconic Atari 2600 joystick is easily recognized due to its iconic design. This controller embodied simplicity with only one button and a single joystick. Nintendo's Wii remote changed the landscape by incorporating motion controls. It opened a whole new world of family friendly and social interactive possibilities while following the principle of simplicity.

Flight simulator controls, such as those created by the companies Thrustmaster and Logitech, are specialized machines that fit the complexity of games like *Microsoft Flight Simulator* (Microsoft). Often specializing to the point of mapping to specific planes such as the Air Bus, they are beautiful examples of complex immersive feedback controls that match the level of enthusiasm and investment of the player community that buys them. Many PC gaming keyboards will map to the complexity of specific games such as *League of Legends* (Riot) to optimize for inputs in fast-paced and competitive esports arenas.

**Difficulty**: Input difficulty should reflect the difficulty of the game's core loop. Initially, controls should be straightforward enough that players can understand and adapt. As players get accustomed to the feel and feedback of the controller, complexity can be gradually added. Then the difficulty should progressively increase in a balanced manner. *Angry Birds* (Rovio) uses a simple finger-pull interaction to mirror the casual physics mechanics. The difficulty comes from the amount of accuracy required in that interaction as the puzzles become more complex. Input doesn't always just involve the shape and the design of the control, it also refers to the way the player interacts with the controller over time. *Marvel vs. Capcom 2* (Capcom), on the other hand, uses a complicated button layout for a variety of attacks. It has a steep difficulty curve that can be rewarding to master, mirroring the competitive difficulty of the game.

**Frequency and Repetition**: High-frequency actions should be mapped to controls that are easy to access and require minimal effort, reducing the risk of user fatigue or discomfort. On the other hand, controls for less frequent actions can be located in less accessible positions. The NES controller was well suited to *Super Mario* (Nintendo) with its D-pad for movement and two buttons for actions (one for jumping and one for both running and executing skills). The repetitive jumping action was easily performed because the button was placed in a way that allowed the player to react quickly and intuitively.

**Feedback**: Feedback is crucial in any control scheme. Haptic feedback in particular can offer an extra dimension of immersion. It should be carefully calibrated not to overwhelm the player but to enhance the gaming experience. It can be used to signal events (such as getting hit), confirm actions, or even provide directional cues. The advent of the Sony PlayStation introduced the DualShock controller, notable for its inclusion of two analog sticks and its haptic feedback capabilities, giving a new layer of immersion. Sony's PlayStation 5 DualSense takes haptic feedback to a new level with adaptive triggers and sophisticated rumble technology for increased immersion. Kojima's *Death Stranding* takes advantage of the more complex controls by using the triggers to balance the character's load and mirror the friction required as they carry a backpack laden with goods across rough terrain, a mechanic that ties in closely with the game's themes of burden and balance. By mapping the interaction and feedback of the control triggers to the character actions, the designers are aligning the core loop mechanics to the controls in a thematic and contextual way. This creates immersion while also reinforcing and encouraging mastery.

**Consistency**: It is vital to be consistent in control schemes, both within a game and, if possible, with common standards across games. This lowers the learning curve for new players and improves the overall user experience. It ensures that players who are familiar with a series or a genre can easily pick up a new game and feel at home. Consistent controls also reduce the learning curve for new games, allowing players to focus on enjoying the new content rather than relearning the controls (though designers should never assume that the player has retained this knowledge from game to game- tutorials are still important to the early onboarding experience). The *Street Fighter* (Capcom) series, one of the most famous fighting game franchises, provides an excellent example of consistency in control schemes. Across all games in the series, the basic mechanics remain the same. For instance, the motion to use Ryu's Hadouken (a quarter-circle forward plus a punch button) has remained consistent since the original *Street Fighter II*. This consistency means that players can easily perform their favorite moves when going from one game in the series to another.

While not every controller design has been successful, each one has taught us valuable lessons about how to adhere to the principles of good design. It's crucial to test your controls with real players and make adjustments based on their feedback. This can help you uncover issues that weren't apparent in the design phase and lead to a more refined and player-friendly control scheme (Figure 4.4).

**FIGURE 4.4**  Controller evolution.

# Difficulty and Accessibility

A deep understanding of player **habit formation** can be a powerful tool in the designer's arsenal. By creating feedback loops that both challenge and accommodate player habits, a game can continuously evolve. We should never mock our players for wanting a more accessible experience. Modes like the "chicken hat" in *Metal Gear* (Konami) contribute to the toxic community that permeates our medium, alienating large groups of players by showcasing their choice in the form of an absurd hat on Solid Snake's grizzly head. While I agree with the common saying that "a game designed for everyone is a game designed for no one," I see this adage used too often as a way to justify treating our players poorly.

The more difficult a game is, the more agency we should afford the player in terms of how they can overcome its challenges. *Psychonauts 2* (Double Fine/Microsoft) does a masterful job of giving players flexible difficulty options, allowing them to change multiple settings, even turning off damage for tougher battles. This eliminates stress and reduces the mental load for the player, allowing them to enjoy the game's delightful puzzles and world.

Playing with the concept of difficulty by having a deeper understanding of cognitive errors and behaviors also creates opportunities for designers to innovate. By understanding how the brain processes information, designers can craft increasingly engaging puzzles or challenges. *Dead Space* (EA Motive) provides a unique example when its control scheme is momentarily inverted during an intense sequence, providing a jarring yet memorable experience. By understanding that consistency is a key part of habit formation, and by changing the control scheme during a high-stress situation, they increased the level of difficulty exponentially (this cognitive error is called a double control slip). Adding another layer, the intentional use of perceptual confusion—where objects or elements look strikingly similar—can elevate the challenge in hidden object games or visual puzzles.

Addressing **accessibility** is an essential facet of inclusive game design. Such thoughtful design choices make sure that a diverse player base can relish the game experience without impediments. It's crucial to note that a one-size-fits-all approach does not apply when it comes to accessibility. I could write an entire book about accessibility options and choices in games, but here are a few key elements to consider:

## *Visual options*

- **Color Blindness:** It's estimated that around 300 million people in the world are color blind. That's a lot of players who could potentially be affected by your color choices in design. *Fortnite* (Epic) incorporates a colorblind test with its iconic llama to cater to players with color vision deficiencies.
- **Flashing Images:** Flashing images and colors can trigger seizures in players with epilepsy. In general, it is better to avoid content that rapidly flickers or changes color, but if you do need it for your visual effects or animations, make sure it doesn't flash more than three times per second.
- **Text Size:** The text in UI and subtitles is often too small for players with vision impairment, so allowing players to change the font size can have a big impact on the experience. This can also help mitigate some of the issues that occur with rendering your game in different screen ratios or resolutions.

- **Contrast:** High contrast modes can help players with vision impairment navigate the complex visuals in many games, particularly open-world ones.
- **Dark Modes:** Similar to many apps on our phones, games can help prevent eye strain with dark modes or brightness settings.

## Auditory options

- **Audio Cues:** Blind players can navigate the space and action in games with well-designed auditory cues. This could include incorporating a voiceover that describes the actions and inputs or creating spatial auditory cues that give feedback as they navigate the world.
- **Mono Options:** Many players have limited hearing in one ear, so stereo sound can often halve their experience. Offering a mono option allows these players to hear all the sounds in the game. This is especially important in genres like horror or action, where a missed audio cue can make the difference between success and failure.
- **Audio Settings:** Volume and frequency settings can have a big impact on the experience for players with tinnitus, sensory processing issues, or audio impairment. Many games now have options to eliminate high- or low-frequency noises, or specific tinnitus filters.

## Motor options

- **Landscape or Portrait:** Players who play with tablets or larger phones can often have arthritis or other issues that prevent them from being able to hold the phone vertically for long periods. Supporting both modes can help mitigate this.
- **Input Options:** Controllers often have complex combinations of inputs, requiring players to hold down triggers while hitting buttons simultaneously. They also assume a certain hand size and shape. Giving players options for which buttons they can use for inputs allows them to customize their experience to accommodate their different motor needs.
- **Adaptive Controllers:** Many gaming hardware companies have begun to create adaptive controllers for players with limited mobility. Xbox's adaptive controller was created with input from groups like AbleGamer and SpecialEffect. It is heavily customizable, with more than 20 different ports for adding additional controls, and works on both Microsoft PCs and the Xbox One. Quadstick is a company that makes different controllers for quadriplegic gamers, converting mouth sensor inputs into the appropriate signals for PCs and many modern consoles.

## Content options

- **Content Warnings:** One of the beautiful things about games is their ability to transport players into immersive worlds, but for players with trauma, this immersion can trigger anxiety attacks, painful memories, or fear responses. Having content warnings at the beginning of your game can help your players anticipate these issues so they can use the tools and resilience they've built to navigate them while playing your game.

- **Content Modes:** Some games take content warnings a step further, giving the players options to turn off specific content that may be triggering. For example, *Grounded* (Obsidian) has an arachnophobia mode that allows players to turn off features of the main enemy, giant spiders. This allows players to adjust the enemy's shape until they are comfortable enough to engage. Peaceful (also sometimes known as vegan) mode is becoming a popular option in survival games such as *The Forest* (Endnight) for players who want to avoid killing or eating animals.

Different players have varied needs, and thus, it is vital to offer a range of options that cater to diverse requirements. Combining the methods we discussed while exploring a range of customization options can help you connect the needs of your players to the intention of your game. This demonstrates an inclusive design ethos, acknowledging and respecting the varied abilities and preferences of players. By creating intuitive experiences in our games, we are allowing players to spend the majority of their cognitive load on the very reason they booted them up- to play. In the next chapter we'll explore methods of guiding them through the experience.

# BIBLIOGRAPHY

Chen, Jenova. "Designing Journey." *GDC Vault*, 2013, https://www.gdcvault.com/play/1017700/Designing. Accessed 11 July 2023.

Hossenfelder, Sabine. "To Err is to Play: Human Error and Game Design." *YouTube*, 5 March 2020, https://www.youtube.com/watch?v=JyuR2fKvQ20. Accessed 24 August 2023.

Lewis-Evans, Ben. "To Err is to Play: Human Error and Game Design." *GDC Vault*, 2018, https://www.gdcvault.com/play/1025283/To-Err-is-to-Play. Accessed 29 December 2023.

Norman, Don. *The Design of Everyday Things: Revised and Expanded Edition*. Basic Books, 2013.

Norman, Don, and Tamara Dunaeff. *Things That Make Us Smart: Defending Human Attributes In The Age Of The Machine*. Basic Books, 1993.

Portnow, James. "The Real Core Loop - What Every Game Has In Common - Extra Credits." *YouTube*, 25 September 2019, https://www.youtube.com/watch?v=mGL5YGcAxEI. Accessed 24 January 2023.

Stabley, Justin. "Why developers are designing video games for accessibility." *PBS*, 11 May 2023, https://www.pbs.org/newshour/arts/why-developers-are-designing-video-games-for-accessibility. Accessed 4 November 2023.

Tassi, Paul. "One Year Later, 'Elden Ring' Announces 20 Million Copies Sold." *Forbes*, 22 February 2023, https://www.forbes.com/sites/paultassi/2023/02/22/one-year-later-elden-ring-announces-20-million-copies-sold/. Accessed 29 December 2023.

Tremblay, Kaitlin. "Storytelling with Verbs: Integrating Gameplay and Narrative." *YouTube*, 17 March 2020, https://www.youtube.com/watch?v=ontNUxSLhb8. Accessed 11 July 2023.

# Guiding the Player Experience

# 5

---

## INTRODUCTION

---

When we design a game's actions, we ask a lot of our players. They need to learn the skills required to overcome the obstacles and challenges we lay in front of their goals and achievements. Understanding how they learn—and creating tools and systems that reinforce that learning—is key to creating an immersive and engaging experience. In this chapter, we'll dive deep into learning techniques as well as the emergence that occurs when we weave these methods together to form memorable experiences.

### What You Will Learn in This Chapter

- Player goals
- Onboarding and Tutorials
- Holistic world and level design
- Emergent narrative

---

## ITERATIVE LEARNING THROUGH PLAYER GOALS

---

Games, by their nature, are **goal-oriented** activities. They are beautiful motivation engines. They draw us in with their challenges and promises of victory. Player goals are one of our primary design tools for driving engagement, but they can also be leveraged to guide the player through their journey. As they learn, their senses pick up the details of the landscape around them—this is **perception**. **Memory** is the mental map (or model, if you will) that they craft from those details, and the map will constantly update as new information flows in. **Learning** is the act of traversing the landscape,

DOI: 10.1201/9781003342977-8

charting new paths, and understanding the terrain's nuances. And goals? They are the destinations, roadside attractions, and the peaks your players will strive to conquer.

The **perception-memory-learning triad** is the vehicle that drives you toward these goals (yes, I'm using a road trip metaphor here, if you couldn't tell already, I love to travel). In games, effective goal-setting often involves these three processes, each serving a critical role in guiding and motivating the player. Consider perception as the gateway. It's the first contact the player has with a goal, the billboard indicating the miles (or kilometers) left to the intended destination. Whether it's a shimmering princess castle in *Super Mario Bros.* (Nintendo) or the elusive chicken dinner in *PlayerUnknown's Battlegrounds* (Krafton), the goal must be perceptible and enticing to draw the player in. Perception cues are the roadside attractions along the way—they can be visual, auditory, or textual, subtly nudging the player toward the goal.

From the eerie shadows of *Limbo* (Playdead/Double Elven) to the serene landscape of *Journey* (thatgamecompany), these worlds are not mere backdrops; they are intentionally orchestrated stimuli designed to steer players' attention, evoke emotional responses, and provide contextual clues: *I perceive light and shadow. I perceive the horizon. I perceive the tower in the distance. The subtle flicker of a torch, the distant roar of a monster, the gentle rustling of leaves.* These elements all serve as cues that guide the player, inviting them to notice, explore, and act.

Of course, perception is only the beginning of our road trip. Once the goal is perceived, memory allows players to retain and recall their objectives over time—the mental map that they form as they travel. It is the echo stating that the princess is in another castle or the understanding of the impending consequences in the ever-encroaching last circle in a battle royale game. Memory is the thread that weaves discrete game sessions into a continuous, meaningful experience. It is the mental stage whereupon the past informs the present, patterns are recognized, lessons are remembered, and skills are honed. Without memory, the player would be lost, the goal forgotten as soon as it's out of sight.

Learning is the bridge between perception and memory. It is the process through which players understand how to achieve their goals—the joy of discovering how to navigate a labyrinth, the thrill of mastering a complex combo move, or the satisfaction of figuring out a boss's attack pattern. These moments of insight and understanding transform the perceived goal into a tangible and achievable target.

Memory operates on three distinct levels: sensory, working, and long-term. **Sensory memory** relates to immediate stimuli that last for only a fraction of a second. **Working memory** temporarily holds a limited amount of information in an accessible state. **Long-term memory**, as the name suggests, is responsible for storing information over an extended period. Understanding perception and memory is not merely an academic exercise for designers; it is a vital craft skill. Effectively introducing new features or mechanics requires a delicate dance between perception and these three layers of memory. We designers must skillfully introduce and reinforce game mechanics to help players understand, master, and remember them.

Consider introducing a new mechanic in a platformer game, such as the ability to double jump. Initially, the player perceives a visual or textual hint (sensory memory), followed by a safe space to experiment with this mechanic (working memory). Gradual challenge escalation and the mechanic's repeated application engrave it into the player's long-term memory. In other words, the player is shown the mechanic, then given environments to safely repeat and experiment, and finally given several increasingly difficult challenges to master.

*Thomas Was Alone* (Bithell Games) turns geometric shapes into compelling characters (my personal favorite is Claire the square) that the player must use to navigate increasingly complex spatial puzzles. As new characters are introduced, so too are new mechanics, each serving as a goal for the player to master. Each character possesses a unique ability, and understanding these abilities is crucial for navigating the game's platforming levels. The game gently guides the player, ensuring they understand one mechanic before introducing the next. By carefully orchestrating the learning process, *Thomas Was Alone* transforms the simple act of jumping from platform to platform into an engaging exercise of goal-oriented problem-solving.

In Nintendo's iconic *Metroid* series, the labyrinthine world of Planet Zebes doesn't merely exist to be explored; it serves as a pedagogical tool. Each room, each enemy, each power-up, they are all cues, invitations to perceive, remember, and learn. As players traverse the alien landscape, they encounter obstacles they can't overcome with their current abilities. These roadblocks form an implicit goal: acquire the ability needed to progress. Once the requisite skill is obtained (say, the Morph Ball), players remember the previous obstacles and return to overcome them.

*Deathloop* (Arkane) is a masterclass in iterative learning. The game's core mechanic—the time loop—turns failure into a learning opportunity by encouraging players to experiment, adapt, and gradually master the game's challenges. Difficulty in *Deathloop* is fluid, a function of player choice and strategy, and each loop is a new chance to test hypotheses and refine strategies. The game's world is a sandbox that supports a wide array of approaches. For example, players can choose to face challenges head-on, or they can use their growing knowledge of the game's systems and cycles to manipulate the environment, enemies, and time itself to their advantage.

In terms of perception and memory, *Deathloop* shines with its distinct visual and auditory design. The game's striking color palette, the vibrant contrasts of light and dark, and atmospheric weather effects all serve not just as a distinct aesthetic but also as subtle perceptual cues. These cues guide players, signal danger, indicate progression, and help players build a mental map of complex, interconnected environments. Sound, too, plays a crucial role, providing aural clues about unseen threats or the proximity and activities of the game's memorable characters. These characters, rich with personality, serve as both narrative anchors and distinct, memorable goals that the player must strategically eliminate.

# Learning Through Onboarding and Tutorial Design

**Tutorialization** is the art of teaching players how to navigate the game world, and it requires a delicate balance between **guidance** and **autonomy**. In every game that I have worked on, the onboarding and tutorial designs were among the features that were iterated upon the most. And when you think of how much a game changes over its development, that makes sense. As the experience changes, the ways that we guide players through that experience must also change. When you are planning the development of your game, make sure that you have resources at the end of your production cycle to support this. It will provide both your team and your players with a better experience.

Understanding how your players learn is an essential part of creating the bridge between their comprehension and the challenges you present to them in your games. **Educational psychology** is, fundamentally, an intersection of various fields such as neuroscience, developmental psychology, and pedagogy. The purpose of educational psychology is not just to distill the raw scientific knowledge of how we learn and grow but also to uncover its application in real-world contexts. These applications are models of understanding that inform us about how students acquire knowledge, skills, and attitudes. As with any intricate system, there's no one-size-fits-all solution to teaching players. The key lies in the interplay. Human learning is both a deeply personal and widely communal experience.

In the early years of educational theory, John Locke propounded the idea of the mind as a "tabula rasa" or blank slate. This was a radical shift in perspective, prioritizing experience over innate knowledge in human development. Locke's theories underscored the importance of environmental influence, an idea central to later educational philosophies and methodologies. If we think of game onboarding as a safe environment for experimentation and influence, we are essentially mapping the mechanics to this slate. But how best to do so?

Anyone who has struggled with rote memorization of facts or wakefulness during a long classroom lecture will likely agree that learning through contextualized practice is a faster way to develop deeper knowledge and learning. Introduced by Italian physician Maria Montessori, the **Montessori** method leverages a carefully crafted environment that encourages self-guided exploration and learning. The method's essence is found in the marriage of freedom and structure, an arena that empowers the child to independently discover and interact with their surroundings. In a Montessori classroom, children are given materials and tools within prepared environments to solve problems independently and collaboratively with minimal instruction. This allows them to experiment and fail within a safe environment (an open world, or sandbox, if you will).

In *Spiderman: Miles Morales* (Insomniac), Miles is introduced to new combat mechanics and acrobatic techniques by Peter Parker through a tutorial space represented in a holographic training program. This not only creates a safe space for the player to learn and try out these techniques, but it also offers a nice bit of character development as Peter and Miles geek out and banter throughout the successes and failures (we'll talk more about crafting banter in a later chapter).

The concept of **self-determination theory** (SDT) dovetails nicely with the Montessori approach. SDT suggests that humans are driven by three basic psychological needs: competence, relatedness, and autonomy. In the context of game design, these needs translate into the player's skill mastery (competence), their connection with the game world or other players (relatedness), and their freedom to make meaningful choices (autonomy). These needs are not external motivators; rather, they are fundamental aspects of our human nature. When these needs are nurtured—as they are in the Montessori method—learning becomes a self-propelled endeavor. The child is no longer a passive vessel waiting to be filled but an active, autonomous participant in their learning journey. Intrinsic and extrinsic motivations are key components of SDT when it comes to driving self-propelled behavior, something we will discuss more in Chapter 6.

In well-crafted game tutorials and onboarding experiences, players are encouraged to explore and experiment within the game environment, organically building understanding. The game serves as the environment and the players as learners who absorb knowledge from their interactions. In a game, players are often expected to learn and evolve their understanding as the game progresses. When designers craft game tutorials, this principle guides them to create experiences that respect and empower the player. The player achieves **competence** through incremental challenges and feedback, allowing them to grasp game mechanics at their own pace. The game nurtures **relatedness** through compelling narrative or social elements, allowing the player to forge strong emotional connections. And designers ensure the player's **autonomy** by providing meaningful choices and agency, making the player an active participant in their gaming journey.

*Hitman Go* (Ubisoft) offers one of my favorite examples of gentle onboarding in controlled environments. In this turn-based strategy game, the player guides Agent 47 through a series of grid-based puzzles, and the game's tutorial is elegantly woven into the gameplay. Without any explicit instruction, players are gradually introduced to the core mechanics. By placing the player in carefully designed initial scenarios, the game indirectly guides the player to understand how movement and enemy behaviors work. This gentle, implicit approach allows players to learn and construct their understanding through direct interaction with the game environment (Figure 5.1).

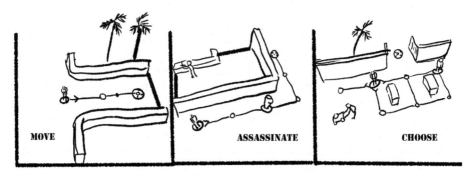

MOVE                    ASSASSINATE                    CHOOSE

**FIGURE 5.1**  Hitman go.

In *Horizon Zero Dawn* (Guerrilla), the player is introduced to the gameplay actions and interfaces in an elegant and contextualized way that also gives them key insights into the backstory of the world their character, Aloy, inhabits. The game begins with Aloy as a child learning to hunt. By having the player embody the identity of a child learning a new skill, the tutorial prepares them to learn; it also prepares them to be open to failure by referencing existing mental models. Since children are more likely to fail—through learning in a socially acceptable way, the player's threshold of tolerance for failure is most likely higher than it would be in a fighting game where they are playing a muscle-bound combatant. Embodying a child also requires the player to slow down and take their time since the avatar's legs are shorter than what is usually expected in an action video game. This is helpful because the control scheme for aiming and shooting in *Horizon Zero Dawn* is quite complicated, involving multiple inputs and careful timing. The slower pace gives the player time to learn and master it. The player is also able to learn about the world's culture and values through Aloy's communications with her adoptive father, which provide helpful background context. Because their relationship leverages many player's existing mental models of parents teaching their children, the informational dialogue feels natural, rather than coming across as an expository lore dump.

The tutorial brings an unexpected twist for the player when Aloy falls into a hole, finding the ruin of a previous civilization. There, she also discovers a piece of technology. This technology creates a visual interface that does double duty as the game interface for a variety of functions that include hinting, quest actions, receiving audio files, and analyzing the world around her. By giving Aloy this tool while having her explore the remnants of its associated technology, the designers have created a playground for the player to safely explore its functions while simultaneously serving backstory. This playful and narrative-rich solution truly immerses the player while leveraging existing mental models to reduce friction and teach them about the interactions within the game.

*Portal* (Valve) is another shining example of a game that masterfully integrates iterative learning. This first-person puzzle-platform game presents players with a series of challenges based on using a portal gun to create interdimensional portals. The brilliance of Portal's tutorial lies in its gradually increasing complexity and its embrace of trial and error. The narrative even reinforces the idea of playful experimentation by making the player's identity related to that of a test subject. As the player progresses, the game subtly guides them through the mechanics, starting from simple spatial puzzles and gradually introducing more complex elements like momentum conservation (Figure 5.2).

**FIGURE 5.2**   Portal.

# NARRATORS AS PLAYER GUIDES

Narrators can serve as a crucial bridge between the story and the player, creating an emotional, thematic, and experiential connection to the unfolding tale. In classic storytelling structures, a narrator often acts as a guide by providing context or shaping the reader/viewer/listener/player's perceptions. Narrators act as mediums through which tales are told, and they can vary in their level of objectivity, presence, and reliability.

In games, I like to think of narrative as either **explicit**, where specific voiceover or text directly tells the story, or **implicit**, where the narration perspective is applied as the storytelling perspective for the player. These perspectives offer different values depending on the type of game you are making and the type of stories you want to tell.

There are many different styles of narrator, each with its own unique qualities and limitations. Let's take a look at a few.

## First-Person Narrator

A first-person narrator uses "I" or "we" and provides a subjective view of the plot. In an example from classic literature, Herman Melville's *Moby Dick* uses Ishmael as a first-person narrator, and he shares events from his perspective. While game experiences are often unnarrated, first-person is a ubiquitous perspective due to the desire to put the player in the forefront of the action. While "I" or "we" is used infrequently, the actions and perspective act as the lens through which the narration occurs. The first-person perspective is a camera angle used in many shooter and action games, but we can also see it in calmer experiences such as walking simulators or environmental puzzles. In *Firewatch* (Campo Santo), for example, players assume the role of Henry; the story is conveyed through his eyes, and his emotions, perspectives, and interactions shape the narrative. While most of the dialogue comes from another character through his walkie-talkie, it is always Henry's perspective from which the story is told.

## Second-Person Narrator

A second-person narrator directly addresses the reader or the protagonist using "you," "yours," and "yourself." This relatively rare perspective creates an immersive and confrontational narrative style, and N.K. Jemisen's *Broken Earth* trilogy offers an excellent literary example. *Baldur's Gate 3* (Larian) makes extensive use of the second-person point of view to emulate the feeling of a Dungeon Master telling an evolving adventure for the player and their party of companions. Many older text adventures also use second-person narration, letting you know what your choices are and whether they result in you being eaten by a Gru. This level of abstraction creates opportunities for richer subtext, allowing the player to fill in the gaps with their imagination.

## Third-Person Limited

Third-person limited provides an external perspective but only describes the experiences and inner thoughts of a single character (e.g., Harry Potter in J.K. Rowling's series). Third-person narrators use "she," "he," and "they" pronouns. *Thomas Was Alone* (Mike Bithell) uses the third person in a unique way to imbue geometric shapes with personality and story by describing their innermost feelings and desires, demonstrating how the narrative voice can bring depth and emotion to the most minimalistic of characters and settings.

*Bastion* (Supergiant) employs a dynamic third-person narrator to enrich its story-telling. Rucks, the narrator, doesn't merely recount events but responds in real time to the player's actions, creating an engaging and immersive experience. While the player is experiencing the events by assuming the role of the main character "The Kid," Rucks' deep, gravelly voice provides context, lore, and commentary, intertwining player agency with a structured narrative. His reliability, while not overtly called into question, gently nudges the player to consider perspective and objectivity, given that he shares the story from a particular, personal viewpoint.

## Third-Person Omniscient

This narrator—who also uses "she," "he," and "they" pronouns—has a god-like perspective and can offer insights into the thoughts and experiences of all characters, moving fluidly through time and space. (A classic literary example is the narrator in Leo Tolstoy's *War and Peace*.) The perspective works well for games that include significant player agency or rely on procedural systems to convey the story. The *Civilization* series (Firaxis) often uses well-known voice actors such as Leonard Nimoy or Sean Bean as their narrators. This lends a feeling of history and gravitas to the omniscient narration. *The Sims* (EA/Firaxis) series could also be seen as having a third-person omniscient perspective as players oversee and manage the lives of all characters. By granting direct access to all characters' actions, needs, desires, and thoughts, the game makes the player the narrator of the story, rather than a single character.

### BREAKING THE FOURTH WALL

Have you ever had moments where a game becomes self-aware, directly addressing you, the player? This concept is known as "breaking the fourth wall" and originates from theater, where there are traditionally three physical walls on stage; the "fourth wall" is the invisible barrier between the actors and the audience. When an actor "breaks" this wall, they acknowledge the audience directly—either by speaking to them or recognizing their existence in some other way. In essence, the actor rips apart the illusion of the play's world being separate from ours.

We see this a lot in film and TV. Ferris Bueller, for example, speaks to the audience. So does Deadpool, who seems to love nothing more than taking a katana to that fourth wall. Like any narrative tool, though, it can be overused or used poorly. You've got to strike the right balance. Too much fourth wall breaking can make a game feel gimmicky and pull players out of the immersive experience. But when it's done right, it adds another layer to the narrative, turning the game from a simple interactive experience into something more—something that not just includes us but directly engages us.

The **willful suspension of disbelief**, a phrase coined by poet Samuel Taylor Coleridge, refers to an audience's willingness to shelve judgment about the narrative's implausibility to fully engage with a work of fiction. It's about over-looking the impossibility of a man flying in a red cape or a young wizard casting spells and accepting the fiction's internal logic for the sake of immersion.

On the other hand, Johan Huizinga's concept of the "**magic circle**," intro-duced in his book *Homo Ludens*, refers to the psychological space that's created when we play a game. Inside this circle, normal rules of the real world are set aside and the game's own rules take precedence.

So, what happens when we break the fourth wall in this context?

Breaking the fourth wall can push against both the player's suspension of dis-belief and the game's magic circle. When used in a clever and meaningful way, it can be a playful act of disruption that intentionally jolts the audience or player out of their immersive state, reminding them that they're participating in an artificial experience.

In games, fourth wall-breaking moments are like nothing else. They can blur the line between fiction and reality, reminding us we're in a constructed world even as we sink deeper into that world. In the context of suspension of disbelief, breaking the fourth wall could be seen as a rupture, a tear in the fabric of the story that allows the real world to seep in. It's a deliberate act that forces us to confront the fact we're interacting with fiction. It's a paradox that can be playful and poi-gnant if handled correctly.

*Love Quest* (Tokuma Shoten) is a self-aware and satirical JRPG that continu-ously breaks the fourth wall, starting from the very beginning of the game. The player, embodying a protagonist whose fiancée has been kidnapped, is allowed to decide whether they want to rescue their supposed beloved with a simple YES/NO prompt. If they answer "NO" enough times, the game will simply end, rolling to credits and a final cutscene that depicts the player attempting to return the game after receiving the dissatisfying ending and only getting 200 yen for it. This kind of cheeky and self-aware fourth wall breaking can often make up for the willful suspension of disbelief through novelty and wit.

In the context of the magic circle, breaking the fourth wall pushes the bound-aries of the game space. It reminds players that they are just that: players. In BioShock (Irrational), the phrase "Would you kindly" is used as an in-game com-mand, but it also serves as a commentary on the linear structure of video games and the player's obedience. This narrative twist essentially serves as a fourth wall break since it forces the player to reflect on their own lack of agency within the video game structure. When Psycho Mantis in *Metal Gear Solid* (Kojima// Konami) mocks you for playing *Castlevania* (Konami) or when the narrator in *The Stanley Parable* (Galactic Cafe) comments on your choices, they're effec-tively stepping outside the magic circle, breaching the game's reality to directly interact with you, the player, in your reality.

It's a risky move because it can disrupt the immersive experience. When done well, it can also elevate the narrative. It can make us question the nature of games and stories, reflect on our roles as players or viewers, and blur the line between fiction and reality in mind-bending, innovative ways. When used poorly, however, it can pull us out of the experience. This is particularly relevant in tutorial design, where talking directly to players with instructional text not only breaks immersion and the magic circle but can also leave players feeling infantilized and talked down to.

# Unreliable Narrator

An unreliable narrator presents the story in a way that raises questions or inspires doubt. This narrator asks readers to engage critically with the narrative and is used in works like Edgar Allan Poe's *"The Tell-Tale Heart."* In this story, the narrator's skewed perspective—his unreliable recounting of events—is central to understanding the plot. In Shakespearean works, the Fool often speaks in riddles and paradoxes, providing commentary and revealing truths that others cannot or will not see.

*The Stanley Parable* (Galactic Cafe) cleverly experiments with the idea of an unreliable narrator. It also incorporates elements of metanarrative, whereby the game is self-aware and directly comments on its own structure and the nature of video game storytelling. The narrator (voiced wryly by Kevin Brighting) attempts to criticize and even mislead the player's actions, revealing that he can't be trusted. Because of this, the unreliable narrator evokes a complex relationship between player, character, and storyteller. Just like the Fool in *King Lear*, who uses wit and paradox to comment on events and reveal truths, game narrators can elucidate deeper themes and challenge player perceptions, making them not only participants but critical observers of the unfolding stories.

*Portal* (Valve) takes a different approach with its AI antagonist, GLaDOS, which serves as a guide and commentator throughout the game. Though not a traditional narrator, GLaDOS embodies characteristics of the unreliable narrator by misinforming and manipulating the player, fostering a sense of mistrust and tension that enhances the gameplay experience. This mechanism is akin to the subversion found in cinematic tales in which deceptive characters or narrators, such as Keyser Söze in *The Usual Suspects*, foster a palpable tension between perceived reality and hidden truths.

# Objective Narrator

An objective narrator offers a fly-on-the-wall view of events without delving into the characters' thoughts or emotions, instead focusing purely on observable phenomena. *Prince of Persia: The Sands of Time* (Ubisoft) features a protagonist who also serves as the narrator by recounting his adventurous tale, sometimes even addressing the player directly and rewinding time when "misspeaking" (when the player dies), crafting a narrative where the narrator's reliability and control over the story are central themes. The narrator never dives fully into the character's thoughts, they only recount the action as it unfolds. Similarly, the Greek Chorus found in classic dramas comments on and interprets the action for the audience, offering a collective, often moralistic perspective on the unfolding drama. Narrators in games can also instruct the player, offer insight, or cunningly misdirect, adding layers of complexity and depth to the player's experience.

## Stream-of-Consciousness Narrator

This narrative style attempts to depict the continuous, chaotic flow of thoughts in a character's mind, famously used in Virginia Woolf's *Mrs. Dalloway*. Similarly, *Hellblade: Senua's Sacrifice* (Ninja Theory) immerses players in the protagonist's mind, vividly portraying her mental turmoil and struggles through a stream-of-consciousness narrative style.

### GETTING YOUR PLAYER TO READ INSTRUCTIONS

In his delightfully named GDC Talk "How I Got My Mom to Play *Plants vs. Zombies*," game designer George Fan speaks extensively (and hilariously) about tutorialization. He and I agree that it is better for the player to learn by doing rather than reading, but sometimes we need to use text. This might be for practical reasons, like not having enough time in the production schedule to create another onboarding loop, or it might be for design reasons, such as providing additional context. Whatever the reason, if you need to have text on the screen, then it is important for your players to actually read it. And anyone who has worked on a game or website will tell you that this can be a very difficult task. Fan suggests that when players need to read, limiting the text to eight words or less in a single sentence ensures that they pay attention. In general, I've also found this to be a good rule, although less is always better!

Creating accessible text is the first step. If they can't read the text easily, they won't just skip it, it will make them frustrated and less open to learning. UX designer Anna Brandberg cites a number of best practices around fonts and text in her keynote Devcom talk "The Psychology of Play: The Power of Understanding Your Players," stating, "You don't want players squinting trying to read something tiny. Make sure fonts are legible, [with good contrasts]. Consider that there's such a massive part of your player base that have different accessibility needs, and accessibility means so many different things. "

Understanding visual hierarchies and weights can help you guide your players to the most important text. These principles can be used to create designs that effectively guide the viewer's attention, making the information more digestible and the user's interaction more intuitive. The Nielsen Norman Group has published extensive videos and resources to help designers understand hierarchy concepts, but here's a quick overview of the basics:

## VISUAL WEIGHT:

- **Contrast:** Elements that contrast with their surroundings will appear heavier and draw more attention.
- **Size:** Larger elements generally have more visual weight than smaller ones.
- **Color and Brightness:** Bold or bright colors tend to add visual weight to an element.
- **Complexity:** A more complex element has greater visual weight compared to a simpler element.
- **Position:** Elements positioned in familiar focal areas, such as the center or along reading direction, may carry more visual weight.

## VISUAL HIERARCHY:

- **Alignment and Positioning:** Aligning elements and positioning them strategically can create a flow that guides the viewer's eye through the design.
- **Scaling:** Using different sizes can denote importance, with larger elements typically seen as more important.
- **Color and Contrast:** Utilizing contrasting colors can create a hierarchy by drawing attention to specific elements.
- **Repetition and Consistency:** Repeating visual elements creates unity and can reinforce a specific part of the hierarchy.
- **White Space:** Utilizing space effectively can separate or emphasize elements, aiding in establishing a hierarchy.
- **Typography:** Using different fonts, sizes, and styles can establish a hierarchy, guiding the viewer through the text content (Figure 5.3).

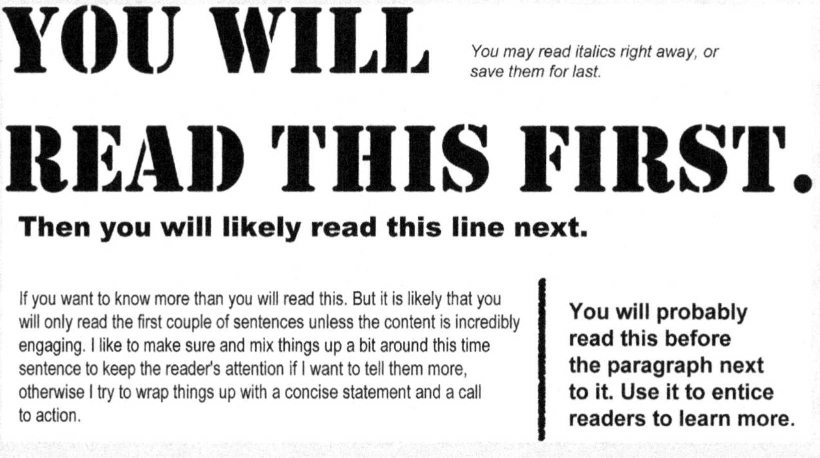

# YOU WILL

*You may read italics right away, or save them for last.*

# READ THIS FIRST.

## Then you will likely read this line next.

If you want to know more than you will read this. But it is likely that you will only read the first couple of sentences unless the content is incredibly engaging. I like to make sure and mix things up a bit around this time sentence to keep the reader's attention if I want to tell them more, otherwise I try to wrap things up with a concise statement and a call to action.

**You will probably read this before the paragraph next to it. Use it to entice readers to learn more.**

**FIGURE 5.3**   Text visual hierarchy.

# SCAFFOLDING AFFORDANCES

I've talked about affordances in several previous chapters and how they indicate and facilitate the purpose and action of an object. When you wake up in the morning, for instance, the handle on your coffee or tea pot suggests, or affords, an opportunity for you to pour a hot beverage. In an MMORPG, a tank's big and bulky armored design affords their purpose of absorbing damage for the rest of the party. But in the context of interaction, an affordance can either be open or closed. The extent in which an affordance is **open** dictates the amount of agency and interactivity the player has. The extent an affordance is **closed** dictates the limitations on their level of interaction.

Open affordances can be likened to invitations for exploration, letting players engage with an object or system in many ways. They don't limit or prescribe specific interactions but instead offer opportunities for creativity, discovery, and personal interpretation. This gives the player a large amount of agency but also requires an advanced understanding of the game rules. A *Minecraft* (Mojang/Microsoft) block, while seemingly simple in its design, affords the creation of many different expressions and interactions.

Closed affordances, on the other hand, provide a more restricted and guided experience. They are clear and precise, indicating exactly how an object or system should be used. Designing closed affordances typically leads the player down a particular path, reducing the possibility of error or misinterpretation. In *Bejeweled* (Popcap), the player can match any jewels in a pattern of three or more, but they may only do so by swapping that jewel with another next to it.

In tutorial design, I like to categorize and plan based on when I open up the affordances for further experimentation and risk. By starting with the more structured guidance of closed affordances, players build the necessary skills and confidence to handle more open-ended challenges later on, gaining confidence and mastery. Transitioning from closed to open affordances allows players to apply what they've learned in unique and creative ways, enhancing engagement and replay value. This shift helps in creating a natural difficulty curve, where players are slowly introduced to more complex challenges.

This approach is particularly evident in Metroidvania-style games, which portion out design challenges in an engaging and challenging way while signposting future unlocking mechanics through environmental and level choices. In the initial levels, these games guide the player through specific paths and teach essential mechanics such as jumping, attacking, and climbing. The design restricts where the player can go, helping them to focus on mastering basic skills. As the player progresses and becomes more comfortable with the basic mechanics, the games begin to open up, offering more complex challenges.

*Hollow Knight* (Team Cherry) employs both closed and open affordances when introducing mechanics. By presenting obstacles and tantalizing glimpses of potential skills, the game heightens the player's sense of exploration, accomplishment, and wonder. Early levels are filled with high ledges, vertical shafts, and walls that are too high to scale. Then, the player encounters enemies that demonstrate the Manis Claw ability in the Mantis Village (note the use of repetition here to reinforce learning), which is part of the Fungal Wastes. This acts as a preview and educates the player on how the ability might work. Once the player obtains that ability later, those previously unreachable paths become new avenues of exploration. The game does not spell this out explicitly but instead relies on the player's memory and curiosity.

# HOLISTIC LEVEL DESIGN

In many games (but not all), players explore the rules, motivations, and systems by also exploring the world. This world could be as simple as counters on a grid representing soldiers on a battlefield or as complicated as the vast realms of an open-world RPG. Holistic level design refers to the process of considering a game's levels not just as individual, isolated challenges but as interconnected parts of a larger whole. This perspective emphasizes the importance of coherence and continuity across a game's levels, with each one contributing to the overarching themes, narratives, and gameplay mechanics of the whole.

Indulging in the artistic elegance of level design is akin to wandering through a well-planned city or a meticulously arranged garden. Christopher Totten likens game spaces to architectural spaces in his wonderful book *An Architectural Approach to Level Design*, weaving a compelling argument that level design is, in essence, digital architecture. Through this lens, level designers are architects who build structures from polygons and textures rather than bricks and mortar. They do not merely construct spaces for players to traverse; they choreograph experiences, sculpt narratives, and—crucially—signpost goals. I highly recommend reading this seminal work from cover to cover, but I'd like to highlight a few key concepts that are essential to consider when designing intuitive levels.

In Totten's architectural view of level design, games are not just playgrounds, but places imbued with **meaning** and **purpose**. The space players navigate in a game is not arbitrary. It's a crafted experience, a narrative written in space and form, paths and obstacles, light and shadow. Level design, therefore, is a form of storytelling. It shapes player behavior, guides exploration, and sets challenges. Goals, in this context, are the story's narrative beats, the milestones that mark the player's progress and motivate their journey.

**Visual goal-setting** in level design is a conversation between the game and the player, spoken in the language of architectural and visual cues. It is an art and a science, a balance of revealing and concealing, of guiding and letting loose. Visual goal-setting involves using architectural elements and visual cues to guide players toward their objectives. They are the digital equivalent of a towering cathedral in the distance or a striking monument at the city center, visible from various points. A level designer, acting as an architect of experience, uses **visual cues**, **spatial layout**, and **environmental storytelling** to establish goals and guide players toward them.

Jesse Schell takes this concept further, drawing on the world of theme park design. He introduces the term **architectural weenie**, which was coined by Walt Disney and refers to a visually intriguing element that serves as both a landmark and a goal. Cinderella's Castle at the center of Disney World is perhaps the most famous example.

In the context of level design, weenies also act as visual goals, beckoning the player toward them and providing a sense of direction. In *Elden Ring* (FromSoftware), the player is introduced to an enormous tree that is visible from nearly every point of the game world. It acts as both a goal and a vehicle for narrative state changes and progress as the player navigates the game's grueling and exciting challenges.

## DESIGNING ENVIRONMENTS FOR OPEN AND IMMERSIVE WORLDS

In his book *An Architectural Approach to Level Design*, game design professor Christopher Totten discusses several architectural and design principles that developers can adopt to create game spaces that facilitate immersion and exploration. Understanding and leveraging these principles when mapping your world to your story can help facilitate emotional and intuitive experiences for your players:

**Landmarks and Sight Lines:** Landmarks, like towering castles or uniquely shaped mountains, can draw the player's attention and guide them to points of interest. Clear sight lines enable players to see these landmarks from a distance, enticing them to explore. These can be used to highlight key points in your story map in a visual and diegetic way.

**Pathing and Zoning:** Carefully designing the layout of paths and zones can subtly guide players through the game world. For example, a winding path that leads into a forest might hint at hidden treasures or encounters waiting to be discovered. This can help them find side content or keep them on the main story path.

**Scale and Density:** The game world's scale and the density of its points of interest can greatly influence the player's experience. A larger world might evoke a sense of grandeur and adventure, while a denser world might encourage more detailed exploration. Try to match your scale and density to your story map when possible.

**Environmental Storytelling:** The environment itself can tell a story and hint at the kinds of narratives the player might find. For instance, a burned-down village might suggest a tale of conflict and tragedy while a thriving town full of NPCs might promise stories of daily life and community.

**Affordances and Signifiers:** Affordances are what the environment allows the player to do, and signifiers are signals about how the player can interact with the environment. For example, a brightly lit doorway might signify that it can be entered, leading the player to a new narrative thread.

**Risk-Reward Structures:** Areas that are more difficult to reach or navigate might contain more valuable rewards or more significant narrative revelations, encouraging the player to take risks and venture off the beaten path.

By using these architectural and design principles, game developers can create open map story structures that guide players to different points in the story in an organic, immersive way. They can make the exploration of the game world an engaging narrative experience in and of itself, allowing players to create their own unique narratives through their choices and actions. Level design is mapping space, and when done meaningfully that space can reinforce the story and emotion maps.

A holistic approach also includes considering how every element of a level, from its architectural layout to its aesthetic details, can contribute to the player's experience. This might involve considering how a level's visual design supports its gameplay mechanics or how the placement of enemies and resources can create a sense of pacing and tension. Designer Steve Lee speaks extensively about his experience creating these kinds of levels in his insightful GDC talk "An Approach to Holistic Level Design." Working on titles like *BioShock Infinite* (Irrational), and *Dishonored 2* (Arkane), he talks about the value of using sound, visuals, space, and light to guide the player in his masterfully designed levels. Let's take a closer look at one of these games and how it leverages holistic thinking.

Arkane Studios is known for creating games that offer players a high degree of freedom and flexibility in how they approach challenges. Their levels are often designed to support a variety of gameplay strategies, from stealth and avoidance to direct combat. Additionally, they often feature interconnected layouts that encourage exploration and reward players for learning the intricacies of the game space. Their game *Dishonored 2* provides a masterclass in goal-oriented level design. Visual and auditory cues dot the landscape, subtly guiding players, while memory and learning solidify their understanding of the world and its mechanics. Its semi-open-world levels are replete with visual cues. These cues, whether a towering structure, a tantalizingly open window, or a barely visible rooftop path, highlight potential routes and objectives. They serve as promises of what can be achieved, encouraging exploration, experimentation, and strategic planning.

The city becomes more than a backdrop; it's a character. It shapes the narrative, guides players' behavior, and sets challenges. Each level, a carefully crafted narrative in and of itself, contributes to the game's grand composition. Similarly, the soundscape of *Dishonored 2* is a purposeful composition. The humming of the wind, the distant chatter of citizens, and the clanking of machinery all contribute to a rich, immersive auditory environment that alerts, informs, and orientates the player. The use of color, light, and atmospheric effects also plays a pivotal role. Golden sunlight bathes the streets of Karnaca, revealing its vibrant yet decaying beauty. Conversely, the gloomy interiors of the Clockwork Mansion, punctuated by harsh artificial light, contribute to an oppressive, unsettling atmosphere. These elements aren't merely aesthetic choices. They are design elements that impact gameplay by emphasizing stealth mechanics, influencing the player's strategy, and subtly guiding their path.

# DIEGETIC UI AND NARRATIVE

Once we have fully released a player into the world to explore and experiment, we want to keep their immersion levels high. **Diegetic** UI and narrative allow us to continue giving the player feedback about their goals and obstacles without fully breaking that immersion. Diegetic UI refers to the user interface elements that are integrated into the diegesis (the fictional world). This can include in-game menus, maps, health bars, and other on-screen displays that are part of the game world and serve to enhance the player's immersion in that world.

In the classic adventure game *The Legend of Zelda: Ocarina of Time* (Nintendo), the player accesses their inventory and maps through a menu system integrated into the game's world. The menu appears as a backpack the player character carries, and items are stored and retrieved from it in real time as the player progresses. In the *Fallout* series (Obsidian/Bethesda), the player accesses health and information using the Pip-Boy they wear on their arm.

Diegetic UI can enhance player immersion and provide valuable information in an integrated and believable manner within the game world. Diegetic narrative, on the other hand, refers to the story or plot that unfolds within the diegesis. Metaphorizing gameplay elements and systems into world-integrated items heightens immersion, ensuring that the game's story unfolds within the actions and fabric of the world. This process creates and reinforces player immersion.

The main difference between diegetic UI and diegetic narrative is that the former is a tool for the player to interact with and navigate the game, while the latter is the story that the player participates in. While they both serve to enhance the player's experience and immersion in the game world, they serve different purposes and affect the player in different ways.

In a game with a diegetic UI, the player may use an in-game map to navigate the world and keep track of their progress. Meanwhile, the diegetic narrative may involve the player navigating or changing the game world through their narrative choices. While the map is a tool the player uses, the story is what the player participates in and what drives their experience. Games with complex environments and levels to navigate work best when those elements are designed intuitively, but we can't make assumptions about the player's ability to navigate on their own. These methods, especially in open-world titles or those requiring level navigation, are an intrinsic part of design philosophy, ensuring that all players, regardless of their physical capabilities or familiarity with gaming, can experience and enjoy the content to the fullest.

Diegetic UI integrates navigational and informational components directly into the game world in a manner that is coherent with its narrative and aesthetic. For example, *Dead Space* (Motive) projects the player's health, ammo, and other essential info directly onto the protagonist's suit. Even the game map and objective screens are projected into the game world in a believable way. This not only aids immersion but also provides essential information in an easily accessible and intuitive manner, ensuring that players do not have to navigate complex menu systems. This can be particularly helpful for those with cognitive impairments.

Games like *The Witcher 3: Wild Hunt* (CDProjekt Red) employ dynamic mini-maps that assist in guiding the player through vast open worlds while also allowing them to set their own waypoints, offering a level of customization in navigation. These features enable players to traverse large, complex environments with clearer direction and purpose, ensuring that potential barriers related to spatial awareness and decision-making are minimized.

Diegetic narrative prompts are cues that naturally occur within a game's environment or story, providing guidance to players in a subtle, immersive manner. For instance, in *The Last of Us* series (Naughty Dog), visual and auditory cues such as lights leading down a path or distant sounds of characters conversing subtly guide players through the world without being obtrusive. These cues are particularly beneficial for players who might struggle with more traditional navigation methods, offering an organic means to suggest directions or points of interest.

Helpful companion NPCs can provide navigational assistance while simultaneously enhancing storytelling and emotional engagement. They blur the lines between diegetic UI and narrative. Elizabeth in *BioShock Infinite* (Irrational/2K) assists the player by not only providing resources and identifying threats but also nudging them toward the correct path or objectives, facilitating smoother navigation through the game's expansive environments. Elizabeth's presence and interactions are seamlessly woven into the narrative, ensuring that her guidance feels natural rather than coming across as an overt assistance mechanism. The wolf in *Final Fantasy 16* (Square Enix) takes this one step further, actively guiding the player to objectives when prompted. By wrapping a complicated hint and guidance system into a companion character, designers can contextualize complex text or interface elements into an experience that is both intuitive and entertaining for the player.

# EMERGENT NARRATIVE

We've talked a lot about guiding the player experience in this chapter, but I'd also like to take a moment to talk about the player driving the experience. Games are unique in their ability to empower players to change and impact the rules and systems of the world they are playing in. When these changes are reflected through story and narrative, we designers refer to it as **emergence**.

Marc LeBlanc introduced the concept of emergent narrative in video games at the 1999 Game Developers Conference. It refers to storytelling that arises from the gameplay experience rather than from a pre-written script or plot. It implies that the story emerges primarily from the player's interactions with the game mechanics and environment—and less so from the predetermined narrative structure imposed by the game developers. Game designer Doug Church, in his presentation "Abdicating Authorship," emphasizes relinquishing traditional authorial control to facilitate emergent narratives. He suggests that developers' inclinations to exert total control over the narrative and gameplay experience can inadvertently inhibit the player's ability to fully immerse themselves and shape the game world. Church suggests that by stepping back and allowing players more agency to influence the narrative, developers enable the creation of a more organic and player-centric storytelling experience, where each decision carries palpable weight and consequence within the game's evolving story.

Emergence, from my perspective, revolves around three primary principles—**agency**, **complexity**, and **feedback**—that collectively enhance the user's immersion and engagement by permitting narratives to unfold in response to player choices and interactions.

# Agency

Agency refers to the degree of control and influence a player has over actions or decisions within the game. In the context of emergent narratives, agency empowers players by validating their choices and actions, which, in turn, have tangible impacts on the game world and the unfolding story. The storyline evolves and branches in different directions based on player-initiated actions and decisions, creating a personalized narrative experience. We'll talk more about the player-as-character in a later chapter, so for now, let's focus on the actions and verbs associated with this agency, rather than the drivers that form player identity.

Games, as I have said before, are beautiful motivation engines. And the player experiences these motivations primarily through the actions and verbs within the game. Agency allows the player to feel like they have control over these actions to influence and direct the story of the game world. This is a strong motivator for many players, and often results in a large amount of replayability. When discussing emergence, the most prominent and impactful verb is **choice.** It is the player's choices that contribute to their feeling of agency; that, in turn, contributes to immersion and believability when paired with complexity and feedback.

In the popular series *The Sims* (Firaxis/EA), players have a large amount of agency over what the characters in the game can do. These games are often referred to as "dollhouse sims" for this exact reason. In his 2018 GDC talk, Matt Brown discusses this system at length. Players can choose the extent to which they control their characters, and the amount of choice in terms of actions available is often wide and varied. When a player doesn't feel like taking full control of an NPC, it will employ a simpler version of agency on its own that is driven by a combination of prior player decisions and the interlocking systems of wants, fears, and wishes.

On the surface *The Sims* seems simple. A player creates characters, gives those characters actions to complete, and tries to keep them as happy and fulfilled as possible. What is intriguing about *The Sims* is the story that emerges over time through the systems and relationships that the game uses to determine the results of the player actions. Often, it can result in hilarious events like; "My character went to her boyfriend's party only to find that everyone invited was also dating him, so the entire party was spent with people sobbing in various areas of the house." Or for those of us that were tiny goths in our youth… "I removed the ladder from my character's pool and. he drowned, 'oh dear.' I wonder what will happen when I bargain with Death? Oh… I can propose to Death. Well, this complicates things, doesn't it?"

While these examples may seem superficial on the surface, they become more interesting when you think about how these stories emerge. The player interprets characters crying at a party to equate the fact that the relationships between characters are more complicated than they originally thought. Or they wanted to see what happened when they removed an affordance from a potentially deadly situation and then they're delighted/horrified by the results. They haven't been explicitly told these facts, but they have inferred from the events that occur. In other words, the player is building a story around the systems and actions within the game.

# Complexity

Let's think about a simple choice in our everyday lives for a moment. I enjoy both coffee and tea in the morning, but I rarely drink both. When I decide what to drink, there are a variety of factors that go into the decision: how awake I am, what I'm eating for breakfast, how sensitive I feel to caffeine, and more. That is one layer of complexity—the **space** in which the choice is being made. The second layer comes from how I **execute** that choice. Do I start by warming up the water or by choosing my beverage? What cup do I take from the cabinet? Even a simple choice such as my morning beverage routine can explode in complexity depending on how much agency I want to have in the decision-making process.

We as designers must act as filters for the player. This means determining which interactions and actions are most important, which affordances are open in terms of how the choice is executed, and what we decide to obfuscate in levels of abstraction so the player can "fill in the blanks" with their imagination. Games with higher complexity tend to offer a richer soil from which emergent narratives can grow, providing a multitude of ways for the story to develop and conclude. They can also become mired in detailed interactions or deeply connected systems that have unexpected consequences. Therefore, we as designers must choose where complexity reinforces immersion.

*Baldur's Gate 3* (Larian) increases complexity by opening affordances through the unlocking of skills, abilities, classes, and equipment. The resulting player agency blossoms over time, creating a wonderful sense of a living world that can be influenced by their actions. This is particularly evident in its turn-based combat systems, allowing the player to navigate the challenges in the game in creative (and often surprising or hilarious) ways. The combination of these experiences result in emergence that gives the player the feeling of having a large amount of agency. Let's look at a few examples from my most recent completed campaign:

- The charming vampire rogue Astarion shoots down a chandelier with a single arrow. It lands on top of an ogre, killing it instantly.
- The geeky sorcerer Gale turns a friendly NPC moon maiden into a gaseous form to prevent her from getting killed in battle. After the battle is completed, the NPC is understandably upset for being turned into gas without her consent, and attacks our party.
- An enemy NPC is doing brutal damage to my party with a grenade-spawning spear. My rowdy ranger player character summons a bear to disarm and defeat the soldier. When the spear falls on the ground it becomes involved in turn-based combat (even after the enemy is knocked out) and continues to annihilate our party by spewing bombs until my character picks it up.
- The friendly tiefling soldier Karlach is disarmed by an enemy. All she has in her inventory is a few potions and a large salami. She defeats the enemy by beating it with the sausage.

- Our party is surrounded by angry demons in a fiery dungeon. Gale casts sleet, which results in a silent movie Buster Keaton-esque sequence of snarling monsters pratfalling onto their backs as they try to desperately get within range while we attack them from a safe distance.

If this dizzying array of options were available to the player at the very beginning of the game, it would require a lot of their mental energy to understand and the sheer number of choices and options available would be overwhelming. By creating systems that gradually open the affordances of each character available, the designers were able to create an experience that empowers them with the knowledge of how to creatively solve problems and create memorable moments.

The higher the complexity, the higher the opportunity for immersion and agency—but also frustration and confusion. Complex systems result in unexpected behaviors or stories at best and game-breaking bugs or dead-ends at worst. With every layer of complexity, you should add additional time for iteration and playtesting, along with accompanying tools.

# Feedback

Feedback encapsulates how the game communicates the player's actions back to them. This dialogue between the player's actions and the game's responses is vital for creating a dynamic and evolving narrative. Effective feedback mechanisms provide players with a clear understanding of how their actions have influenced the game world and altered the narrative trajectory. Strong feedback also aligns the player's intentions with the outcomes of their actions, thus strengthening their connection and immersion within the game. If done correctly, feedback can surprise and delight players by showing them that the choices that they make in the game have consequences, reinforcing the illusion of meaningful choice.

Strategy and 4X games are a great genre to dig into to find examples of feedback in emergent gameplay to the dynamic and intricate systems that inform and drive player decision making. *Frostpunk* (11 Bit Studios) is a city builder that takes place in a fictional 19th century, where a volcanic winter has hit the globe. Throughout the game the player must make difficult decisions to ensure that their small band of survivors that they oversee survives and grows into a bustling, if not thriving, settlement. The game provides feedback in a variety of ways as the player makes these decisions. Visual feedback is provided through the expansion of the village and the changing landscape as resources are gathered and infrastructure is built. Narrative feedback is provided through emotional events that show the consequences of the player's choices—a law allowing child labor may result in an accident that results in an emotional exchange with a grieving mother, whereas a law building a child shelter results in a letter of heartfelt thanks. This kind of feedback increases the feeling of agency the player has, as it reinforces the idea that their actions have direct effects on the world. And sensory feedback, such as visual or auditory, can take complex systems and contextualize them in a way that is much easier for the player to understand and digest.

## MEANINGFUL AND PERSUASIVE GAMES

Ian Bogost's concept of procedural rhetoric, as introduced in his book *Persuasive Games: The Expressive Power of Video Games*, argues that video games are not just a form of entertainment but also a form of rhetoric that can be used to make arguments and persuade players through the processes and mechanics they use. He explains that video games use "procedural representation" to express meaning and convey ideas through the processes and rules that define gameplay, and the player's interaction with these mechanics becomes a form of argument and persuasion. In other words, the systems and mechanics in a game can be just as important as its story, graphics, or sound in making an argument and influencing players. Many games use their platform to make arguments about ethics, politics, and more. We'll look closely at an example later in this section.

You may recall that I quoted Brenda Romero in Chapter 2, and I'd like to reiterate her message here: "The mechanic is the message." When choosing the verbs and actions that make up your game, keep this profound and simple statement in mind—the choices you make in these core player actions will form the meaning and persuasive arguments of your game and its narrative.

 Let's look at *Papers, Please* (Lucas Pope) as an example. In the game, the player takes on the role of an immigration inspector and must make decisions about who to admit to the country. The mechanics of the game, such as checking passport stamps, searching for contraband, and balancing finances, represent arguments about the morality of immigration control. The decision-making complexity gradually grows with the mounting number and intricacy of rules, making the act of validating documents increasingly difficult and pressure-laden as players progress.

As the player navigates the growing complexity of the game's rules, their perception of choice becomes less black-and-white. The choice space is notably limited and morally charged—players must make decisions that not only impact the game world but also carry ethical weight, like deciding between following oppressive regulations or subverting them to enact small measures of kindness or justice. The ever-changing rules that the player's character must enforce as an immigration officer do not always reflect the player's perception of the world around them. By keeping the affordances closed as the world and rules become more complex, the game creates a feeling of disenfranchisement directly through the gameplay. And as the choice space feels more limited, the feedback of the available affordance—the stamp—becomes more weighted in its impact and physicality.

By confronting players with moral and ethical dilemmas within a circumscribed choice environment, *Papers, Please* inherently prompts reflection upon real-world sociopolitical issues, thus inviting them to draw parallels between the fictitious realm of Arstotzka and tangible historical and contemporary contexts. This clever utilization of procedural rhetoric thereby transforms *Papers, Please* into a poignant commentary on oppression, morality, and the complexities embedded within bureaucratic systems.

# Using Abstraction to Keep Emergence Believable

Integrating a level of abstraction into a game's narrative provides fertile ground for the player's imagination to sow seeds of their own interpretations and stories. Games like *Journey* (thatgamecompany) masterfully integrate abstraction into their designs. Instead of providing explicit narratives or objectives, it merely guides the player through its world and allows them to imbue the experience with personal meaning. This meaning is represented directly through the mechanics reflecting the personal experience of the player. The narrative gaps aren't seen as deficiencies but rather as intentional spaces for the player's creative engagement and immersion.

Some players find high abstraction and agency to be liberating and engaging, while others find it disorienting or lacking in direction. *Minecraft* (Mojang) offers vast player agency and operates with high abstraction, allowing players to create, explore, and survive in a blocky, procedurally generated world that has no prescribed narratives. For some, this is the epitome of immersive and engaging gameplay; others crave more structure and explicit storytelling.

Abstraction can also be used to mitigate ludonarrative dissonance—specifically, an abstract narrative structure. Abstract narratives offer a canvas broad and vague enough to accommodate various player-driven stories and actions without directly contradicting predetermined narratives. This is a delicate balancing act; the game must include enough narrative structure to guide and motivate the player but also provide sufficient space for their agency to genuinely impact and shape the unfolding story. Successfully tailoring these aspects can significantly enhance the player's experience by encouraging them to both engage deeply with the available narrative and to imaginatively interpret the journey.

### ON EKPHRASIS AND ABSTRACTION

**Ekphrasis** is a literary description of or commentary on a work of visual art (such as a painting, sculpture, or architecture). It involves creating a written or performed representation of a visual image, often with the intention of evoking the sensory and emotional experience of viewing the artwork. The term "ekphrasis" comes from the Greek word "εκφράζεσθαι," meaning "to describe" or "to interpret."

Ekphrasis has a long history. It dates back to ancient Greek and Roman literature, where it was often used as a means of explaining or interpreting works of art for a wider audience. In the Renaissance, ekphrasis was used as a means of expressing the ideals of the time, such as humanism and the revival of classical learning. In the modern era, poets and writers have used ekphrasis to explore the relationship between the visual and literary arts. They've also used it to challenge traditional notions of representation and interpretation.

Ekphrastic writing can take many forms, from poetry and prose to critical essays and reviews. It can also serve different purposes, such as preserving a work of art for posterity, evoking the sensory experience of viewing it, exploring the themes and ideas it embodies, or offering a critique of its style or content.

"*Ode to a Grecian Urn*" by John Keats is a classic example of ekphrasis in which the poem's speaker describes a Grecian urn and reflects on the time-less beauty and mystery of its images. Keats uses vivid imagery and imaginative language to bring the urn to life and evoke the emotions and thoughts it inspires

"O Attic shape! Fair attitude! with brede
Of marble men and maidens overwrought,
With forest branches and the trodden weed;
Thou, silent form, dost tease us out of thought
As doth eternity: Cold Pastoral!"

Video games are, as an experiential medium, ripe for ekphrastic interpretation. In August Smith's *The Mario Kart 64 poems,* each poem is an ode to a different track or course in Nintendo's iconic game, but as the poems progress the author brings in memories and external elements, giving the reader a glimpse of his experience of playing the game. Adolescent love and loneliness become pervasive themes in lines such as, "I want to encircle you like a ring of emerald turtle shells, vigilant, deadly, letting no one come too close."

Designers can leverage ekphrasis in a variety of ways to reinforce and supplement abstraction. *Monument Valley* (ustwo) is set in a fantastical world inspired by the architecture and designs of indigenous peoples as well as the work of graphic artist M.C. Escher. The player must navigate through impossible structures and manipulate the environment to reach their goal, all while appreciating the world's breathtaking visuals. By having the player solve visual puzzles inspired by Escher's work, they are creating an ekphrastic experience that synthesizes the act of viewing and interpreting that work.

In the indie itch.io game, *Ekphrasis: a game about looking at things* (Martha Hipley), the designer uses pixelated artwork to abstract famous works of art and the act of viewing them in a museum. The text narration offers the player a win-dow into the internal thoughts of their character as they look at the works on display. The pixelated graphics create a sense of removal and impartiality that contrasts with the intimate reflections of the player character. By adding the layer of abstraction, the designer is creating space for the player to bring in their own reflections, walking (metaphorically) hand in hand with the player character as they explore the museum together.

# Tying the Principles of Emergence Together: Case Studies

Now that we've dug into the various principles of emergence, I think it is time for us to take a gestalt view. Emergence is more than the sum of these principles, it is the tapestry that appears when they are woven together. Let's delve deep into a few games that weave our principles of abstraction, agency, complexity, and feedback into active experiential narratives for players.

## Hades

In the dark, mythologically rich caverns of *Hades*, players navigate through a dynamic narrative maze that extends far beyond the limitations of scripted storytelling by pairing predetermined narrative beats with emergent, player-driven experiences. This dual narrative approach grants players an influential presence within the game as their choices, successes, and failures carve out a personalized storyline through the Underworld.

At the helm of this personalization is the agency the game awards to the player, which is granted through the vast array of choices that pepper both combat and progression. The main protagonist (and player character) Zagreus doesn't merely exist within a static, unchanging world. The game's unfolding narrative tapestry is molded by his journey, weapon choices, and strategy for each attempt to escape the Underworld. Players weave through myriad experiences, crafting their personal combat styles and influencing character interactions, thus affecting subtle story arcs alongside the main plotline.

The complexity of the game emerges in the various loops of play upon each failed attempt. The combat increases sharply in difficulty, requiring the player to gain mastery over a variety of techniques and tools. These combat mechanics are abstracted in a way that is grounded in the context of the Greek mythology that is the backbone of the game's world building and story (as we discussed in Chapter 3).

*Hades*'s celebrated, sharp mechanics aren't solely confined to the game's combative aspects. For example, non-playable characters act as a narrative mirror, adjusting their dialogues, demeanors, and revelations based on the player's unique journey. The Underworld subtly shifts in response to Zagreus's actions, whether it's through the lament of a failed escape attempt or the shifting allegiances and relationships among the gods and spirits inhabiting it.

Intricacy breathes life into the cavernous depths of the Underworld, embedding both its systems and its narrative within a complex web of potential player experiences. A rich blend of systemic and narrative complexity enriches each attempt to escape, introducing varied challenges, enemies, and opportunities to strategically mold Zagreus's abilities through divine boons.

## 80 Days

*80 Days* (Inkle) blends meticulous design with a vibrant, emergent narrative structure. Navigating through a steampunk-inflected reimagining of the world author Jules Verne created in *Around the World in 80 Days*, players assume the role of Passepartout, valet to the punctilious Phileas Fogg. They embark on a race against time in a world that spins on the axis of player choice and chance encounter. The game's narrative tapestry is both broad and beautifully detailed, offering many paths through a complex, responsive world, all while ticking against the relentless clock of an 80-day deadline.

With every mode of transport they choose, every city they visit, and each interaction they have, the player is granted significant agency, forging a path that is uniquely their own. As Passepartout, players decide the course of their global journey while also navigating nuanced micro-narratives within each city and transport route. Conversations held, items purchased, and relationships forged can significantly influence the unfolding adventure, contributing to an emergent narrative that burgeons from each decision, making every circumnavigation of the globe distinctively individual.

*80 Days* transcends mere choose-your-own-adventure dynamism with its robust feedback system because the world reacts, remembers, and reshapes itself in response to the player's actions and decisions. The cities visited and the characters encountered respond to Passepartout's (and, by extension, the player's) actions, offering new opportunities or closing off paths based on previous choices and relationships.

The game delicately juggles a remarkable complexity that enhances the replayability and depth of the narrative experience. The intertwining story arcs, character interactions, and potential routes create a dense network, each journey offering new stories to explore and fresh adventures to undertake. This complexity is not merely spatial; it is also deeply embedded in the game world's sociopolitical and cultural narratives, which reflect themes of colonization, gender, and technology. As a result, players are invited to navigate a labyrinthine narrative that is as thought-provoking as it is entertaining.

## *Dwarf fortress*

*Dwarf Fortress*, a creation of Tarn Adams and Zach Adams, emerges as a dense, sprawling, and deeply intricate simulation that beautifully embodies the essence of emergent narrative in the gaming realm. Set in a procedurally generated world of abstracted graphics (in early iterations of the game, the various elements were represented by ascii characters, whereas with the more recent Kitfox publication they are represented with pixel art) where dwarves endeavor to build and sustain their fortress amidst a host of challenges, the game doesn't prescribe a narrative. Instead, it births stories from the complex, interwoven mechanics and systems at play. Each playthrough is not a journey through a predetermined tale—it's an unfolding player-driven saga crafted from decisions, calamities, and unexpected moments of triumph.

From the start of the game, *Dwarf Fortress* hands the reins of agency to the player not in the form of a scripted protagonist but as an omnipotent force guiding the fledgling dwarven colony. The player's role encompasses decision-making at various levels, from strategic resource management to the minutiae of daily life within the fortress. Through this granular decision-making, tales begin to weave themselves. The player's choices around resource allocation, construction, and interaction with the environment and other entities foster a rich tapestry of stories that are entirely emergent and deeply personalized.

Intricate feedback mechanisms enhance the player's immersion and sense of impact within the world. The dwarves, driven by their individual personalities, needs, and skills, respond to the environment and player's decisions, dynamically shaping the narrative as they forge relationships, develop skills, and sometimes meet an untimely demise. In the ebb and flow of successes and failures, a multifaceted narrative emerges, always unique and spontaneously crafted from the melding of mechanics, systems, and player input.

But it's the profound complexity of *Dwarf Fortress* that truly becomes the loom upon which emergent narratives are woven. The game doesn't confine itself to simple binary outcomes or linear paths. Instead, it plunges into a deep algorithmic complexity that affects everything from the dwarves' physical and psychological traits to the fluctuating environment around them. This complexity breathes life into a world that is chaotically organic. Here, narratives are not merely player-derived; they spring from the complex interplay of innumerable variables, each dwarf's tale intertwining with another, crafting epics of survival, despair, and unexpected triumph. The abstraction of graphics and story representation through text creates a bridge between this complexity and the player's imagination.

When our players pick up our games, they are not just playing, they are learning. And by understanding the ways in which they learn and retain that knowledge, we can guide their experience in a way that is intuitive and immersive. This can be done through intentional goal-setting, iterative learning through play, guidance that gives them the autonomy to explore, and worlds and characters that lead them in that exploration. In the next chapter we'll explore motivations and how they can engage and delight players in the long term.

# BIBLIOGRAPHY

Bogost, Ian. *Persuasive Games: The Expressive Power of Videogames*. MIT Press, 2010.

Brandberg, Anna. "The Psychology of Play: The Power of Understanding Your Players". Devcom, 2023.

Brown, Matt. "Emergent Storytelling Techniques in The Sims." *YouTube*, 2 July 2018, https://www.youtube.com/watch?v=YjuOSgPdtS0. Accessed 14 January 2024.

Budke, Alexandra, and André Czauderna (2020) "How digital strategy and management games can facilitate the practice of dynamic decision-making." *Education Sciences*, 10:4, 99. DOI: 10.3390/educsci10040099.

Coleridge, Samuel Taylor. *Biographia Literaria*. edited by Adam Charles Roberts, Edinburgh University Press, 2014.

Dealessandri, Marie. "Adapting your game's vision to benefit your players." *GamesIndustry.biz*, 21 August 2023, https://www.gamesindustry.biz/adapting-your-games-vision-to-benefit-your-players. Accessed 14 October 2023.

Fan, George. "How I Got My Mom to Play Through Plants vs. Zombies." *GDC Vault*, 2012, https://www.gdcvault.com/play/1015541/How-I-Got-My-Mom. Accessed 1 August 2023.

Gordon, Kelley. "Visual Hierarchy." *YouTube*, Nielsen Norman Group, 22 June 2023, https://www.youtube.com/watch?v=8OTbyWndY9M&t=0s. Accessed 1 August 2023.

Hudson, Kent. "Player-Driven Stories: How Do We Get There?" *YouTube*, 27 December 2018, https://www.youtube.com/watch?v=qie4My7zOgI. Accessed 14 October 2023.

Huizinga, Johan. *Homo Ludens: A Study of the Play-element in Culture*. Angelico Press, 2016.

Jagoda, Patrick. *Network Aesthetics*. University of Chicago Press, 2016.

Keats, John. *Ode on a Grecian Urn (Complete Edition)*. E-Artnow, 2019.

Kreimeier, Bernd. "Puzzled at GDC 2000: A Peek Into Game Design." *Game Developer*, 2000, https://www.gamedeveloper.com/design/puzzled-at-gdc-2000-a-peek-into-game-design. Accessed 14 October 2023.

Kroenke, Pawel. "How a Time Loop Influenced 'Deathloop's' Narrative Design." *GDC Vault*, 2022, https://www.gdcvault.com/play/1027796/How-a-Time-Loop-Influenced. Accessed 1 August 2023.

Lee, Steve. "Level Design Workshop: An Approach to Holistic Level Design." *GDC Vault*, 2017, https://www.gdcvault.com/play/1024301/Level-Design-Workshop-An-Approach. Accessed 1 August 2023.

Menzel, Jolie. "Level Design Workshop: A Narrative Approach to Level Design." *GDC Vault*, 2017, https://www.gdcvault.com/play/1024302/Level-Design-Workshop-A-Narrative. Accessed 1 August 2023.

Rilke, Rainer Maria. *Sonnets to Orpheus*. Translated by M. D. Herter Norton, W. W. Norton, 2006.

Russell, Jayme. "Burning Rubber, Tearing Reality: A Review of August Smith's The Mario Kart 64 Poems." Fanzine, 16 February 2017, http://thefanzine.com/burning-rubber-tearing-reality-a-review-of-august-smiths-the-mario-kart-64-poems/. Accessed 28 January 2024.

Schell, Jesse. *The Art of Game Design: A Book of Lenses*. CRC Press, 2019.

Smith, August. *The Mario Kart 64 poems*. Cool Skull Press, 2015.

Szczepanski, Leszek. "Building Non-linear Narratives in 'Horizon: Zero Dawn.'" *GDC Vault*, 2017, https://www.gdcvault.com/play/1024158/Building-Non-linear-Narratives-in. Accessed 1 August 2023.

Totten, Christopher. "Level Design Workshop: An Architectural Approach to Level Design: Creating an Art Theory for Game Worlds (and So Can You!)." *GDC Vault*, 2018, https://www.gdcvault.com/play/1025176/Level-Design-Workshop-An-Architectural. Accessed 1 August 2023.

Totten, Christopher W. *An Architectural Approach to Level Design*. CRC Press, 2019.

Wang, Huei-Hsin. "What is Visual Weight?" *YouTube*, 19 July 2023, https://www.youtube.com/watch?v=o3mCcnN61GY. Accessed 1 August 2023.

Yin, Stephanie. "Rules of Go - Part 1." *YouTube*, 9 April 2018, https://www.youtube.com/watch?v=eNpJF0BzUig. Accessed 14 October 2023.

# PART 3

# Emotion

# Motivation and Engagement

# 6

## INTRODUCTION

As we've discussed in previous chapters, games are great engines for translating context, action, and emotion into motivation and engagement. When we, as designers, create and publish our games, we extend our hand to the player, inviting them into our worlds. But who are we extending that hand to? And why do they want to play? What drives the player to purchase, install, and play your game? Is it a way to engage with their friends? To relax and escape? To prove they can be the best? Answering these questions early in your design process, along with understanding how these motivations relate to each other, is essential for creating an engaging and coherent experience.

### What You Will Learn in This Chapter

- Understanding player motivations
- Crafting player personas
- The difference between intrinsic and extrinsic rewards
- Motivating with luck and emotion
- Understanding and avoiding dark user patterns

## PLAYER MOTIVATIONS

We discussed in earlier chapters how trying to find and define the fun in your game can quickly complicate your development process. Fun can be hard to define because it means different things to different individuals (and games don't need to be fun for players to love them). Understanding what motivates your players, however, is a much clearer way to connect your game design with what they will find engaging.

When modeling player **motivations**, it is important to closely examine the needs you identified in your hypothesis crafted during research and development. These needs should be the primary drivers that motivate the player, and they should tie closely into the game's actions and core experience. When modeling motivations in your game, there are a variety of methods you can use.

Tracy Fullerton, veteran game designer and director of the Game Innovation Lab at the University of Southern California, has done extensive work on exploring player motivations in game design. In her book *Game Design Workshop*, she emphasizes the importance of understanding player motivation as a foundation for designing engaging experiences. She breaks these motivations into several key categories:

- Challenge
- Exploration
- Fantasy
- Expression
- Social Interaction
- Progression and Completion

Quantic Foundry's player motivation model uses research to build out a framework for understanding the needs of a wide range of players. Created by surveying and interviewing over a million players, the framework breaks motivations into six key categories

- Action
- Social (Competition and Community)
- Mastery
- Immersion
- Creativity

Note that both Fullerton and Quantic Foundry discuss **social** motivation. Like Fullerton's social interaction motivation, Quantic Foundry's social motivation focuses on players having experiences together. Therefore, this motivation relies on interpersonal relationships and play, allowing players to engage with one another as well as with the game's systems and actions. However, Quantic Foundry takes it further by specifically breaking social motivation into two main areas: competition and community.

In addition to identifying their six motivation types, Quantic Foundry suggests that there are key relationships, which they call "clusters," that work well together:

- Action and Social
- Mastery and Achievement
- Immersion and Creativity

If we take this clustering one step further by creating distinctions between the different social motivations and adding Tracy Fullerton's categories, the clusters could look like this:

- **Thrill Seeker:** Action, Challenge, and Social Competition
- **Completionist:** Progression, Mastery, and Achievement
- **Escapist:** Immersion, Fantasy, and Exploration
- **Architect:** Social Community, Expression, and Creativity (Figure 6.1)

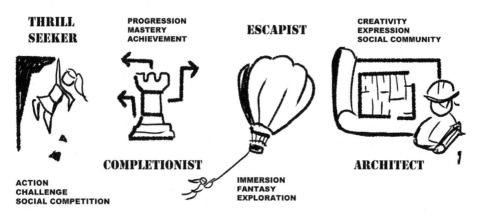

**FIGURE 6.1**  Motivation clusters.

**Action** is a motivation that focuses on events and experiences that result in surprises, chaos, destruction, and thrills. The rush of adrenaline when players reach a finish line, leap over a chasm, or overcome an opponent. This motivation relies on intense moment-to-moment activity and quick decision-making, often (but not always) requiring dexterity and fast reflexes. Examples of features that serve the action motivation are survival crafting systems, time-based battle royale matches, player versus environment (PVE) combat, and intense platforming puzzles.

Because of the focus on intense moments in games that leverage the action motivation, it is important to pace that intensity with short sessions or quiet breaks to avoid player burnout. This could take the form of an online lobby or a quiet bonfire.

**Challenge** is the drive to overcome obstacles, solve puzzles, and master complex game mechanics. This motivation can drive players to improve their skills and achieve a sense of accomplishment. Players who are motivated by challenge often enjoy steep changes in difficulty curves to prove their level of mastery, and they appreciate clever puzzles and mechanics. Examples of challenging features include puzzles or activities that are completed under tight time constraints or require a large amount of skill or dexterity. Roguelikes, intense boss battles, and platformers often map to this motivation beautifully.

*Celeste* (Maddy Makes Games) is a 2D platformer where players need to navigate complex levels with precision and dexterity. As the protagonist, Madeline, navigates the challenges of Celeste Mountain, the game leverages the challenge motivation to create a beautiful metaphor for overcoming self doubt, anxiety, and depression.

For many players, games offer an opportunity to connect with others through **social competition**. Examples of socially competitive features include leaderboards and player-versus-player matches. Games have leveraged social competition as a motivation for as long as they have existed, pitting players against each other to showcase their skills. But studies show that social competition can positively affect reaction time and learning.

In a 2015 paper written by Brynne DiMenchi and Elizabeth Tricomi, participants played carnival water gun video games that required a large amount of precision and attention. They were divided into groups, one of which was tested against themselves in the form of playing against the clock, while the other was told they were playing against a participant they had met earlier in the study. Participants in the competition cohort had improved reaction times, tolerance for sustained effort, and recall. Since these skills have a high impact on performance in action and challenge games, social competition can act as a potent enhancer when used by savvy designers.

*Titanfall* (Respawn) is a competitive first-person shooter that combines intense combat, parkour movement, and giant mechs (robots). It is a fantastic example of the Thrill Seeker cluster. One of my very favorite moments in this game was in an intense deathmatch battle where my mech was about to blow up. I ejected as it exploded and used the momentum to land on a nearby enemy's back to "rodeo" their pilot by shooting the mech's weak spot at close range to get the final point for my team before time ran out. The intense action and social competition combined with the challenge of time pressure was a potent mix of motivations memorable enough for me to continue to recount this moment many years later.

**Progression** is a form of motivation driven by the satisfaction of making progress, ticking off tasks, or completing collections. As someone who loves ticking off the boxes on my to-do lists, I personally find this motivation compelling. One of my favorite games for fulfilling it is *Spiritfarer* (Thunder Lotus). The cozy nature of this game belies the complexity and nuance of its collection and quest systems, wrapping them in character collection, crafting, and boat upgrades. In *Spiritfarer,* the protagonist Stella uses this boat to ferry souls into the afterlife. By pairing a compelling story with strong visual progression, the designers reinforce progression and completion motivations in interesting and accessible ways.

**Mastery** focuses on the player's need to be mentally challenged and overcome those challenges to gain a sense of **achievement**. This motivation relies on engaging the player's mind through solving difficult problems or making deep strategic decisions. Examples of mastery features include real-time strategy, challenging puzzles, or complex physics problems. This motivation often requires a large investment of the player's time and energy, so it is important to build engaging systems that help sustain their attention long term.

*Gitarooman* (Liona Interactive/Koei) is a challenging and delightful rhythm game where the player is pitted against a variety of musicians, each showcasing a distinct style, in notoriously difficult musical battles. This game is notoriously difficult. The curve is steep, and the complex series of inputs requires a strong amount of manual dexterity. Each boss (of which there are only five) has a distinctive style that requires many attempts to overcome. This mastery loop results in a strong sense of achievement every time the player makes progress in the game, similar to the sense of achievement musicians get when they learn a new song.

Speed running is another fantastic example of the Completionist motivation cluster in action. The speedrunning community focuses on fully completing games as quickly as possible. Successful speedrunners use a combination of mastery, ingenuity, and memory to play notoriously long games like *Legend of Zelda: Ocarina of Time* (Nintendo) or difficult games like *Cuphead* (Studio MDHR) in under 30 minutes. *Good Games Done Quick* is an organization where these streamers raise money for charity, allowing them to share their achievements in a way that benefits various causes. This potent mix of intrinsic self-driven motivations showcases the strengths of this cluster.

The **immersion** motivation focuses on players escaping into the narrative, characters, and environment of the game world. Examples of immersive features include character relationship systems, role playing, or narrative choice. Players who are motivated by immersion are the most likely to be affected by ludonarrative dissonance if the world, story, and characters do not align with the game's core actions and motivations.

Many Escapist players are driven by the motivation and desire to immerse themselves in **fantasy** by taking on roles or living experiences beyond their everyday lives. While the most obvious examples are narrative-rich roleplaying games, this motivation also applies to the fantasy of, say, running a restaurant or owning a farm. Because a high level of immersion is required to successfully drive this motivation, it is important to avoid breaking the fourth wall to address players directly or interrupting their play with pop-up tutorials, ads, or features.

**Exploration** is the desire to discover new worlds, uncover hidden secrets, or learn new things. This can involve physically exploring a game world, but it can also include exploring a game's mechanics or narrative possibilities. Players who are motivated by exploration generally prefer complicated, abstract, or open systems and worlds (emergence) that they can delve into. They often find that strict rules or overly inhibitive constraints are frustrating.

While there are many wonderful roleplaying games that come to mind when we dive into the Escapist cluster, an unexpected example can be found in *Sable* (Shedworks). In this coming-of-age tale, the player has full agency to explore the Mœbius inspired world as they try to find the perfect mask for their coming-of-age ritual. The immersive desert environment, underscored by a beautiful soundtrack by the indie band Japanese Breakfast, create an enigmatic fantasy world that is filled with rich emergent stories. In *Sable*, the game is not about the destination, it is about the journey.

Players in the Architect cluster leverage the game systems in creative and expressive ways, and then share these creations with their community. **Social community** features can include trading systems, communication systems, and collaborative team play. Successfully integrating this motivation into your game often requires a deep understanding of social dynamics. Additionally, it is important to incorporate systems that keep your players' experiences safe and inclusive. Social interaction can also include parasocial relationships such as those with companion NPCs or game masters.

**Trust** is the cornerstone of all social interactions in gaming but is particularly important in building social communities. It's what allows players to band together, share resources, and overcome challenges. But trust, like everything else, exists on a spectrum—it can be built or broken, it can flourish or falter. Raph Koster eloquently details how designers can leverage the trust spectrum to build a ladder of systems that facilitate social interactions in his excellent blog articles on the subject (Figure 6.2).

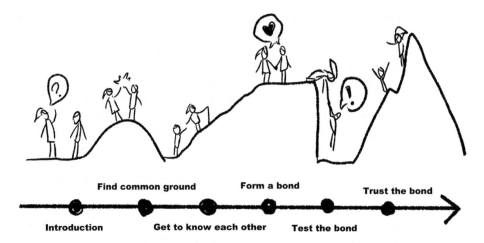

**FIGURE 6.2**   Raph Koster's Trust spectrum.

Players come to trust each other not merely by virtue of shared quests but also through shared emotional experiences. The exhilaration of a hard-won victory, the despair of a crushing defeat, the amusement of a shared joke—these emotions, and the trust they foster, become the building blocks of the game's social fabric. Essentially, we are creating friendships.

In order for social relationships in games to blossom into friendships, the game needs to fill certain social needs. It's hard enough to make friends in the real world, where body language, facial expression, and voice tonality reinforce social cues and bonds. Games that rely on social motivations as primary drivers must recognize that the actions and systems in the game need to provide the space and actions to foster the building and reinforcement of social bonds. During the 2014 game design retreat Project Horseshoe, a talented group of game designers (Lauralyn McWilliams, Terry Redfield, Patricia Pfizer, Vijay Thakkar, Jonathan Hamel, Yuri Bialoskursky, Dan Hurd, and Joel Gonzales) took a closer look at forming friendships in games and identified several key factors related to creating and strengthening these relationships:

- **Meaningful communication:** The ability to sharing thoughts and feelings with others in a safe space
- **Humanize:** The ability to foster empathy, understanding, and patience for others
- **Proximity:** The availability of shared spaces, with opportunities for social recognition and spontaneous interactions
- **Shared Experience:** The creation of interpersonal and group identities through common experiences
- **Group Reliance:** The availability of opportunities to help one another, so that the shared effort of the group yields greater results than that of the individuals
- **Status Expressions:** The ability to demonstrate and recognize individual status, and exchange (or share) items that convey that status accordingly

Note that status **expression** is a key factor here. Status expression can mean a lot of things. Whether it is a group of players working together to impact the game world through their action or a single player showing their friends the latest skin they earned, expression is a powerful motivator that directly ties to player agency. Players can customize their characters, design and decorate a guild hall, or make narrative choices that reflect their (or their character's) personal values or moral compasses.

**Creativity** focuses on players being able to express themselves within the game. This motivation relies on experimentation and creation. Examples of creative expression features include crafting systems and sandbox builders. This motivation requires a lot of flexibility due to the amount of self-expression and choice involved, so planning your design systems with scalability in mind is key. This motivation is similar to Fullerton's expression motivation; however, a notable difference is that expression includes making decisions that impact the game world in meaningful ways while creativity focuses more on creating and experimenting.

The *Animal Crossing* series (Nintendo) is a classic example of a game that serves the Architect motivation cluster, but it is *New Horizons* where we really see this combination shine. This installment of the series has many familiar features such as crafting, decoration, and quest completion, but players found new ways of connecting with one another through the ability to visit each other's islands. This feature was particularly helpful during the game's release, which happened in the midst of the COVID-19 pandemic. Players that were unable to see each other in person found innovative ways to use the game as their primary social space, playing games, chatting, and even hosting weddings.

Hopefully it is becoming clear to you how powerful these motivation clusters can be when used to drive your game design. It is vitally important to understand the balance you wish to hit between these motivation clusters as you set up your design systems within the game world. In her insightful GDC Talk "World Design for Different Player Types," designer Raylene Deck digs deeply into the Quantic Foundry model to show how level designers can tap into the motivation clusters when building out their worlds. Digging into lessons learned during her time at Bioware and Bungie, she details how a greater understanding of these clusters can help designers avoid pitfalls and engage their players long term.

**Action** players might appreciate intricate combat arenas in games like *Doom* (id), where rapid decision-making and split-second reflexes are the keys to survival. These players would find an adrenaline-fueled thrill in surmounting overwhelming odds and emerging victorious.

**Social** players appreciate shared worlds to explore, common objectives to collaboratively complete, and spaces that facilitate inter-player dynamics can form the heart of the level design for these social butterflies.

**Mastery** players seek complex systems to understand and conquer, be it the complex stealth assassination scenarios in the *Hitman* (IO Interactive) series or the intense competition in *League of Legends* (Riot). Level designs catering to these players often present challenging obstacles that reward strategic thinking and tactical skill. Hard-to-reach locations, optional boss fight arenas, and intricate puzzles can be excellent tools in designing for mastery players.

**Achievement** players crave progress and a sense of accomplishment. They are the players who will strive to unlock every achievement, find every collectible, and explore every nook and cranny. For them, completion is the goal. Level designs for these players might include numerous hidden collectibles, detailed completion statistics, and rewards for thorough exploration, like in *The Legend of Zelda: Breath of the Wild* (Nintendo). These players will also enjoy the complex navigational puzzles of *Deathloop* (Arkane).

**Immersion** players seek to be lost in another world, become part of a narrative, and live another life. Rich, detailed game worlds like Thedas in the *Dragon Age* (BioWare) series provide the canvas for these players to paint their stories. Detailed lore, atmospheric environments, and non-linear narratives are potent tools for designing levels and worlds for immersion players.

Lastly, **creativity** motivated players are likely to engage in user-generated content, customizable characters, and flexible environments

Understanding these motivations allows us as designers to tailor our level and world designs to our intended audience. After all, games are a conversation between designer and player, and understanding our players' motivations helps us speak their language.

Motivation is a framework, a lens through which we can view our game world and ask, "Who is this for? How can I make this a more engaging, more fulfilling, more personal experience for my players?"

For example, Deck highlights how the introduction area of the Hinterlands in *Dragon Age Inquisition* (Bioware), included more than 20 hours of content catering to the immersive fantasy cluster. This world showcased the rich open world of the game, but became a bottleneck for players in the progression and completion motivation cluster. These players felt like they had to complete all 20 hours of content available in the area before moving on to the rest of the game, thus delaying their access to key plot points, new characters, and new equipment. This became such a problem that the development team encouraged players to move past the Hinterlands area on social media.

Deck details how the area of Crestwood, from the exact same game, better balances between the different motivation clusters by providing the player with an easy to follow and central narrative that is constrained by the evolution of the environment and landscape over time. This combination of slowly opening closed affordances and providing consistent feedback creates a potent combination of engaging systems for players in multiple motivational clusters.

# INTRINSIC VERSUS EXTRINSIC REWARDS

Now that we have gained an understanding of these motivations and their clusters, it is time to put them into action. A great way to do this is through rewards. To appropriately cater to the motivations of your players, it is helpful to understand the reward systems and tools available to you, as a designer.

**Intrinsic rewards** are psychological rewards that players receive based on the enjoyment, satisfaction, and personal fulfillment that come from playing a game. These are the feelings of satisfaction, accomplishment, and enjoyment that come from the act of playing the game itself. They're closely tied to player motivations. For example, the joy of finally cracking a tough puzzle is an intrinsic reward that appeals to players who are driven by challenge or completion. On the other hand, the pleasure of uncovering a game's lore will appeal to those driven by exploration or immersion.

**Extrinsic rewards** are tangible rewards or prizes the game bestows upon the player, often for accomplishing specific tasks or challenges. Rather than tying directly to motivations, they often act as enhancers or components of the systems that reinforce motivation. In *Fortnite* (Epic), the Battle Pass system offers an array of extrinsic rewards. As players accumulate points from playing matches, they progressively unlock rewards like new skins, emotes, or gliders. These act as components for expression, and they also reinforce intrinsic social motivations by becoming what I like to call "brag swag."

A well-designed game balances intrinsic and extrinsic rewards, creating a rhythm of play that satisfies immediate intrinsic motivations while also offering the promise of meaningful extrinsic rewards over the longer term. The key is to understand your players and their motivations and to design your reward systems in a way that acknowledges and reinforces what your players value most about your game.

# Quests as Motivation and Reward Systems

One way of connecting these rewards to different motivations is contextualizing them through quests. By aligning design systems with these motivations and carefully balancing the reward types and grounding them within the game's world and narrative, we can create engaging challenges on a gameplay level while also resonating with players on a deeper emotional level.

The joy of discovering a hidden location or revealing a piece of the world's lore are intrinsic rewards. The quest narrative should transport the player into the game world, allowing them to live out experiences they can't have in their everyday lives. This reinforces immersion in the game's narrative and the ability to affect its direction. In *The Legend of Zelda: Breath of the Wild* (Nintendo), one of the game's greatest intrinsic rewards is the freedom of the open world, driven by quests discovered by the player through exploration. The game's open world is crafted in a way that encourages curiosity. Players can climb virtually any mountain, cross any field, and discover secrets hidden in the landscape. The joy of discovery and the fulfillment of curiosity provide strong intrinsic motivation.

The emotional journey that arises from a game's narrative quests can be a powerful motivator for players. They can include character progression, like unlocking new abilities that reflect the character's growth within the story and reinforcing parasocial motivations. A well-crafted narrative elicits a wide range of emotions, from fear and sadness to joy and triumph. This emotional engagement can be a strong motivator, driving players to keep playing so they can see how the narrative will unfold and how their relationships with other characters will develop. Or, they may continue playing simply to continue experiencing the emotional highs and lows that the game provides.

Extrinsic rewards in quests could be unique items found only in these locations or information that will help in future quests. The resulting systems will not just be tasks to be completed—they'll be meaningful journeys that players want to undertake.

## NPC dialogue and quests: the balance of effort and narrative payout

In quest design, non-playable characters (NPCs) often serve as the primary channel through which the narrative unfolds. These characters provide context, drive plot development, and offer tasks or quests for the player to undertake. However, when creating NPCs and their associated quests, it is crucial for designers to consider the balance between the effort a player puts into the game and the narrative payout they receive.

The fundamental principle to grasp is that the depth and volume of narrative content should be proportional to the player's gameplay effort and the NPC's importance within the storyline. In other words, the more significant an NPC's role or the more effort a quest demands, the richer the narrative experience should be. The number of dialogue lines spoken by an NPC should be proportional to the level of effort the player is expected to give in the NPC's world via quests or companion lines.

Striking the right balance between gameplay effort and narrative payout is crucial for maintaining player engagement. Players will feel unrewarded if they invest a significant amount of time but receive minimal story development. Conversely, overwhelming players with too much dialogue or story as part of a minor task can lead to fatigue or disinterest.

## Considerations for balancing gameplay effort and narrative payout

- **Pacing:** Ensure that narrative developments occur at a pace consistent with the player's progress. It's essential to provide narrative "breathing room" between major plot points. *The Last of Us Part 2* (Naughty Dog) paces its narrative with exploration, combat, and quiet moments. After intense sequences, players often find solace in calm, dialogue-rich scenes—like the guitar-playing moments between Ellie and Dina—allowing for emotional processing and character development.
- **Variety:** Not every quest needs to be epic, and not every NPC must have a tragic backstory. Some NPCs can offer light-hearted, humorous, or even mundane interactions, creating a richer, more varied world. The side quests in *The Witcher 3: Wild Hunt* (CD Projekt Red) are varied, ranging from heart-wrenching tales like "The Bloody Baron" to light-hearted ones like helping trolls with their painting.

- **Choice & Consequence:** Giving players agency in how they engage with NPCs can deepen their investment in the story. For example, the ability to choose dialogue responses can lead to different narrative outcomes, making the story feel tailored to the player's decisions. *Detroit: Become Human* (Quantic Dream) thrives on player choice. For instance, as the android Connor, players can decide to be empathetic or strictly professional, which in turn affects his relationship with his human partner Hank and, ultimately, Hank's fate.
- **Quality over Quantity:** It's essential to focus on the quality of narrative content rather than sheer volume. It's better to have a few well-crafted, engaging dialogue lines than pages of uninspired text. *Firewatch* (Campo Santo) is dialogue-heavy, but it doesn't feel overwhelming. That's because the quality of conversation between Henry and Delilah—their depth and emotional intensity—makes players invested in their relationship, even without a vast open world or dozens of side quests.

The narrative content provided by NPCs and quests should reflect and honor the player's investment in the game. By carefully calibrating the balance between gameplay effort and narrative payout, game designers can create a compelling and rewarding experience for players.

# Luck as Motivation in Reward Systems

Balancing intrinsic and extrinsic rewards while intertwining them with elements of luck can create a rich, layered reward system. For instance, combining luck-based loot drops (extrinsic) with the thrill of overcoming a tough enemy (intrinsic) can offer a compelling mix of rewards that cater to a range of player motivations. The key is to ensure that players feel their efforts are recognized and valued while also sprinkling in just enough uncertainty to keep them on their toes. With the right balance, designers can create a game that not only rewards players but makes the act of playing its own reward. Richard Garfield, the legendary designer of *Magic: The Gathering*, offers valuable insights around this balance in his lecture, "Luck in Games." Garfield notes that while luck can make a game more exciting and accessible, it's crucial to balance it with skill. Too much luck can make players feel like their decisions don't matter while too little can lead to stale, predictable gameplay. He highlights how luck serves as a critical balancing element in games, allowing new players to have a chance against more experienced ones, which can make games more accessible and enjoyable.

Garfield breaks luck in games into two main types

**Input Luck** (also known as "luck of the draw"): This type of luck comes into play before the player makes a single decision. A classic example is the hand of cards you're dealt at the start of a round. Input luck can add an element of unpredictability and excitement to a game.

**Output Luck** (often seen in dice rolls): This type of luck happens after a player makes a decision, affecting the outcome of that decision. The chance that your perfectly planned move in a board game might be thwarted by a poor dice roll is an example of output luck.

The role of luck in achievement and rewards systems is a nuanced one. On one hand, incorporating elements of luck can heighten the sense of anticipation and excitement as players hope for a favorable outcome. On the other hand, players may become frustrated or feel that their skill and effort are not adequately recognized if rewards feel too arbitrary.

Consider the loot system in a game like *Borderlands 2* (Gearbox) versus *Final Fantasy 14* (Square Enix). The random chance of acquiring rare gear from defeating enemies creates a sense of suspense each time the player vanquishes a powerful foe. The procedural guns generated in *Borderlands 2* offer significant variety (we'll talk more about this in a later chapter), but that variety can lose novelty due to the lack of impactful changes in their statistics. In *Final Fantasy 14*, however, there is a higher amount of luck associated with getting bespoke and rare items. This uncertainty, this element of luck, makes obtaining a coveted item more rewarding.

It's crucial to balance this luck with systems that reward skill and effort. If a player puts significant time and energy into a challenging quest or boss fight, they expect a commensurate reward. If the outcome feels too luck-dependent, it can lead to frustration and imbalanced engagement. Bungie experienced this when they released, and subsequently removed, the loot cave for their multiplayer game *Destiny*. In their GDC talk "User Research on Destiny," the developers detailed how the players would spend hours in this environment killing enemies due to the perceived lack of difficulty in receiving rewards, neglecting other more compelling (and often more rewarding) content. The key to avoiding this is to understand your target players' motivations and then carefully balance elements of luck against elements of skill to cater to those motivations. By doing so, you create engaging experiences that resonate with your players by offering moments of surprise, achievement, shared laughter, and thrilling tension—all the ingredients of a memorable game.

## KNOW YOUR DARK PATTERNS

In the realm of user experience (UX) design, emotional design plays a significant role. This doesn't only apply to games—it also extends to all digital interfaces. When UX design is leveraged to seamlessly guide users toward beneficial actions, it can create an enjoyable and memorable user experience. When used manipulatively, however, it may result in what Harry Brignull terms "**Deceptive Patterns**." Also known as dark patterns, these are design choices that leverage an understanding of psychological principles in a way that facilitates exploitative actions or behaviors. They can infiltrate game design in a myriad of ways, often subtly influencing player behavior to the game's or company's benefit rather than enhancing the player experience.

Including these dark patterns in your games can result in player frustration and churn (i.e., rage quitting), so it is important to have a solid understanding of how they can occur. Let's take a look at some common deceptive patterns and how they show up in games.

**Comparison Prevention:** This largely shows up in situations around in-game purchases or trading systems where players can't compare what they are buying with similar packages or products. This can be seen frequently in many third-party sites that auction or randomly reward in-game items, but can also happen in many in-game social trading systems.

**Bait and Switch:** A player may be led to believe they're engaging with one game mechanic or feature, but the outcome of that engagement is entirely different than what the player expects. As an example, a button that's expected to provide a power-up might instead lead to an in-game store or ad.

**Fake Scarcity:** The player feels forced to purchase or pursue something in the game because it is presented as being falsely limited in supply.

**Disguised Ads:** Games may incorporate ads or in-app purchases that are disguised as game content. For example, an icon that appears to be an in-game reward or resource might be an ad or link to an in-game purchase.

**Preselection**: A game might intentionally direct a player's attention away from certain options and instead direct it toward another, default, option.

**Obstruction:** Games might make it easy for a player to enter a specific game state but make it challenging to exit. For instance, it could be simple to sign up for a recurring subscription for in-game perks, while cancellation is buried beneath layers of menus or requires contacting customer service.

**Forced Continuity**: This happens when a free trial of a game or premium service transitions into a paid subscription without the player's explicit consent or notification, leading to unexpected charges.

**Friend Spam:** Some games will ask for access to a player's social media or email contacts under the pretense of a social function, such as adding friends or sending gifts, but then use those contacts to send unsolicited messages or invitations.

**Confirmshaming:** This dark pattern attempts to guilt the user into opting in to something. The option to decline is worded in a way to shame the user into compliance. In games, this could manifest as manipulative messaging like "No, I don't want the super powerful bonus pack" as a way to opt out of a purchase or subscription.

**Hidden Costs:** This occurs when a game hides extra costs at the start of the purchase process, revealing them at the very end. For example, a game might advertise an in-app purchase at a certain price, but once the player goes to make the transaction, additional costs are added, such as taxes and service fees.

In-game design, the use of dark patterns can seriously harm the player experience, leading to frustration, dissatisfaction, and a sense of deception. If the player feels manipulated, they may disengage from the game, potentially leading to decreased player retention and negative word-of-mouth. Confirmshaming, for instance, can make players feel guilty or manipulated, while hidden costs can cause surprise and frustration and Friend Spam can lead to breaches of trust when players find they've shared more information than they intended.

Furthermore, when dark patterns intersect with elements of chance or luck, such as in randomized loot box mechanics, they can prey on the player's desire for rare items or achievements, sometimes leading to harmful behaviors like excessive spending.

Instead of resorting to such techniques, game designers should strive to create player-centric experiences by building mechanics and systems that are fair, transparent, and respectful of the player's autonomy. This upholds ethical standards, and it can also lead to more sustainable success by fostering trust and cultivating a positive relationship with the player community. Designers must strike a careful balance between elation and shame when motivating players with luck, emotions, and experience.

# PLAYER PERSONAS

A game, like any product or service, is designed for people, and people are complicated and diverse. This is a good thing! It allows us to make experiences as varied and unique as our players. Each player brings unique motivations, backgrounds, and experiences, so how can designers cater to this complexity and diversity?

Player **personas**, fictional but realistic representations of key player segments, allow us to empathize with and design for different player types. One of our key jobs as designers is to make sure our systems meet our players' needs and motivations, and player personas, which are grounded in understanding player motivation models, are an excellent tool to help us do this job. Each persona is a character sketch grounded in data and research, and it embodies a different cluster of player motivations and behaviors. Motivation models are invaluable when using personas because they provide a systematic way of mapping the personas to associated engagement types.

Why are personas important? They allow us to step into the player's shoes by making the abstract "player" concept concrete. This facilitates easy communication among members of the design team. Instead of talking about "the player," we can talk about Alex, who loves strategic challenges, and Sam, who craves social interactions. This makes our discussions more specific, our designs more focused, and—ultimately—our games more enjoyable for players.

When crafting personas, designers essentially craft a narrative of potential user experiences based on real data and research. Creating a persona isn't about designing for yourself or an imagined "ideal player." Rather, it's about designing for real people, with all their complexity, diversity, and (sometimes contradictory) motivations.

Let's examine what player personas might look like for one of my favorite game series, Mass Effect (BioWare), viewed through the lens of the motivation models we previously discussed

- **Alex the Completionist**: Alex is motivated by achievement, progression, and mastery. She wants to complete every mission, find every collectible, and max out her character's abilities. She enjoys doing speedruns of the game for charity fundraisers. During regular play sessions, she spends time on the Normandy (the player's spaceship) between missions, meticulously deciding which upgrades to invest in. A well-tuned difficulty curve with strategic decision-making along key milestones will keep her engagement high throughout her experience.
- **Sam the Architect**: Sam is primarily driven by social, expression, and creativity motivations. They spend a decent amount of their time in the game's multiplayer mode, but when they look for deeper social connection, they love the dialogue and team-building aspects of *Mass Effect*. They also like to shop at all the different stores and decorate Shepard's room on the Normandy. They are motivated by gaining an understanding of the game's world and characters in addition to working collaboratively with others. They spent 30 minutes with the character creator making sure their Shepard was absolutely perfect before starting the game.
- **Charlie the Thrill Seeker**: Charlie loves fast-paced, thrilling gameplay, so his motivations are action, challenge, and social competition. He enjoys the game's combat sequences and tense moments. Charlie focuses on completing missions and beating difficult opponents. He also engages deeply in the game's multiplayer mode, albeit for different reasons than Sam.
- **Emily the Escapist**: Emily loves to immerse herself in rich worlds and stories, so she is likely to engage deeply in the character relationship systems, digging into lore and dialogue. She's driven by fantasy, immersion, and exploration motivations. The game's romance options are also a large source of motivation for her. She is less interested in the action, so the story-focused difficulty setting, along with options to solve problems in ways other than fighting, are deeply rewarding for her.

Each persona has a unique journey (we discussed journeys in Chapter 4) based on their motivations, so these personas help designers predict player behavior and possible areas of frustration and churn. In essence, crafting player personas isn't just about predicting what players will do. It's also about foreseeing potential issues and addressing them early on, ensuring an engaging and enjoyable experience for all players. A player like Alex, driven by achievement and mastery, would find joy in conquering missions, gathering collectibles, and optimizing character abilities. In contrast, someone like Sam, who enjoys social interaction and immersion, would be drawn to dialogues, relationship building, and lore discovery. Then there's Charlie, who's all about action; his journey would emphasize thrilling battles and adrenaline-pumping sequences.

Understanding these diverse journeys is essential for designing a game that caters to various player types. It's about identifying where a player might stumble or lose interest—the so-called pain points. For instance, an action lover like Charlie might find lengthy dialogues frustrating, suggesting a need for optional or action-integrated dialogues.

Of course, it isn't the goal to design for all players—the goal is to design for *your* players. Research (as discussed in Chapter 2) helps you understand who your players are and what motivates them while personas help you remember and design for those players. If you use research, motivation clusters, and personas in your design process, you'll be well on your way to creating games that are enjoyable, engaging, and user-centered. In the next chapter we'll dive into unlocking and mapping the next driver in our motivational engine-emotion.

# BIBLIOGRAPHY

Barry, Isaac, et al. "Group Report: Making Friends While Killing People." *Project Horseshoe*, 2014, https://www.projecthorseshoe.com/reports/featured/ph14r6.htm. Accessed 03 02 2023

Brignull, Harry. *Deceptive Patterns: Exposing the Tricks Tech Companies Use to Control You.* Harry Brignull, 2023.

Deck, Raylene. "Level Design Workshop: World Design for Different Player Types." *GDC Vault*, 2019, https://www.gdcvault.com/play/1025881/Level-Design-Workshop-World-Design. Accessed 10 January 2023.

DiMenichi, Brynne, and Eldad Yechiam. "(PDF) The power of competition: Effects of social motivation on attention, sustained physical effort, and learning." *ResearchGate*, 1 September 2015, https://www.researchgate.net/publication/282047273_The_power_of_competition_Effects_of_social_motivation_on_attention_sustained_physical_effort_and_learning. Accessed 9 March 2024.

Fullerton, Tracy. *Game Design Workshop: A Playcentric Approach to Creating Innovative Games.* CRC Press, 2018.

Garfield, Richard. "Richard Garfield - "Luck in Games" talk at ITU Copenhagen." *YouTube*, 14 September 2013, https://www.youtube.com/watch?v=av5Hf7uOu-o. Accessed 20 June 2023.

Hopson, John. "User Research on Destiny." *YouTube*, 8 April 2017, https://www.youtube.com/watch?v=izZcrG4WqGI. Accessed 3 February 2024.

Koster, Raph. "On Trust (part I) – Raph's Website." *Raph Koster*, 4 February 2006, https://www.raphkoster.com/2006/02/04/on-trust-part-i/. Accessed 3 February 2024.

Koster, Raph. "The Trust Spectrum – Raph's Website." *Raph Koster*, 16 March 2018, https://www.raphkoster.com/2018/03/16/the-trust-spectrum/. Accessed 3 February 2024.

Quantic Foundry. "Gamer Motivation Model." *Quantic Foundry*, April 2019, https://quanticfoundry.com/wp-content/uploads/2019/04/Gamer-Motivation-Model-Reference.pdf. Accessed 10 January 2023.

Tassi, Paul. "Destiny's 'Loot Cave' Showcases Bungie's Lingering Endgame Problems." Forbes, 22 September 2014, https://www.forbes.com/sites/insertcoin/2014/09/22/destinys-loot-cave-showcases-bungies-lingering-endgame-problems/. Accessed 3 February 2024

Wen, Leana, et al. "The pandemic canceled their wedding. So they held it in Animal Crossing." The Washington Post, 2 April 2020, https://www.washingtonpost.com/video-games/2020/04/02/animal-crossing-wedding-coronavirus/. Accessed 9 March 2024.

# Emotion Mapping and Player Journeys

# 7

## INTRODUCTION

Emotion is a powerful part of the motivation engine, but without intentional design, the emotions we try to evoke in our games can feel false, forced, or confusing for our players. Emotion and story maps are powerful tools that allow us as designers to map out a player's emotional journey as they engage with the narrative, helping us track and compare the player's intended experience with the actions and interaction of the game.

### What You Will Learn in This Chapter

- Creating Emotion Maps
- Personas and Emotion Maps
- Mapping emotion to player input
- Story Forms—linear and branching

## EMOTION AND STORY MAPPING

Margaret Kerrison's *Immersive Storytelling for Real and Imagined Worlds* is a guide to creating immersive narratives for a variety of mediums, including games, film, and literature. One of the book's key themes is the importance of using emotion to guide stories and create meaningful experiences for audiences. Emotion mapping allows designers to plan out the player's feelings and the game's desired intensity at key moments within the gameplay experience. We talked about mapping a player's journey through goals and guidance in Chapter 5; combined with emotion and story mapping, they create

DOI: 10.1201/9781003342977-11

a potent trifecta (or triforce for Zelda fans) of tools for understanding the overall game experience.

As a refresher, the player's **journey** refers to the player's total experience as they interact with a game. It begins the moment they first hear about the game, continues through their initial interactions and proficiency development, and carries on to eventual mastery, tracking the game verbs along the way. Similarly, emotion mapping involves understanding the emotional journey a player walks while playing a game, including the frustration they feel during challenges, the connections they make with characters, and the elation of unlocking achievements. Story mapping involves understanding the narrative journey the player walks, the characters they meet, places they visit, and challenges they overcome.

Including these combined maps in the full UX player journey can help designers create a coherent experience across the game's various systems and actions. It also helps prevent cognitive and narrative dissonance. A good emotion map will ebb and flow, offering the player breaks in the emotional story in the same way that we offer them breaks in the intensity of gameplay. Emotions can cause cognitive overload much like intense action and complex interactions can; when the emotional and intensity experiences are out of sync, it often compounds the "overload" effect.

To map this combined journey, we must adopt an empathetic mindset by placing ourselves in the player's shoes. This mapping process has several steps, not unlike what you'd see in other UX and design thinking approaches.

## Charting the General Emotional Journey

The first step in the mapping process is charting the player's emotional journey. Player emotion mapping focuses on capturing the player's emotional experience throughout the game. It identifies the emotional high and low points the player is expected to experience while playing. This journey is often depicted by a line graph with game progression on the X-axis and emotional intensity on the Y-axis. Throughout the game, players are likely to experience a range of emotions from confusion and frustration to joy and triumph (Figure 7.1).

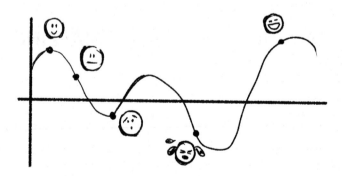

**FIGURE 7.1**   Emotion mapping.

It's crucial to map these emotional highs and lows since they can (and should) greatly impact the overall player experience. Mapping the player's emotional journey might help you find opportunities to enhance positive experiences. It will also allow you to identify points of friction—places where players may get stuck or frustrated. In addition, mapping lets you avoid pitfalls like placing high-stakes action or emotion directly after a vital plot point. (you don't want the player to be crying while fighting an intense boss, and yes, this has happened to me before). By giving them a few moments and the proper space to process the story point, you increase the likelihood that they will remember it when they move on to the action. Of course, your map is just a tool to help you get a general idea of the emotional journey; individual player experiences will vary widely depending on play style, decision-making, and personal reactions to the game's events. We'll talk a bit more about how you can map this to your personas in the next section.

Let us take a look at each step by looking at *Mass Effect 2* (BioWare), as an example (Figure 7.2).

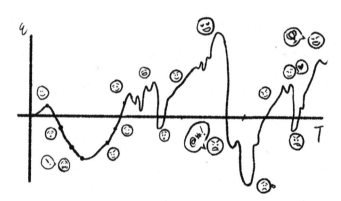

**FIGURE 7.2**  Shepard mapping.

1. **Beginning (High Stakes, Shock, Curiosity, Anticipation):** 😕🔍 As the game begins, there is a mix of curiosity and anticipation. Players are introduced to the game's setting, characters, and initial conflict through a series of intense sequences where the player's ship, the Normandy, is attacked, and the protagonist, after getting her crew to the escape pods safely, is blasted out into space. As she plummets down to the planet below, burning up as she enters the atmosphere, the player can't help but ask, "is the last we see of our beloved hero, Commander Shepard?"

2. **Character Building & Early Quests (Excitement, Engagement):** 😲 Commander Shepard awakens in a strange place. (Whew, she's alive!) But as she is being debriefed, the facility she is in is attacked! She must find allies and defeat the enemies. Excitement and engagement levels rise as players learn the combat systems, build a team of misfits, and start building their character's abilities.

3. **Revelation of the True Threat (Shock, Determination):** 😨 😐 The true threat is revealed by the mysterious Illusive Man, (the man who is responsible for resurrecting Shepard): this threat is the Collectors, an alien race hiding behind the Omega-4 relay. This brings about a sense of shock, which is quickly replaced by determination. The player's mission becomes clearer, and they're motivated to press on. They are given the goal of forming a team and gaining the tools needed to defeat their new enemy.

4. **Crew Member Loyalty Missions (Concern, Attachment):** 😟 🌱 Shepard scours the galaxy for her elite team, and as she builds her crew, she begins to form relationships with them. As players embark on loyalty missions for their crew members, they can experience concern, empathy, and even desire for these characters as they grow more attached to them.

5. **Collector Mission (Triumph, Horror, Fear, Revelation):** 😨 💀 Shepard and her crew head to a colony that is being attacked by the Collectors. They successfully rout the enemy but cannot stop the colonists from being abducted. The Illusive Man sends them to a disabled Collector Ship to investigate. There, the crew not only finds information on the Collectors and how to defeat them but also discovers that the ship is not disabled, but filled with enemies. The mission on the Collector Ship heightens the player's tension and fear as they fight through hordes of difficult enemies. Once the mission is completed, this turns into a sense of triumph and revelation as they realize they now have the information they need to truly defeat their enemy.

6. **Suicide Mission Preparations (Anxiety, Determination, Affection):** 😨 👊 Preparations for the final Suicide Mission elevate the player's anxiety levels as the crew attempts to retrieve the IFF necessary to get their ship through the Omega-4 relay. As Shepard and her away teamwork to acquire the IFF, the crew on the Normandy are attacked and abducted by the Collectors. Things look hopeless as the team approaches the Collector Base. However, the determination to save humanity helps players push through. They also realize that their entire crew may not survive the challenges to come, and they have the opportunity to spend some final quiet (and ahem, not so quiet) moments with those they have formed their closest relationships with.

7. **Suicide Mission & Climax (Tension, Elation):** 😨 💀 The crew of the Normandy believes they are ready to take on the enemy and head to the location of the Collector ship. They head into the Omega-4 relay with their newly acquired knowledge and IFF. The player makes some difficult choices around which of their crew will handle key roles in the mission. As the team works to save their abducted comrades and defeat the Collectors, they have to use all the skills they have acquired to come through victorious. The Suicide Mission is a tense ordeal, but completing it—especially if the player manages to keep their entire crew alive—leads to a great sense of accomplishment and elation.

8. **Endgame & Reflection (Satisfaction, Anticipation):** 😌 😊 After the climax, players may feel a deep sense of satisfaction. The emotional journey wraps up with reflection and anticipation of future adventures (in *Mass Effect 3*).

This sequence captures a general progression but is by no means definitive. There are also many ways of capturing this beyond graphs and charts—I will often, for example, create a music playlist to supplement my journey maps. Music is amazing at evoking mood and emotion in abstraction, and I've found that it can often communicate in ways that words and images cannot.

Because player agency foments complexity, it can often be impossible to fully and accurately depict the player journey. The key is to focus on key moments and reinforce the maps with learnings acquired through playtesting. Ideally, an emotion map considers these variations, providing a multifaceted look at the player's journey. For example, you can create different player journeys based on your different personas.

## Integrating Player Personas

Player journey mapping and player personas play a critical role in understanding and designing for your players' emotional experience. In Chapter 6, we used motivation mapping as a base for creating personas, and for the sake of simplicity, we'll do that here.

Let's briefly revisit these motivations

- **Action:** Enjoyment derived from fast-paced gameplay and excitement
- **Challenge:** Pursuit of difficult obstacles to overcome
- **Mastery:** Enjoyment from developing skills and strategy
- **Social:** Preference for interacting and/or competing with other players
- **Progression:** Enjoyment from completing tasks and collections
- **Fantasy:** Preference for escapism and roleplaying
- **Exploration:** Enjoyment from discovery and learning
- **Achievement:** Pursuit of in-game goals and recognition
- **Immersion:** Interest in the game's story, characters, and atmosphere
- **Creativity:** Pursuit of experimentation and creation
- **Expression:** Enjoyment from making the game world their own

Now, let's look at our persona examples for the *Mass Effect* series from Chapter 6, but through the lens of emotion, rather than interaction:

- **Alex the Completionist**: Alex is motivated by achievement, progression, and mastery. Alex's player journey includes not only the game's main storyline but also its numerous side quests and the process of character leveling and power optimization. She has also played the game multiple times to experiment with different classes and difficulty levels. Her emotional high points might be completing a difficult mission or reaching a new character level, but her proudest achievement was beating the game in Insanity mode in the Sentinel class. She bought herself an N7 hoodie to celebrate. She'll help Garrus but mostly engages with Shepard.

- **Sam the Architect**: Sam is primarily driven by the social, expression, and creativity motivations. They love the dialogue and relationship-building aspects of *Mass Effect*. They spend a lot of time talking to crewmates on the Normandy, building relationships, and delving into their personal stories. They particularly enjoy talking to Mordin, Joker, and Tali'Zorah. Their player journey revolves more around these interactions than combat scenarios. Sam's emotional high points might be reaching a new relationship level with a character or uncovering a previously unknown piece of lore, with the highest point coming when they complete the game with their entire crew and team alive and well. Their favorite storyline is the Citadel DLC because they love the goofy interactions between the characters and the teamwork required to complete the missions.
- **Charlie the Thrill Seeker**: Charlie loves fast-paced, thrilling gameplay, so he's motivated by action, challenge, and social. He enjoys the game's combat sequences and tense moments. Charlie's emotional journey emphasizes these adrenaline-fueled moments, and he often skips dialogues to get to the action. Although he enjoys the game, he only plays it once, returning occasionally to the multiplayer mode to get another taste of the world. His emotional high points are the climactic battles and action sequences, such as the boss fight against the Thresher Maw or the giant Reaper. He identifies with characters such as Wrex, Grunt, and Jack.
- **Emily the Escapist**: Emily loves to immerse herself in rich worlds and stories, so she is likely to engage deeply in the character relationship systems, digging into lore and dialogue. She's motivated by fantasy, immersion, and exploration. The narrative and relationship choices in *Mass Effect* allow her to express a certain level of creativity and agency in the game, and she enjoys experimenting with the story through multiple save points. She feels ownership over these choices and often refers to different types of "Shepards" she has created: FlirtShep, FightShep, LudditeShep, and more. For Emily, the game's emotional high comes when she completes a romantic story arc with her chosen character, Thane, and she has written popular fan fiction about the experience. She also completes multiple playthroughs, so surprising emotional twists and turns reward her efforts, although she restarts entire sections of the game if a character dies. If the combat becomes too difficult for her, she may quit the game entirely.

When we map these personas to the player's emotional journey, we as designers, better understand how different players might experience their game. By considering various perspectives during design, we can cater to a broad range of player motivations, thus enhancing the overall player experience.

Player personas can also help uncover areas of ludonarrative dissonance early in storycrafting. Consider an immersion-driven player like Emily. Encouraging her to make decisions that contradict her character's established values could break her sense of immersion. Keeping Emily's persona in mind, developers can strive for consistent and meaningful narrative choices, aligning gameplay more closely with the narrative and minimizing ludonarrative dissonance.

# Identifying Player Touchpoints

Every point of interaction between the player and the game is a **touchpoint.** This includes downloading the game, opening it for the first time, completing a tutorial, engaging in a challenging level, and even interacting with game-related content outside of the game itself. In Chapter 4, we talked about mapping game verbs to interactions in the player's journey. It's also important to do this with touchpoints through the lens of the emotional journey.

In *Mass Effect 2*, player touchpoints evolve as the player progresses through their emotional journey. These touchpoints include gameplay mechanics, the game environment, non-player characters (NPCs), and the dialogue system, among others.

In the beginning, touchpoints are largely designed to teach the player about the game's mechanics and rules. Early combat encounters and quests are simpler, designed to familiarize players with the combat system and the game's decision-making process. Players also encounter various NPCs, getting to know the key characters and gaining a sense of the game world's political and social structures.

As the game progresses, the touchpoints become more complex and meaningful. Combat encounters grow tougher, requiring players to use advanced tactics and make full use of their abilities. Their decisions start to have far-reaching consequences, affecting the game world and the story's outcome. At the same time, relationships with NPCs deepen and players can engage in detailed conversations with their crew, explore their crewmembers' backstories, and even pursue romantic relationships.

*Mass Effect 2*'s dialogue wheel is a particularly unique touchpoint. This isn't just a tool for selecting conversation options; it's a way for players to shape their character's personality and relationships. Early on, it introduces the player to the concept of "paragon" and "renegade" responses, essentially choices that are more compassionate or more pragmatic, respectively.

As the emotional journey intensifies, the dialogue wheel plays a significant role in reinforcing player choices. Tough situations often present moral dilemmas where the "right" choice isn't always clear, mirroring the growing tension and stakes in the game's narrative. For instance, players may need to decide whether to support a crew member's personal desire for revenge or advocate for a more lawful solution during a loyalty mission. Such decisions can affect the crew member's loyalty; this, in turn, can affect the game's ending, thereby amplifying the player's feelings of tension, concern, and attachment.

During the game's final stages, the dialogue wheel is critical in determining the outcome of the climactic Suicide Mission. The player's earlier decisions, reflected through the dialogue wheel, can dramatically affect which crew members live and which ones die, reinforcing feelings of satisfaction or regret based on their choices. This solidifies the dialogue wheel as not just a touchpoint but a pivotal aspect of the player's emotional journey. Seemingly simple choices like these—the touchpoints that represent player input and choice, have ripple effects throughout your game, so tracking them is essential.

## CASE STUDY ON IMMERSIVE EMOTIONAL PLAYER TOUCHPOINTS: BROTHERS: A TALE OF TWO SONS

*Brothers: A Tale of Two Sons* (Starbreeze) is unique because of its control scheme, narrative, and emotional resonance. In this game, the player simultaneously controls two brothers, each of whom is tied to one-half of the controller. This is not just a gameplay gimmick—it is a tool that masterfully reinforces the narrative by bonding the player with the characters and the characters with each other. The physical input (controls) becomes part of the player's journey, merging the game's mechanics with its storytelling.

The game starts by establishing the narrative context: the brothers' quest to find a cure for their sick father. Then, it introduces the unique controls. Each thumbstick and trigger on the controller allows the player to control one brother. Initially, this feels counterintuitive and unfamiliar, sometimes causing feelings of frustration or confusion—which mimics the brothers' own feelings of uncertainty as they embark on their journey. The player must adapt and persevere, much like the characters.

As the player navigates the game's puzzles and challenges, they develop a level of competence with the controls. They also discover that each brother has unique abilities; the older is stronger and can swim, whereas the younger is more nimble and can squeeze into tight spaces. Players begin to realize that progress requires coordination and cooperation between the brothers, just as the brothers themselves realize their need for each other. This mechanical bonding enhances the emotional connection between the player and the characters.

As the player masters the controls, they feel a sense of accomplishment and a sense of connection with the brothers. Then, comes a pivotal and heartbreaking narrative moment—the older brother dies. With the loss of the brother comes loss of input. Mechanically, the player can now use only half of the controller, a poignant and persistent reminder. The loss is not just built into the narrative; it's also in the gameplay mechanics. The physical void on the controller mirrors the emotional void in the story, and it is absolutely heartbreaking.

At the game's end, the younger brother faces a swimming challenge. Up until now, he has relied on his older brother to swim. His fear of water is a constant theme throughout the game. Naturally, the player tries to use only the younger brother's control, but he drowns. The solution? The player must use the older brother's trigger, a beautiful mechanical metaphor for drawing on the courage and strength of his lost brother. This challenges the game's established control scheme and provides a powerful, emotional conclusion to the journey.

Through *Brothers: A Tale of Two Sons*, we see how the player's journey extends beyond the on-screen narrative. The game's control scheme parallels the emotional journey, creating a sense of empathy, loss, and triumph. It's a brilliant example of how the emotional journey can be deeply influenced by the physical input, turning a game into a moving, memorable experience.

# Outlining the Player's Narrative Path

Kurt Vonnegut (one of my top 10 favorite authors) has a unique approach to storytelling, and his theory on mapping story shapes is both insightful and humorous. He included his insights about the shapes of stories in lectures and interviews throughout his career. One of the most popular examples comes from a lecture based on his rejected thesis for the University of Chicago's Anthropology Department. Vonnegut describes stories in terms of their shapes, which he plots on a graph. He refers to the vertical axis as the Fortune, or G-I axis, which runs from good fortune to ill fortune. The graph's horizontal axis represents the story progression from beginning to end.

## *Mapping popular story types*

- **Man in Hole:** At the start, things are going average for the protagonist. Then, they get into trouble (fall into a hole). By the end, they get out of trouble and end up better off than they were at the start. This creates a U-shaped graph. Action movies like *John Wick* or *Die Hard* use this map frequently (Figure 7.3).

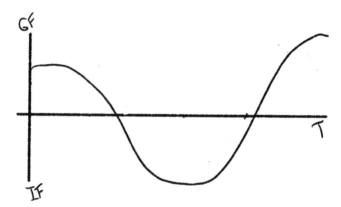

**FIGURE 7.3**   Man in hole.

- **Boy Meets Girl:** The protagonist begins in a state of neutrality then gets something they desire (like a romantic partner), loses it, and finally regains it. This graph's shape is similar to the "Man in Hole" graph but has a slight bump at the first moment where the protagonist first receives what they desire. This is the majority of story arcs for romantic comedies (Figure 7.4).

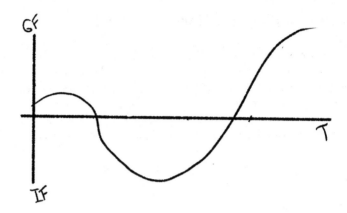

**FIGURE 7.4**  Boy meets girl.

- **From Bad to Worse (Kafkaesque):** The protagonist starts off in bad shape, and things just keep getting worse. This creates a downward line on the graph. A nice example of this story map can be found in the satirical horror movie *Cabin in the Woods* (Figure 7.5).

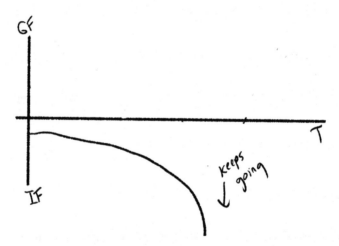

**FIGURE 7.5**  From bad to worse.

- **Which Way is Up?:** In this story map, the main character's fortunes rise and fall multiple times, with no clear trajectory. It creates a more complex and less predictable shape than any of the other story types. Complex dramatic movies and series such as *Downton Abbey* or *Game of Thrones* follow this map. Shakespeare's *Hamlet* is another classic example (Figure 7.6).

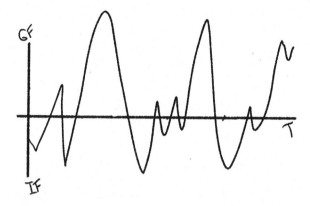

**FIGURE 7.6**  Which way is up.

- **Creation Story:** The world and characters emerge from chaos to create order and peace (Figure 7.7).

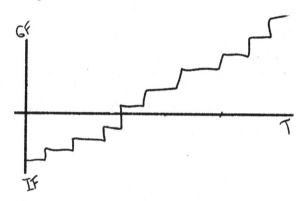

**FIGURE 7.7**  Creation story.

- **Old Testament:** The world and its characters go through cycles of good and bad fortune that slowly cycle downward (Figure 7.8).

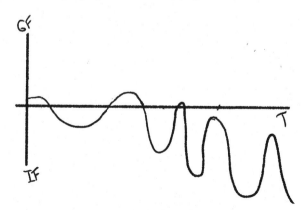

**FIGURE 7.8**  Old testament.

- **New Testament:** The protagonist has exceptionally good fortune until something terrible happens. They must work hard and often make sacrifices to find their path to redemption. The movie *Shawshank Redemption* is a classic example of this story arc. This is also a popular arc for coming of age storylines (Figure 7.9).

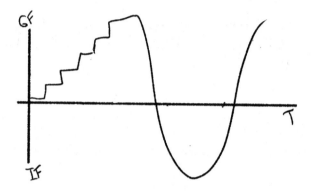

**FIGURE 7.9**   New testament.

- **Cinderella:** The protagonist starts lower than low, they have hit bottom. Then suddenly a change of fate occurs and they skyrocket into bliss. As you can imagine, this story derives its main inspiration from its namesake, but there are many popular rags to riches stories throughout history that follow this arc (Figure 7.10).

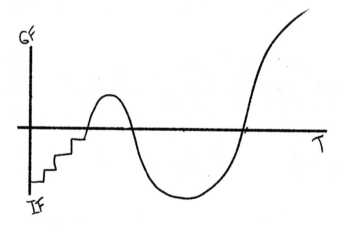

**FIGURE 7.10**   Cinderella.

Often, Kurt Vonnegut's own works don't fit neatly into the simple shapes he has identified—which is part of what makes them so unique and beloved. His narratives frequently subvert traditional expectations. For example, *Slaughterhouse-Five* jumps around in time, blending moments of good and ill fortune in a non-linear way. It reflects protagonist Billy Pilgrim's own experiences of being "unstuck in time (Figure 7.11)."

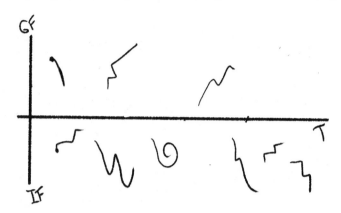

**FIGURE 7.11**   Slaughterhouse five.

As we mentioned with emotion mapping, player agency can make mapping these stories complicated. But using simple visual methods like Vonnegut's G/I axis to explore video game narratives provides a unique lens that is easy to replicate and explore. Let's delve into some examples and see how they might fit:

| GAME | STORY SHAPE | KEY PLOT POINTS |
| --- | --- | --- |
| **Super Mario Brothers (Nintendo)** | Boy Meets Girl (again, and again, and again) | • Mario meets Princess Peach<br>• Peach is captured by the evil Bowser<br>• Mario journeys to rescue Peach<br>• Mario defeats Bowser<br>• Peach is in another castle<br>• Mario defeats Bowser....again<br>• Peach is in another castle…again<br>• Repeat until world map is explored<br>• Mario (finally) rescues Peach |

*(Continued)*

| GAME | STORY SHAPE | KEY PLOT POINTS |
| --- | --- | --- |
| **Tomb Raider (Crystal Dynamics)** | Woman in Hole | • Lara Croft's expedition to Yamatai has been funded and she sets forth to the island.<br>• Shipwreck! Lara is stranded on the island.<br>• The island is inhabited by violent settlers and cultists.<br>• Lara dies… a lot… and violently… as the player attempts to escape the island.<br>• Lara finds her friends, escapes from the island, and sails home. |
| **Final Fantasy 12 (Square Enix)** | Which Way is Up? | • The story starts in the city of Rabanastre, which is under Archadian occupation. Vaan, the protagonist, dreams of becoming a sky pirate.<br>• As the plot unfolds, Vaan gets involved in a tangled web of political intrigue, war, and resistance, teaming up with a wide variety of complex characters.<br>• The characters face multiple setbacks and challenges, from the betrayal of their allies to confrontations with powerful foes.<br>• Although the main threat is thwarted by the game's end, the world and its political landscape have changed significantly. |
| **Civilization (Firaxis)** | Creation Story | • The world is new and filled with roving bands of barbarians. You and your band of settlers must find resources and establish colonies.<br>• As the ages pass, you discover new technologies, form societies, and build your empire.<br>• You reach the height of civilization and get ready to explore the cosmos. |
| **Forgotten Anne (Throughline Games/ Square Enix)** | New Testament | • Anne is an enforcer who keeps order in a place known as the Forgotten Lands, raised by the ruler of the world Bonku.<br>• She discovers that a rebellion is taking place and attempts to thwart it.<br>• Anne learns that the power source in her world stems from destroying the beings who live in it.<br>• Anne allies with the rebels and discovers true friendship.<br>• Anne chooses to sacrifice herself to save the world and its inhabitants. |

*(Continued)*

| GAME | STORY SHAPE | KEY PLOT POINTS |
|---|---|---|
| **Forgotten Anne (Throughline Games/ Square Enix)** | Old Testament | • Anne is an enforcer who keeps order in a place filled with forgotten items, raised by the ruler of the world Bonku.<br>• She discovers that a rebellion is taking place and attempts to thwart it.<br>• Anne learns that the power source in her world stems from destroying the beings who live in it.<br>• Anne discovers that she herself is a forgotten object and hungers to return to the real world.<br>• Anne sacrifices the Forgotten Lands to allow her and Bonku to return to the "real world." |
| **Hatoful Boyfriend (Hato Moa/ Mediatonic)** | Cinderella | • An epic war of birds and humans results in the world being populated by sentient birds. Our protagonist is one of the few remaining humans, a boisterous hunter gatherer who lives in the wilderness.<br>• The protagonist is invited to join the prestigious bird academy St. PigeoNation's Institute as the only human.<br>• She meets eight different birds that, if she makes the right decisions, she could have her dream relationship with. |
| **Cinders (Moacube)** | Cinderella, Subverted (sometimes) | • Cinders is a young woman raised by her stepmother with her two step sisters. Her father has passed away and she has become the house maid due to her stepmother's cruelty.<br>• There is a ball coming up and everyone is talking about it.<br>• Based on the decisions that the player makes and how they want to roleplay, Cinders can have adventures that end in everything from marrying the prince of her dreams to traveling the world to becoming an independent business woman. |
| **Dream Daddy (Game Grumps)** | Boy Meets Boy | • A single dad moves to a new town with his daughter.<br>• He meets other dads in his new neighborhood<br>• He pursues one or more of the dads<br>• There is flirtation, connection, conflict, then a moment that reunites them<br>• He celebrates his daughter's birthday with his new partner |

(Continued)

| GAME | STORY SHAPE | KEY PLOT POINTS |
|---|---|---|
| **Dream Daddy (Game Grumps)** | Boy Meets Boy, then things get Kafkaesque | • A single dad moves to a new town with his daughter.<br>• He meets other dads in his new neighborhood<br>• He pursues one or more of the dads but<br>• Dads start disappearing around the neighborhood<br>• After investigating the disappearances, the player uncovers a cult that is sacrificing dads, led by their love interest! |
| **Disco Elysium (ZA/UM)** | Old Testament | • The protagonist, a detective, wakes up in a hotel room with a terrible hangover and no memory of who he is or how he got there. (He starts off at "ill fortune.")<br>• The player makes choices that either improve or worsen the detective's situation, echoing the fluctuating fortunes characteristic of the "Which Way is Up?" shape, but continuously moving along a downward trajectory.<br>• The story unravels as a complex case involving murder, political tensions, and personal traumas.<br>• The detective solves the case but is unable to find redemption. |
| **Disco Elysium (ZA/UM)** | From Bad to Worse (Kafkaesque) | • The protagonist, a detective, wakes up in a hotel room with a terrible hangover and no memory of who he is or how he got there. (He starts off at "ill fortune.")<br>• As the game progresses, the player makes choices that worsen the detective's situation consistently. He is horrible, the world is horrible, everything is horrible.<br>• The detective continues spiraling into despair. |

As you can see from some of our examples, player agency can make things get complicated quickly. Since games allow players to influence narrative outcomes, they don't often fit neatly into traditional story shapes. Still, Vonnegut's model provides a fascinating starting point for analyzing them. Like Vonnegut's own stories, games often defy expectations, offering complex, multifaceted narratives. Therefore, we need more complex maps.

## LEARNING FROM FILM TO CREATE CINEMATIC EXPERIENCES

One of the magical things about games is the level of agency, immersion, and interaction they provide to the player. This level of interaction can, however, make narrative dialogue and cinematics seem disruptive or annoying when the timing is off. Fortunately, the film medium demonstrates many clever ways to explore the perception of time and the linearity of story.

## ORDER

Game designers can shuttle viewers back and forth along the narrative timeline by playing with order. In Christopher Nolan's film *Memento*, the protagonist's anterograde amnesia is portrayed through a narrative that progresses both backward and forward, twisting the viewer's perception of order. Similarly, the game *Twelve Minutes* (Annapurna) uses repetitive time loops to reveal information to the player as they run out of time in each instance. It takes direct inspiration from psychological thrillers in the film medium, including *Memento*.

Her Story (Sam Barlow) takes the idea of order one step further by granting the player agency over which video clips they see. This is accomplished through an open and searchable database, bringing the verb "investigation" to the very forefront of the game, aligning and counterpointing it with the order in which the player experiences the narrative.

## PACING

Pacing is the speed and cadence at which a narrative unfolds. The frenetic, fast-paced action sequences of George Miller's film *Mad Max: Fury Road* pull the viewer along at breakneck speed, while Yasujiro Ozu's film *Tokyo Story* luxuriates at a slow pace that mirrors the unhurried rhythms of everyday life. Cinema also uses shot sequences that create rhythm and supplement pacing and duration. The suspenseful buildup leading to the shower scene in Alfred Hitchcock's Psycho illustrates the powerful use of rhythm to enhance narrative tension. Hitchcock once said that he enjoys "playing the audience like a piano," and in *Psycho*, he does this masterfully by manipulating the film's rhythm. Its sequences are long in the beginning and gradually get shorter, using more and more cuts before reaching the frenetic pace of over 70 short shots in the three-minute shower scene.

Racing games like *Forza Motorsport* (Microsoft) use a quick pace to heighten tension and excitement. This sense of speed affects the player's perception of time and requires them to react quickly. The game uses cinematics as bookends to the racing experience, heightening the player's feelings of tension and drama before and after the race. This helps the player focus on the moment-to-moment gameplay during the race itself.

*Firewatch* (Campo Santo) is a first-person adventure game set in the Wyoming wilderness. The player's only emotional lifeline is the person on the other end of a handheld radio. The game makes extensive use of dialogue and environmental storytelling, building its narrative slowly as the player explores the game's environment and interacts with the other main character via radio. This game, like *Tokyo Story*, emphasizes dialogue and character interaction, focuses on ordinary people in extraordinary circumstances, and is willing to take its time in letting the narrative unfold. There are no high-speed action sequences or explosive moments; instead, the game is driven by conversation and exploration. The player has the freedom to experience the game world at their own pace, which allows for a more meditative, introspective experience than that of fast-paced games.

## DURATION

Duration, the actual runtime of a film versus the timeframe of the narrative it depicts, can be manipulated to startling effect. In the second season of the tv series *The Bear*, the seventh episode ("Review") includes an intense, uninterrupted 18 minute take. As the story unfolds in real time, the viewer is pulled into the frenetic and chaotic action of a small restaurant operation. In contrast, *2001: A Space Odyssey* by Stanley Kubrick encapsulates millennia in a two-hour film, rendering time elastic. In games, we have the benefit of creating a wide range of experiences in terms of duration; some games last for only two hours while others last 200.

## SPEED

Slow motion is often used for dramatic impact in film, elongating the biggest moments so the audience has time to absorb and reflect on them. In games, this effect is usually leveraged for dramatic ends to boss fights or celebratory sequences. Conversely, speeding up time creates an overall sense of tension or indicates a fast elapse of time. If you must subject your players to lore dumps or exposition, speeding up the cinematic tempo can make the experience feel more dynamic while also alluding to a large amount of time passing between the moment of play and the story being told.

The iconic slow-motion bullet-dodging scene in *The Matrix* or the surreal speed manipulation in *Inception* serve to enhance these films' narrative impact and aesthetic appeal while granting greater agency to individual characters. As action heroes move faster, the world slows down to emphasize the power shift. Games like *Superhot* (SUPERHOT team) manipulate time in a similar way. In this game, time only moves when the player does, leading to a unique blend of strategy and action. The *Max Payne* series (Rockstar/Remedy) uses "bullet time" during intense gunfights in gameplay and cutscenes, slowing down the action so the player can react to threats, reminiscent of the slow-motion scenes from *The Matrix* or John Woo's films.

**SIMULTANEITY**

In film editing, simultaneity refers to the video editing technique of switching back and forth between scenes (also known as crosscutting), often giving the impression that the action occurring in different locations is unfolding at the same moment. It adds suspense and develops narrative contrast. *The Godfather* artfully uses crosscutting to display the duality of one of the main characters. As he attends the Baptism of his niece, the film cuts back and forth between the brutal assassinations he ordered as the new head of the family. In a similar vein, cutscenes in *Star Wars: Knights of the Old Republic* (Bioware) show multiple events that happen simultaneously. For example, a scene might cut between characters on different parts of a spaceship who all have unique experiences at the same time, heightening the tension and stakes.

# Story Mapping for Player Agency

A typical game story map is similar to an emotion map, but it highlights the game's key plot points in relation to the actions and experiences. This is particularly important in non-linear or branching storytelling, where player agency introduces significant complexity into the game. The story map should show when new characters are introduced, when key story beats occur, when there are new environments to explore, and so on. The format of these maps depends on the type of game you're making and the story you want to tell. In linear storytelling, the map is fairly straightforward—you simply map any new events and characters to your existing emotion maps, and then you make sure the narrative aligns with the emotions to avoid ludonarrative dissonance.

Games, however, are rarely that simple because the player's journey is rarely linear. They may loop back to revisit levels, make choices that impact the story, take detours to side quests, or perhaps even put the game down for a while before returning to it. You'll want to outline these various paths on your map, considering the different decisions a player may make along the way. Narrative designer Sam Kabo Ashwell's blog post "Standard Patterns in Choice-Based Games" presents a taxonomy of various structures used in branching narratives, specifically within choice-based games. Ashwell breaks these structures into a few categories. Each of these categories offers a different approach to creating an interactive narrative and player experience.

**Gauntlet:** This structure is primarily linear, with players facing a series of obstacles or challenges in a set order. While choices may be available within individual challenges, they do not significantly alter the overall sequence or outcome of events. This type of structure is common in many action-adventure games where the main narrative follows a set path. While the choices do not impact the story, they offer flavor, novelty, and variety (Figure 7.12).

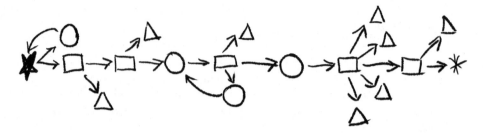

**FIGURE 7.12**   Guantlet.

Choices usually rely on characters or daily life in these games to help manage player expectations. In *Bioshock* (Irrational), the player is prevented with a choice around the characters of the Little Sisters—they can either harvest them or purify them. While this choice is a way for the player to express themselves within the game, it does not impact the plot in a meaningful way.

**Branch and Bottleneck:** In this structure, there are key narrative points where the story branches out, offering different paths and outcomes based on player choices. However, these branches eventually lead back to common points, or "bottlenecks," allowing the story to progress along a relatively fixed path. This structure allows for meaningful player choices while keeping the narrative manageable from a development standpoint (Figure 7.13).

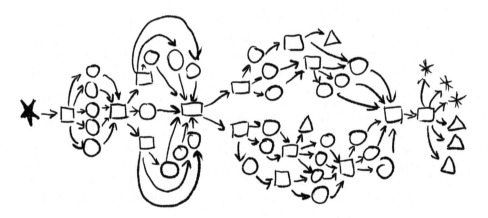

**FIGURE 7.13**   Branch and bottleneck.

In Telltale's episodic games such as *The Walking Dead* or *The Wolf Among Us*, the player is often given choices that have micro impacts on the game but do not change the overall plot. These games are great examples of the Branch and Bottleneck model at play. It is important when using this map to set appropriate player expectations, as choice often leaves the expectation of impact, and having big choices with small impacts can result in frustration.

Point and click adventure games are another great source of inspiration for this map. In *Maniac Mansion* (Lucasfilm), the player needs to use different characters to solve the game's various puzzles, and the game was the first in the industry to utilize cutscenes (a term coined by designer Ron Gilbert) to inform the player about the impact of their choices. The game was also lauded for its five endings, all of which were dependent upon which characters survived the mansion's various traps and terrors.

**Time Cave:** This structure is like a branching tree. Each decision point splits the narrative into different paths, each with its own subsequent decision points, leading to an exponentially increasing number of potential narratives. This type of structure allows for a highly interactive narrative, but it can be difficult to manage due to its complexity (Figure 7.14).

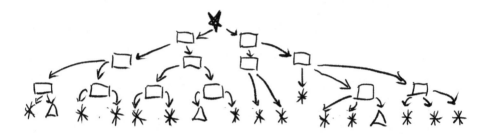

**FIGURE 7.14**    Time cave.

Dating sims are great examples of Time Cave maps, particularly in the otome genre. In these games, the player typically goes through an onboarding plotline that introduces them to the various characters, and then as they make decisions toward who they want to spend their time with the path becomes more focused on that specific character's arc.

*Boyfriend Dungeon* (Kitfox games) takes this a step further, by integrating the weapons upgrade and combat systems into the branching maps. The more time a player spends with their weapon in the dungeons, the more they get to know the character that the weapon transforms into.

This branching system offers high replayability, but requires a lot of upfront design, writing, and asset creation. You as a designer need to be comfortable with the fact that your players will likely only see a fraction of the content you create and adjust your designs accordingly.

**Quest**: In this structure, the game offers a pool of available quests or tasks that players can complete in any order—or even ignore altogether. The overall narrative is shaped by the player's choices and the quests they choose to undertake (Figure 7.15).

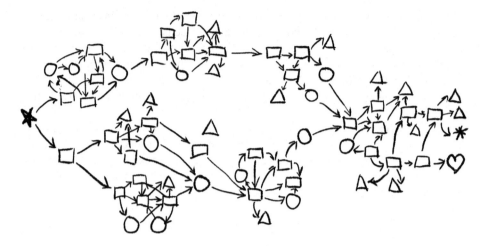

**FIGURE 7.15** Quest.

*Sunless Sea* (Failbetter) is a game that combines roguelike and roleplaying mechanics to create a web of quests that generate what designer Emily Short calls "storylets," short snippets of story that fit into a greater emergent landscape. In the game, the player pilots a steamship that they can use to explore islands throughout the dark expanse of the sunless sea. In this way, the story map reflects the physical map that the player navigates—each quest cluster is represented by an island.

Quest systems offer a large amount of flexibility and player agency, but that can result in complexity. Keeping each quest cluster relatively isolated in terms of impact can help mitigate this complexity. If you want the quests to impact other areas of the game and its narrative, make sure you create the proper tools for testing and troubleshooting those impacts.

Another way to mitigate this complexity is to combine quest structures with a Branch and Bottleneck. In *Baldur's Gate 3* (Larian) the designers intentionally divided the narrative into three distinct acts. By doing this, they were able to lower the number of narrative variables that need to be tracked from storyline to storyline and lower the ripple effects of the quests by gating them.

**Loop and Grow:** This structure is built around a central theme or thread that the narrative keeps circling back to. This allows the player to unlock new knowledge or try new things as they progress (Figure 7.16).

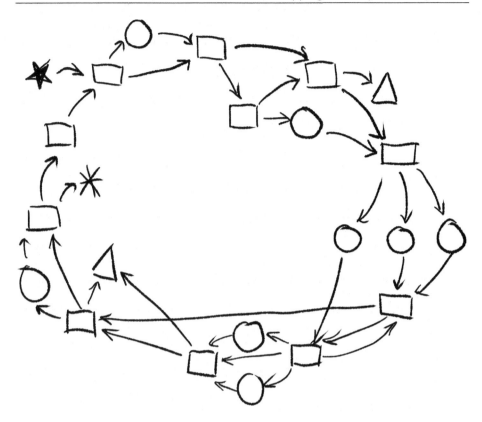

**FIGURE 7.16**   Loop and grow.

We discussed Kishōtenketsu in Chapter 1, and I think it's worth revisiting when thinking about the Loop and Grow structure. You might recall that Kishōtenketsu is a four-act narrative structure common in East Asian storytelling. The four acts are:

**Ki (Introduction):** The characters, setting, and other basic elements are established.

**Shō (Development):** The story develops by expanding on the elements introduced in Ki without introducing conflict.

**Ten (Twist):** An unexpected event occurs, usually something that doesn't directly involve the main narrative.

**Ketsu (Conclusion):** The twist is integrated and the story is concluded, often linking back to the Ki in a surprising or satisfying way.

This structure doesn't rely on conflict or confrontation, making it quite different from the typical Western three-act structure (setup, confrontation, resolution).

In the Loop and Grow structure, a repeating cycle or loop of gameplay (or narrative) grows or changes over time. This happens either by expanding upon the existing loop or introducing new elements (the "grow" part), very much like what happens in the Ki and Shō stages of Kishōtenketsu.

The Ten ("Twist") stage manifests as a significant change or shift in the loop, adding a new dimension to the gameplay or narrative. The Ketsu, or conclusion, mirrors the loop's ultimate growth. This is where the elements introduced in the twist are incorporated into the gameplay or narrative in a way that brings everything to a meaningful conclusion.

*13 Sentinels: Aegis Rim* (Vanillaware) is a game that wonderfully demonstrates the connection between Kishōtenketsu and the Loop and Grow structure. In this game, players switch between 13 different characters, each with their own narrative arc (the loop) that contributes to a larger, overarching story.

The Ki and Shō stages correspond to the introduction and development of each character's story as well as the introduction and gradual mastery of the game's unique combat system. The Ten stage is represented by the various plot twists that occur within each character's story and the overall narrative. These twists often involve revealing surprising connections between characters or unexpected aspects of the game world, which add new layers of complexity to the gameplay and narrative (the "grow" part of the Loop and Grow structure).

Finally, each character's story is resolved in the Ketsu stage, along with the overall narrative. The elements introduced in the twist stage are incorporated into a meaningful conclusion that ties all the individual narratives together and brings the game's complex plot to a satisfying end.

These looping maps are also important to consider for games that operate in a live service setting. However, they should be created and handled somewhat differently for this type of game. Instead of mapping the overall narrative, create maps based on short-term, mid-term, and long-term goals. This allows you to create flexible stories that can cycle and continually engage players as they enjoy the game over time. Because this kind of game rarely has a traditional ending, planning stories based on these different goal levels helps the writing team understand that they need to create cyclical stories to mimic the player's experience within the game. Looking at narrative structures from serial television or stories from outside of the common Western narrative structures can ensure that the story will match this experience.

How does this tie into games like *Fortnite*? *Fortnite* is a live service game that continuously evolves by adding new content, characters, and events. It encourages emergent gameplay, where the players create their own narratives based on their actions and interactions within the game's systems.

Imagine mapping each of *Fortnite's* islands, or seasons, to this looping structure. Like the characters in *13 Sentinels*, each island represents a loop of the story map, and with the end of each season it is the players that are transformed by the experience rather than the plot. And because of the emergent gameplay and the regularly updated content, each player's journey can be unique and unpredictable, adding depth and replayability to the game.

The beauty of live service games like *Fortnite* is that the story doesn't conclude with ketsu; it loops back to ki and the player embarks on a new journey. This cyclical narrative structure, with variations in each cycle, is a key reason why games like *Fortnite* manage to keep players engaged over extended periods of time. The primary difference is rather than the characters evolving over time with each loop, it is the players.

Different story structures offer different balances between player agency and narrative control. Understanding this balance can help developers design narratives that offer satisfying levels of interactivity while still delivering a coherent and engaging story. For instance *Mass Effect 2* mostly uses the Branch and Bottleneck structure with some elements of Quest maps in the form of optional side missions. This allows for meaningful player choices while still maintaining a strong, overarching narrative.

Now, this mapping might sound like a lot of work (and it can be), but it's worth it. It allows you to design a game that not only satisfies the player's goals and desires but also elicits positive emotional responses. It helps you create a game that is not just fun to play but also a joy to experience. When you map out your story through the emotions, personas, and choices, you're not just sketching a path—you're crafting an experience, a story that each player can make their own.

This is why a player's journey is so vital in game development. Like a well-designed object or service in the physical world, a well-designed game should feel intuitive, enjoyable, and rewarding. And just like in traditional UX design, the player journey is at the heart of achieving this. Solid story and emotion mapping allows you to create an experience that aligns your narrative with the player's actions and interactions, creating a consistent and engaging emotional experience. In our final chapter we'll dig into characters and their potential for heightening this emotional resonance and engagement.

# BIBLIOGRAPHY

Ashwell, Sam Kabo. "Standard Patterns in Choice-Based Games | These Heterogenous Tasks." *These Heterogenous Tasks*, 26 January 2015, https://heterogenoustasks.wordpress.com/2015/01/26/standard-patterns-in-choice-based-games/. Accessed 25 July 2023.

Comberg, David. "Why should you read Kurt Vonnegut? - Mia Nacamulli." *YouTube*, 29 November 2018, https://www.youtube.com/watch?v=cwwK7NmfF9w. Accessed 24 August 2023.

Doane, Mary Ann. *The Emergence of Cinematic Time: Modernity, Contingency, the Archive.* Harvard University Press, 2002. Accessed 4 July 2023.

Hadadi, Roxana. "How 'The Bear' Shot Episode 7 in One Take." *Vulture*, 29 July 2022, https://www.vulture.com/article/how-the-bear-shot-episode-7-one-take.html. Accessed 29 March 2024

Kerrison, Margaret. *Immersive Storytelling for Real and Imagined Worlds: A Writer's Guide.* Michael Wiese Productions, 2022.

Vonnegut, Kurt. *"The Shapes of Stories."* Case Western University, 2014.

# Designing Characters

# 8

---

## INTRODUCTION

---

When I ask players about their favorite stories in games, they very rarely respond with a plot synopsis. More often, they talk about characters—either the characters they themselves embody or the ones they form relationships with as they play. They'll talk about jumping over chasms as Nathan Drake in *Uncharted* (Naughty Dog), navigating the desert with another hooded character in *Journey* (thatgamecompany), or their favorite romance in *Dragon Age* (BioWare).

While not every game or story needs its characters to be engaging, it is incredibly difficult for characters to be relevant to players in the absence of story or deeper mechanical ties to the game. Therefore, it is important for game teams to take great care when making decisions around character use and design.

A character can represent an element of the game system, or it can represent the player's identity. Beyond that, characters guide player goals and create deeper emotional motivations. They coax, cajole, and sometimes even compel players into experiencing a wide range of feelings. In other words, well-crafted character designs are masterful emotion engines. When a beloved NPC is in danger, for instance, we feel anxiety. When they betray us, we feel anger or disappointment. When they aid us in our quest, we feel gratitude. These emotional responses motivate players to engage more deeply with the game world and its narratives and keep our beautiful motivational engine running.

## What You Will Learn in This Chapter

- Inspiring emotion with characters
- Supporting game actions with characters
- Aligning character motivations with player motivations
- Character versus caricature
- Character casts that support the game world
- Creating user-friendly character documentation

DOI: 10.1201/9781003342977-12

# CRAFTING CHARACTERS

Creating compelling characters in video games is akin to sculpting a masterpiece from a block of marble—it requires patience, precision, and a profound understanding of the medium's potential. At the heart of this process are three vital principles: depth, emotion, and player agency (Figure 8.1).

**FIGURE 8.1**   Character crafting.

Game designer Caroline Marchal and drama producer John Yorke discuss these principles in their 2018 GDC Talk "How to Create Great Characters: Depth, Emotion and Player Agency." Drawing on her experience designing games like *Heavy Rain* (Quantic Dream) and his seminal book *Into the Woods*, they examine these principles in the context of video game characters, bringing them to life with examples from the gaming landscape.

# DEPTH

Depth in a character is synonymous with layers: backstory, personality, ambitions, fears, and a complex array of traits. Deep characters resonate with audiences because they are relatable figures even though they navigate a fabricated world.

A character's **traits and values** should convey the main descriptors of their personality and beliefs. They should have a unique worldview that reflects their upbringing and shapes their reaction to both the situations they encounter and the world around them. In games, the depth of the character's traits and values should mirror the depth of world-building within the game, reinforcing the world's core tenets while filtering them through the lens of the character's perceptions and personality.

Remember the world-building icebergs we discussed in Chapter 3? Well, character designs should be built like icebergs as well. **Backstory** should explain why the character responds to situations in specific ways. It should also explain how they came to be in their current situation in the game world. Backstory can cover a variety of topics, including

- Background and history
- Relationships and interactions with other characters
- Behavior in unexpected situations
- Wants and needs
- Values and purpose
- Motivations and desires
- Flaws and faults
- Fears and triumphs

As the characters move through the game world and experience the game's actions and goals, their desires can and should change. Changing desires are a great vehicle for narrative feedback; they give the player a sense of progress and agency by reflecting the results of their choices in the characters around them.

Let's take a look at a few classic video game characters and see how far we can get in terms of depth.

| CHARACTER | BACKGROUND | TRAITS | VALUES AND PURPOSE | FLAWS | MOTIVATION | WANTS AND NEEDS |
|---|---|---|---|---|---|---|
| Mario (Super Mario Bros, Nintendo) | Plumber | Athletic, Optimistic | Find the Princess, Defeat Bowser | Princess is always in another castle | Find the princess | Find the princess, Eat mushrooms, Drive karts |
| Pikachu (Pokemon, The Pokemon Company) | Once a wild animal, now a beloved pet/ ally for Ash Ketchum | Determined, Unwilling to give up, Optimistic, Adorable | Make friends, Defeat opponents | Doesn't like to be called cute | Help Ash become a Pokemon Master | Get stronger, play outside, eat treats, spend time with friends |
| Lara Croft (Tomb Raider, Crystal Dynamics) | Former aristocrat turned treasure hunter, on the search for her missing father | Intelligent, Strong, Fearless, Independent, Polyglot, Resourceful | Preserve artifacts, Stand up for the weak | Can't see the bigger picture | Find father, Find treasure | Solve puzzles, Find treasure, Find father |
| Ellie (The Last of Us, Naughty Dog) | Survivor of a deadly pandemic | Strong, Witty, Rough around the edges | Ends justify the means | Struggles with feelings of self worth, Impulsive, Naive | Help create a cure for pandemic | Find love, Help people, Get revenge |

Note that characters do not always have to be complicated to have depth. Sometimes consistency, in the case of characters like Mario, can become iconic. And when consistency is combined with complexity, in the case of characters like Ellie, we can create characters that are realistic, modern, and transcendent.

**Inventory, equipment**, and **skills** are great design tools that can, if used intentionally, integrate your characters into the systems and verbs of the core loop of your game. They are wonderful signifiers for character use and purpose. They should convey the character's main role, the kind of actions they are expected to complete, and their strengths and weaknesses. These aspects can also convey the character's lore and cultural background, grounding them within the game world.

Inventory and equipment serve as an essential palette for bringing color and depth to in-game characters. In a pixelated world where characterization is often limited, tools like armor, weapons, and accessories play a critical role in illustrating a character's personality, their abilities, and how they're perceived by the player. Every item, every piece of gear or accessory, paints a picture of who this character is, how they face challenges, and how they interact with their world. Just as we come to know people by their actions, in games, we often come to know characters by their equipment.

The function of equipment in *Death Stranding*, Hideo Kojima's post-apocalyptic delivery simulator, is practical, often cumbersome, and viscerally tied to the game's survivalist mechanics. The protagonist, Sam, physically lugs his equipment around the world, his staggering load visually representing the weight of his responsibility. Each piece of equipment, from ladders and ropes to the Bridge Baby (BB), reinforces the concept of struggle that Kojima's games are known for. A character burdened with equipment, trudging laboriously up a steep slope, epitomizes the ethos of this game: life in this world is a struggle, and we bear our burdens as best we can. The equipment reinforces and supports the characters and world.

Meanwhile, in *Hades* (Supergiant), the House of Hades's ever-snarky prince, Zagreus, has an array of weapons known as Infernal Arms. Each weapon does more than just provide a new method of combat—it also signifies a different aspect of Zagreus's skill set. The Stygian Blade signifies a classic frontal assault approach while the Heart-Seeking Bow represents a more calculated, strategic fight. But the weapons do more than just affect player perception; they also have a deep impact on gameplay, encouraging players to experiment with various styles and strategies.

Skills not only create opportunities to convey power progression but also translate actions and abilities into personality traits. A character who specializes in healing is likely to be perceived as a caretaker, whereas a strong character who is skilled with multiple weapons may be perceived as a violent warrior. Our mental models, reinforced through our procedural knowledge, create these perceptions.

*Long Live the Queen* (Hanako Games) is a skill-based princess simulator and visual novel. In the game, players can choose how much time each day that they can invest in developing a wide range of hobbies and knowledge from horseback riding to etiquette to military prowess. These choices not only shape the story as the player tries to keep their princess alive and thriving, they begin to form and synthesize her overall personality.

As designers, we can support or subvert these mental models by intentionally pairing skills with character traits and values that either reinforce or contradict them. A combination of skills, or the progression of them as they increase, often signifies a character's class or job. But just like in the real world, their job isn't the whole picture of who they are.

In *Final Fantasy X-2* (Square Enix), the Dressphere and Garment Grid systems serve as the heart of character customization. Here, equipping different Dresspheres (think job classes or roles) doesn't merely alter a character's stats—it also dramatically changes their appearance and even their combat animations. This system offers a unique visual metaphor for each character's ability and style. A player's decision to don Yuna in a Gunner Dressphere does not just augment her offensive capabilities; it also imbues her with a certain gunslinger charm, changing the way the player perceives her. Because this game is a sequel, and the characters and world have been pre-established, the designers can grant more flexibility in the skills and jobs the characters can have. The player's mental model of the character is already fleshed out, allowing them to take in new information.

While it's easy to get lost in the mechanics of hit points and damage stats, the best game designers never forget that equipment serves a dual purpose. These virtual artifacts don't just modify a character's abilities; they also affect the narrative texture, the visual aesthetics, and the broader metaphors at play in a game's digital landscape. Equipment can powerfully inform the player's understanding of and feelings for a character.

In the end, equipping a character is like dressing a stage for a play. Costumes, much like in film and theater, are a vital part of character design in games. They're about more than aesthetics; they convey a wealth of character information— everything from their personality and profession to their cultural background and emotional state. Character concept artist Claire Hummel talks about the importance of costume design as part of the GDC panel "Creating Compelling Characters." She breaks down three key components: expression, aesthetic, and function.

A character's costume is an **expression** of both their personality and their individuality. An armored suit might indicate a warrior while a cloak and dagger could suggest a rogue or thief. Additionally, a costume's **aesthetic** serves as visual shorthand for a character's personality or mood while reinforcing the various design choices of the game world. Bright, extravagant clothing might suggest a flamboyant or confident character while dark, muted tones could indicate a brooding or mysterious personality.

It is important to make costume choices that are informed not only by the characters themselves but also by the world they inhabit. For instance, the color blocking and visual symbols that you incorporate into your costume choices serve the practical purpose of acting as a visual language and iconography that make the character easy to identify. When paired with color choices that are connected to world-building, costumes can also signify guilds, factions, or social classes (Figure 8.2).

**FIGURE 8.2** Character costumes.

The costume's **function** should also give players information about the character's role in the game's world and design. For instance, the materials and cut should convey societal or job rank and status while also giving clues about how the character solves problems. Even subtle details, like wear and tear on a character's outfit, can provide hints about their lifestyle or experiences. Is the clothing crisp and clean or well-worn? Is it heavily decorated or understated?

On a design level, costumes need to be integrated into the game's overall aesthetic and narrative. This means they must be consistent with the world and visual style, thereby contributing to the game's immersive quality. This requires close collaboration between costume designers, character artists, and narrative designers. Therefore, integrating a costume designer into your character pipeline can yield deeper and more immersive experiences. Costume designers can bring their understanding of fashion, culture, and history to the design process, helping to create costumes that are not just visually appealing but also richly detailed and contextually appropriate. This kind of integration can elevate the whole character design process, making characters feel more authentic and helping to further immerse players in the game world.

## ON PROCEDURAL LOOT AND BOWLS OF OATMEAL

Procedural generation stands as a testament to the beauty of efficient creativity. At its heart, procedural generation is a system that relies on algorithms and randomization to create unique elements in a game.

One of the most striking advantages of using procedural generation is the sheer diversity it offers. Each piece of loot or gear is a new surprise for the player, a gift waiting to be unwrapped. This sense of constant novelty keeps players coming back for more, enhancing the game's replayability. This benefit does not come without accompanying impacts on narrative and character, however.

The "1,000 bowls of oatmeal" problem is an analogy for a common challenge with procedural generation. The term is typically credited to writer and game designer Kate Compton. It's the idea that if you generate a thousand bowls of oatmeal using a procedural generator, they will look virtually identical to the observer even though each one is technically unique. The notion of procedural generation tantalizes with the allure of infinite novelty, yet, it's all still just bowls of the same breakfast porridge. That's because the details and variations—one has a few extra oats, another has less milk—aren't meaningful or noticeable to anyone observing or interacting with the oatmeal.

Games like *Borderlands 2* (Gearbox) confront us with the precarious balance between the promise of endless procedural variety and the blunt reality of uniformity. Imagine, if you will, an alien race of gunsmiths cranking out countless weapons using an unseen, inscrutable assembly line. In this industrial cornucopia, individuality is drowned in a sea of relentless similarity. Each one is unique, with its own specifications for damage, accuracy, and rate of fire. And yet the player's interactions with these weapons reveal a cruel truth: in the end, they're all just guns. We expect them to reveal something of our in-game persona—the sniper who favors the deadly accuracy of Jakobs rifles, the shotgun-toting tank blasting through enemies with a Torgue, the tactical player picking off foes from afar with a Maliwan.

But the oatmeal problem grinds against this expectation. The same weapon-producing algorithm that floods the world of *Borderlands 2* with countless guns also dilutes the individuality that we crave in these digital landscapes. When every gun is unique, no gun is unique. One sniper rifle often feels like another despite the slight alterations in specs.

The character we play, who is meant to be a unique protagonist in a vibrant, unpredictable world, becomes merely an avatar wielding a series of interchangeable tools with slightly different statistics, trapped in an inescapable loop of sameness. It's a lot of bowls of oatmeal, really. Although each is unique, it's still just another bowl of oatmeal. Therefore, when using inventory items as part of character design, it is important to balance novelty and scale against the bland uniformity of oatmealification.

# CREATING STRONG CHARACTER DIALOGUE

As we've discussed in this chapter, the best characters have depth—and your characters' dialogue should reflect that depth. Strong dialogue gives players insight into a character's motivations, backstory, desires, and personality using as little text as possible. This can be accomplished by making deliberate choices about tone, cadence, and vocabulary to imbue the lines with meaning.

We humans are social creatures. As we grow, we gain a variety of tools and skills that help us interpret and understand our social relationships. The very best game script writers take that understanding and turn it into meaningful breadcrumbs that lead the player to a deeper relationship with the characters in their game while simultaneously helping the player understand the game's world, rules, and goals The player should feel that every conversation in the game serves a purpose, whether it's revealing key plot points, illuminating character motivations, or providing necessary information for gameplay.

## Authenticity in Character Dialogue

It's not enough for dialogue to merely serve the game mechanics; it must also contribute to character development. When designers have a deep understanding of their characters, this aids in creating unique and compelling voices for each one. Voices are crucial in video games, where players often form emotional connections with characters. Authentic dialogue makes characters feel more real—more human—enhancing the player's empathy and investment. Creating authentic dialogue involves leveraging subtext, regional dialects, cultural idioms, and more. When a game takes the time to develop these aspects of dialogue, it demonstrates a commitment to world-building and contributes to a deeper, more engrossing player experience.

Observation and revision are as important in games as any other written medium, so listening is an essential tool in a writer's arsenal. Listening to the world around you can be an endless source of inspiration that helps you write authentic dialogue by capturing the rhythm, cadence, and idiosyncrasies of real-life conversations. Developers should always be open to revising and refining dialogue based on playtest feedback to ensure it hits the right note. *Oxenfree* (Night School Studio) exemplifies this principle. The game centers on a group of teenagers who experience supernatural events on an abandoned island. The dialogue avoids the stereotypical "teen speak" often found in media and instead focuses on creating realistic, thoughtful conversations between characters.

Even in games where story takes a backseat to action or strategy, good dialogue can enhance the player's connection to the game, making it more memorable and engaging. After all, memorable characters often live on in players' minds long after the game is over, and good dialogue is a key component of creating such characters.

Crafting authentic dialogue that both illuminates characters and propels the story forward is no small task. Screenwriter and television producer Shonda Rhimes dives into this intricate process in her MasterClass, offering invaluable insights.

Rhimes says that understanding the essence of characters is the cornerstone of writing credible dialogue. Therefore, writers must intimately know their characters—their backgrounds, personalities, and motivations. Every word that escapes a character's mouth reflects this intimate knowledge. In other words, dialogue is a manifestation of who they are and what drives them.

## *Variety*

Real people rarely articulate their thoughts in neatly structured sentences with perfect grammar. This is a truth Rhimes embraces. Her fast-paced, snappy dialogue mimics natural speech patterns, complete with stutters, interruptions, and grammatical idiosyncrasies. In Rhimes's world, dialogue is never just idle chatter. It's action. It's the tool characters use to maneuver through their world by persuading, manipulating, charming, hurting, or aiding others. By viewing dialogue as action, we can infuse purpose into our characters' conversations, making them not only more engaging but also instrumental in advancing the story. Each character should possess a unique voice that is shaped by their age, background, personality, and education. Variety isn't just the spice of life—it's also the spice of dialogue.

## *Subtext*

Subtext is the unspoken layer of meaning beneath spoken words. It's the hidden tension, the unsaid words, and the shared history that hums beneath the dialogue. It's the subtle art of leaving things unsaid. Employing subtext infuses complexity and depth into your characters' interactions, offering a more nuanced portrayal of their relationships.

*Night in the Woods* (Infinite Fall) brilliantly captures both of these principles. It successfully depicts the essence of a small, dying town and the people within it by incorporating exceptionally authentic, realistic, and heartfelt dialogue that makes the characters feel genuinely human. Each character has a unique voice that reflects their personality and background while avoiding the pitfalls of stereotypes and clichés. Following these guidelines can help writers navigate the complex process of crafting authentic dialogue while respectfully portraying characters from diverse backgrounds.

Let's break down a few lines of dialogue to get a deeper understanding of how depth, subtext, variety, and authenticity can create memorable moments and characters for our players.

"But loneliness that deep gets into the marrow. Now that I'm here—among friends—I can feel it burning out of me. Little by little, step by step."

—Karlach, *Baldur's Gate 3* (Larian)

*Baldur's Gate 3* is a classic RPG with party-based combat and systems at its core. One of the game's main character development themes focuses on the amount of agency the party members have on their journey to becoming more powerful, brilliantly reinforcing and contrasting the game's key verbs. In this line, the writer quickly conveys a lot of information:

- The dialogue portrays deep vulnerability and character growth. (Depth)
- It shows the progression of trust and relationships. (Subtext)

- It elegantly counterpoints Karlach's burning heart engine with her personal and parasocial growth. (Depth & Subtext)
- It emphasizes her soldier upbringing by using simple vocabulary and a cadence that mimics the marching of soldier's boots. (Variety & Authenticity)

"I can't go to hell. I'm all out of vacation days."
——Burgerpants, *Undertale* (Toby Fox)
With its pixelated graphics and quick-witted writing, *Undertale* is a love letter to video game nostalgia that cleverly challenges player perceptions. It does this, in part, by giving the player limited agency in combat, unlike many of the games *Undertale* derives its inspiration from. There are several moments when the player can choose not to fight the game's other characters. This brings forth possibilities ranging from completing the game without defeating anyone to killing every possible monster. This dialogue only comes up for players who opt for the latter. With this witty phrase, the designer

- Reinforces the game's clever and funny tone. (Authenticity & Variety)
- Reinforces the player's choices in the game by alluding to death. (Subtext)
- References the world in which *Undertale* takes place, the Underground, and draws parallels to another realm often thought of as below. (Depth)
- Emphasizes the character's role as a trader and purveyor of goods while giving players a glimpse into how he handles conflict. (Depth & Subtext)

"A fine bloody banquet. Oh, now I've gone and soiled my cuffs. If a dungeon is our fate, I do hope it contains a change of wardrobe."
—Balthier, *Final Fantasy 12* (Square Enix)
*Final Fantasy 12* is a Japanese party RPG with Shakespearean aspirations. The game's complex political plot is actively narrated by the shrewd Balthier, who often emulates the Shakespearean Fool as he guides the young Vaan. This dialogue brilliantly introduces the player to his character while playfully alluding to the themes of the game by

- Using a laid-back iambic pentameter to emphasize his role as a theatrical narrator. (Variety & Authenticity)
- Alluding to a common joke he makes as the "leading man" of the game through clever fourth wall breaking. (Depth & Authenticity)
- Introducing his personality of a gentleman pirate through a dash of dandy-ism. (Variety & Authenticity)
- Creating a clever pun on equipment and dungeons that winks at the player's experience of the core verbs of the game. (Subtext & Variety)
- Alluding to the political strife with a dash of alliteration for style. (Depth, Subtext, & Authenticity)

"They're all traitors—pigs, rabbits, and dogs. Men without ideals are only animals."
—Iosef Lilianovich Dros (The Deserter), *Disco Elysium* (ZA/UM)
*Disco Elysium* is a murder mystery that features a complex world with a variety of political and social subcultures, each with its own unique philosophies and manners of

speaking. The game presents these subcultures in a nuanced way, refusing to simplify or commodify their beliefs and practices. The game uses dialogue, skill checks, and choice as the primary vehicles for player expression and action. These are executed through the lens of the four primary abilities in the game: Intellect, Psyche, Physique, and Motorics. The overall narrative of the game is dependent upon the player's investment in these skills along with the choices they make. This line of dialogue from a potential murder suspect is one of many that rapidly introduces the player to one of the most nuanced and deep characters in the game. It does this by

- Creating a counterpoint to the game's central theme of nihilism while conveying the backstory and beliefs of the character. (Depth & Variety)
- Alluding to violence and the character's possible role in the murder. (Depth & Subtext)
- Saying a lot with few direct and measured words in a game that tends to use more. (Variety & Authenticity)

# EMOTION

Emotionally engaging characters are the linchpin of unforgettable narratives. When Mario yells "Yahoo!", as he jumps in *Super Mario Galaxy* (Nintendo), it enhances the player's feeling of achievement. When Astarion cracks a dark joke in *Baldur's Gate 3* (Larian), it launches a million thirsty TikTok views. Characters are the most effective and flexible vehicle for emotional motivation in your design toolkit. If games are beautiful motivation engines, characters are beautiful emotion engines.

## Character Expression

Emotional authenticity creates characters capable of experiencing and eliciting a spectrum of feelings. Strong narrative designers utilize many elements to create and represent emotionally compelling characters. We think about how our characters are portrayed through a variety of gameplay lenses. We also leverage visual storytelling, mental models, systems, game verbs and actions, and traditional storytelling to create holistic and whole individuals that the player connects with deeply.

**Animations and poses** should visually convey a character's personality in addition to showing how they react to certain situations or environments, combining body language with game actions. In concept artist Laurel Austin's informative GDC talk on creating expressive faces, she breaks facial animations and expressions into their core muscle movements, showing how they can be combined or emphasized. The nuances of facial expression are the lodestone of emotional conveyance; a single image can suggest more about a character's emotional state than an entire paragraph of dialogue (Figure 8.3).

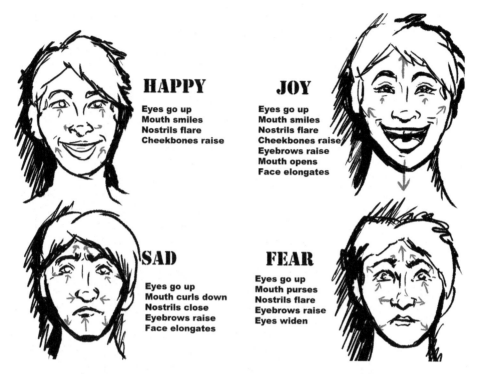

**FIGURE 8.3**   Character expressions.

That being said, it is always important to have a full understanding of the cultural and personal contexts behind an expression before having your character convey it. In the late 1960s, psychologists Carroll Izard and Paul Ekman embarked on parallel investigations around this debate, both using photographs from fellow psychologist Silvan Tomkins's collection. Tomkins was an influential personality theorist known for his work on human emotions. His most notable contribution is Affect Theory, which postulates that humans have a limited set of innate basic emotions. These emotions, according to Tomkins, are hardwired into our biology, are universally shared, and are primarily expressed and recognized through facial expressions. To support his theory, Tomkins amassed a collection of photographs demonstrating various emotional states.

Working independently of each other, Izard and Ekman utilized this photographic collection to conduct similar cross-cultural studies. Both psychologists were interested in testing the theory of universal human emotions and facial expressions. Their procedures were relatively straightforward. They showed photographs to participants from diverse Western and non-Western cultures. The participants were then asked to identify the emotions represented by each facial expression. The compelling discovery across both studies was the striking cross-cultural agreement in interpreting those expressions, suggesting that facial expressions are, to some degree, a universal language—a common human interface, if you will.

Despite these findings, there have been numerous debates around the universality of expression. Therefore, as with many facets of character design, it is important to make your decisions around facial animations and expressions in a way that reflects the game world's culture, the character's background, and the situation the character is facing.

When we smile in public, it may differ from how we smile in private—not just in intensity but also in meaning. Are our public faces universally consistent due to social norms and expectations, or do they merely reflect learned behaviors? Does universality also apply to our private faces, where social constraints might be less prominent? The personalities of humans vary as much as our spectrum of emotion, and therefore the way we react and show these emotions will be different depending on context.

There are also cultural "dialects" in the language of expressions. Does a smile in the United States carry the same meaning as a smile in Japan or Kenya? Not always. People from the United States tend to smile in more situations than others around the world. This is just one of many examples of cultural variances in the execution and interpretation of expressions. This is akin to the affordances in design, where context, background, and usage all shape the player's understanding of a given element. If we think of a facial expression as the signifier of an emotion, that expression carries design weight for both the character and the narrative.

The "uncanny valley" is a term coined by Japanese roboticist Masahiro Mori. It refers to the point at which a person observes a humanoid object, such as a robot or a 3D-rendered video game character, that seems almost, but not exactly, like a real human. The slight off-ness can make the observer feel discomfort, eeriness, or even revulsion.

When facial animations fall short of true-to-life realism while still appearing humanoid, they often elicit players' discomfort or criticism. Even subtle deviations from authenticity can make players uncomfortable and disrupt the immersive experience, demonstrating that our ability to recognize and interpret facial expressions depends not only on the basic emotion being conveyed but also on the cultural and situational context.

Posing and body animations can help mitigate this, as body language often provides the additional context required for us to fully interpret expressive emotional meaning. In his book *Comics and Sequential Art,* Will Eisner creates a microdictionary of gestures that break down body language of expression and emotion into simple and easy-to-interpret forms. See if you can guess which row embodies which emotion in the following image I've created inspired by his work:

Pretty amazing how we can interpret complex emotions and situations from simple scribbles, right? That's the power of posing (Figure 8.4).

**FIGURE 8.4**   Character poses.

## Character Interaction

*Ico* (Team Ico/Sony) is a unique game that tells the story of a young boy, Ico, who finds himself trapped in a mysterious, crumbling fortress. Early in the game, he encounters Yorda, a captive ethereal princess, and the two form an unlikely alliance to escape their shared prison.

The relationship between Ico and Yorda is conveyed through subtle non-verbal cues as the characters speak different languages. There are no prolonged cutscenes or extensive dialogues to describe their bond; instead, it evolves naturally through the player's interactions with Yorda and the environment. The game's most prominent mechanic to exemplify this bond is the handholding mechanic. Ico can reach out and hold Yorda's hand, allowing him to guide her through the fortress, help her over obstacles, and defend her from shadow creatures.

The handholding mechanic adds an emotional depth to *Ico* that creates a strong connection between Ico and Yorda without using a single word, emphasizing their dependence on each other. This simple action, repeated throughout the game, encourages players to feel protective and responsible for Yorda. As they physically navigate the labyrinthine castle together, players also navigate their growing bond by experiencing feelings of companionship, responsibility, and worry.

Despite linguistic and cultural barriers, the silent handholding interaction becomes a metaphor for communication and understanding. It reflects Ico's growing trust in Yorda and vice versa, along with shared hope and their determination to overcome hurdles together. When Yorda's hand slips away from Ico's during perilous situations, it instills a sense of urgency and dread. Similarly, the moments of reunion after separation bring players a strong sense of relief and joy.

Punchdrunk, the pioneering immersive theater company we discussed in Chapter 1, employs similar techniques to engage the audience directly. Among them are one-on-one interactions (1:1s), which are often initiated by an actor who takes a participant's hand, mirroring *Ico*'s handholding mechanic.

The act of handholding in Punchdrunk's immersive productions creates a sense of intimacy and connection between actor and audience member. It serves as a physical bridge, breaking down the metaphorical fourth wall that separates performers from the audience. This act also communicates a silent agreement or consent; the participant either chooses to accept the actor's hand and enters the intimate space or refuses and maintains their observer status.

Once the participant agrees to the interaction, the handholding becomes a tool for guidance and instruction. The actor leads the participant through the space, mirroring the *Ico* mechanic of guiding Yorda through the fortress. The audience member, like Ico, becomes an active participant in the unfolding narrative rather than a passive observer. The participant's journey, decisions, and interactions directly influence the course and outcome of the performance. It brings the audience member into a "player" state in the production, which is a nice segway into our next topic…

# PLAYER AGENCY

One of the delightfully unique aspects of games is the ability to roleplay—to allow players to step into the shoes of another character. We cannot talk about the player's character, however, without addressing the player's agency and identity. Providing agency enhances player engagement, making the game a collaborative storytelling experience. Video games are identity workshops that expand, test, and sometimes transform our sense of self. They allow us to experiment with identities and try on different hats—quite literally in some games. In the comfort of our own homes, we can step into the shoes of a fierce warrior, a cunning rogue, or a wise sorcerer. Games provide us with a risk-free environment in which to explore facets of our personality that may otherwise remain hidden.

In the best game experiences, the player's connection to a character isn't an accident, it's a product of thoughtful design. The motivations and emotions we discussed in Chapters 6 and 7 directly impact and guide the player's identity. It is important to remember that when the player controls a character, they will expect to influence the arc of that character's actions, choices, and story.

Gordon Freeman, the protagonist of *Half-Life* (Valve), is the player's direct proxy. In this game, you don't watch the action happen—you make it happen. This places the player right at the heart of the action, heightening anticipation and anxiety. Freeman's silence (he never speaks) also leaves room for the player to interpret events. Fear, urgency, disbelief—the player directly experiences these feelings, rather than having them filtered through the lens of a predefined character. This leads the player to form a more raw, immersive emotional connection with the game world.

Since he doesn't speak or express opinions, Freeman is essentially a blank slate. This design choice allows players to project their own thoughts and feelings onto him. He's a character with a name and a backstory, yes, but in terms of the player's immediate experience, he's more of an avatar. The silent protagonist style emphasizes player agency. Here, the motivation isn't driven by Freeman's character but by the player's ability to act upon and change the game world. When the player is the hero, the decision-maker, their ties to the character go beyond empathy. They suggest a nuanced player-character connection, a mix of self-perception, wish fulfillment, and immersion. It's a kind of psychological symbiosis that's hard to find in other forms of media.

There's an appeal to this approach because it allows for a more immersive experience. When Freeman witnesses something shocking, there's no voice acting or dialogue to tell the player how to feel. Instead, they project their own reactions onto the character. It's a simple yet effective way to make the player feel connected to the game world. Because of this, Freeman's character aligns nicely with the Thrill Seeker and Completionist motivation clusters. Players must quickly adapt to new challenges, learn from their mistakes, and master various forms of combat and problem-solving.

Commander Shepard from the *Mass Effect* series perfectly encapsulates player agency for the Escapist motivation cluster. Shepard's decisions, made by the player, have far-reaching consequences that affect both the character's evolution and the entire game's story arc. From deciding the fate of an entire alien species to cultivating romantic relationships, the player's agency in molding Shepard's journey is emulated through the choices that they make. This ability to choose not only strengthens the player's emotional resonance with "their" Shepard, it also enhances their connection with the NPCs associated with those choices.

Taking the concept of player agency and character in a very different direction is the god-like character from *Black & White* (Lionhead). In this game, you're not playing as a human character but as an all-powerful deity. Your presence is represented by a giant hand. Being a hand floating above your world distances you from the ground-level action, which can lead to a more analytical, detached emotional state. This displacement creates ambivalence as the game allows—and even encourages—both benevolent and malevolent actions. This omnipotent and omnipresent perspective, combined with moral choices, can give the player feelings of grandeur but also the burdens of responsibility and consequence.

This setup allows the player to engage in an entirely different kind of fantasy fulfillment. They're not just a person in a strange world; they control that world. The god-like character in *Black & White* resonates with the Architect motivation cluster. Players are given free rein to sculpt the world and influence their followers as they see fit, experimenting with different strategies and approaches. They can shape the land, influence their followers, and face off against other gods. The Creatures in the game, large animals that the player can take care of and influence, grow and evolve according to the player's choices. This creates strong feedback for the player's decisions and choices. The nature of the player's actions—benevolent or malevolent—shapes the game world and the way followers perceive the god-like character.

In essence, the player's identity in *Black & White* is tied directly to the choices you make and the consequences they yield, and the characters in the world reflect that identity. The player experiences a god fantasy, a unique sense of power and responsibility that is at once exhilarating and humbling. Here, the appeal is in the game's dynamic and emergent system rather than in a fixed narrative or direct action, but the influence and agency that the player has over the world deepen the connection to the Creatures within it.

## BARKS AND BANTER

Environmental dialogue systems allow designers to reinforce player agency through character expression. "Barks" in video games are short, often reactive vocalizations or pieces of dialogue that characters, especially non-player characters, emit in response to specific events or stimuli within the game environment. This could be an enemy shouting "I've found him!" when the player character is spotted or an ally expressing pain or distress when injured. Barks serve to enhance the game world's realism and dynamism, providing auditory feedback that shows the player that the game's characters are responsive to their actions and the events unfolding within the environment. Barks aren't about developing character relationships or conveying narrative depth; they're about providing **immediate, reactive communication** that alerts players to situational status or changes.

Banter, on the other hand, is dialogue that's inherently connected to character and relationship development. It's crafted to **convey underlying emotions, interpersonal dynamics, and personality through casual conversation** that often occurs independently of direct player input. Whereas barks respond to the player's actions, banter is more about characters interacting with each other—although it may still be influenced by broader player choices or actions within the game.

When designing bark and banter systems, there are a few key principles to take into consideration

### CONTEXT

The contextual appropriateness of banter is pivotal in maintaining player immersion and building the narrative world's credibility. This often necessitates the use of intricate systems that accurately track and respond to a myriad of variables—including character relationship statuses, game-world events, and player choices. This also ensures that they avoid repetitiveness and enhance immersion rather than detract from it.

Good game designers craft conversations that intertwine relationship dynamics with environmental and situational contexts to produce dialogue that feels authentic and timely. When characters respond to real-time events, locations, or player actions with spontaneous and contextually apt dialogue, it not only enhances the game world's liveliness but also cements the player's belief in the characters as sentient entities.

## TIMING

The timing of when dialogue is generated can be just as important as the related context. Barks and banter are fundamentally tied to player agency and actions, serving as immediate feedback or reaction to the player's inputs and decisions. They assist in maintaining the immersive quality of the game world by ensuring that the entities within it believably respond to player actions and environmental changes. Poor timing can result in the context being lost, breaking immersion.

Allowing the player to pick up interrupted dialogue is a key component to timing in designing banter and bark systems. In *Uncharted 4* (Naughty Dog), the story centers around the relationship between the main character, Nathan Drake, and his brother. The dialogue between these characters throughout the game provides context, entertainment, and a deeper insight into their complicated relationship. Nevertheless, the developer ensures that the banter never impedes active gameplay. By creating interruption cues and alternate lincs that facilitate interruption, such as, "Where was I?" or "As I was saying," the dialogue flows smoothly even when Nathan Drake stops to winch the vehicle out of a crevasse or shoot some bad guys.

Speaking of interruption, some games use clever solutions to include the player more actively in banter, including *Guardians of the Galaxy* (Eidos) and *Oxenfree*. While these games have different interactive solutions for this problem, the fundamental design is essentially the same: the player receives a visual indicator that they can participate in the dialogue, with a brief description of response choices, and if they wish, they can contribute to the conversation before time runs out. This kind of system gives the player a more active role in dialogue, and this type of banter can be a nice contribution to branching or relationship choices, even when the player chooses not to participate. The element of choice also allows players who prefer uninterrupted action to continue focusing on the game's action while those who are narratively and socially motivated can further engage with both the action and characters. In addition to inviting player participation, these games are both master classes in party banter. In Guardians of the Galaxy, the amount of character dialogue is staggering. Even so, it manages to feel fluid throughout the experience.

Timing also includes giving the player breaks. It is never a good sign when a narrative designer is uncomfortable with silence. Games that fill every moment with dialogue can break immersion just as quickly as those with poor timing.

**SPECIFICITY**

When writing dialogue, designers and writers must delve deep into character development, using specificity to ensure that exchanges are emotionally resonant, contextually appropriate, and reflective of the ongoing narrative and relationship arcs. Well-executed banter seamlessly conveys backstory, personality, and the dynamics between characters without resorting to overt exposition, tirelessly adhering to the vital storytelling principle of "show, don't tell." Casual, unscripted dialogues can flow between characters to enrich their personalities and relationships within the game, but these dialogues also draw players deeper into the narrative world's emotional and relational depths. This affirms the player's experiential and emotional investment in the unfolding tale. Additionally, it serves to make characters more relatable and endearing to the player, fostering a connection that enhances player investment in the game's narrative and character arcs.

# TYPES OF NPCs

One way to establish and reinforce player agency is through the quests and narrative arcs the player completes through their interactions with non-player characters (NPCs). We talked about using NPC quests to motivate the player in Chapter 6, but NPCs can serve many functions. I'll describe some of the most common NPC types, but this is by no means an exhaustive list.

## The Informed Vendor

This is an NPC whose primary role is to provide rumors about local events or provide the player with items they may need as a vector of the game's economy systems. If a player only speaks to this character occasionally for tidbits of information, their dialogue can be brief and to the point. On the other hand, if this informant becomes central to a major plot twist, their dialogue might expand, delving into their personal backstory or motivations.

## The Local Flavor

These NPCs are purely there for narrative reinforcement, the Greek chorus of your game. They do not even need to be represented physically in the space, you can use discarded letters, photographs, audio logs, and other design tools. Since they don't offer reward or utility, they should be brief, well crafted, specific, and memorable.

# The Cinematic Pillars

These characters are the narrative heavyweights of NPCs, the load-bearing pillars in your story structure. They should be authentic, deep, believable, and memorable. Cinematic pillars can be evil villains, charming scoundrels, or witty narrators that the player sees repeatedly throughout their experience. You can pair these NPCs with powerful extrinsic rewards to reinforce their roles within the game's systems and verbs. They are people, not plot, and they should evolve as the story evolves.

# The Companion

Companions accompany players throughout their journey and offer a deep emotional connection. These characters often have complex backstories, personal quests, and a vast number of dialogue lines. They reflect the player's choices and progress back through their emotional development. The player's effort in building a relationship with them or helping them on their personal quests should be rewarded with an in-depth narrative. We'll talk more about relationship systems in a later section, but note that the depth of these relationships is essential to building strong Companion characters.

# The Minion

These NPCs are purely here to support and follow the player. Whether it is guiding, defending, or healing, these characters often lack depth to focus on their utility. The rigidity and limitations of the interactions as a result of this utility differentiates them from Companions. While lacking in depth, the simplicity and consistency of these characters often make them iconic if they are designed with clarity, heart, and earnestness. Pokemon, the pawns from *Dragon's Dogma* (Capcom), or the companion cube from Portal are all examples of Minions.

# The Quest Giver

Quest Givers offer opportunities or challenges for the player in exchange for rewards or additional content. If an NPC offers a short, simple fetch quest (e.g., "Bring me 10 apples"), the dialogue can be succinct, with a straightforward request and a thank you upon completion. Conversely, for a long, multi-stage quest, the NPC might share a heart-wrenching story, offer context for the quest's significance, and even provide updates or commentary as the quest progresses. Early on in *Red Dead Redemption 2* (Rockstar), a simple chore like collecting debts for Herr Strauss is accompanied by straightforward interactions. But as the player progresses, debt collection tasks lead to profound moral choices, deeper narrative contexts, and consequences affecting camp dynamics. As we discussed in an earlier chapter, proportion in these interactions is key. The narrative depth and extrinsic payout should be equivalent to the effort required for completion.

# DEPTH, EMOTION, AND AGENCY
# IN ACTION IN NPCs

Now that we've explored depth, agency, and emotion, let's see what these design tools look like in action by examining some iconic game characters. The Little Sisters from *BioShock* (Irrational) are young girls who have been genetically modified and conditioned to collect a substance known as ADAM from corpses scattered throughout the underwater city of Rapture. The game ingeniously uses the Little Sisters' innocence, child-like appearances, and vulnerability to elicit the player's empathy and protective instincts. The Little Sisters are Cinematic Pillar NPCs that present an emotional conundrum to the player, reflecting the complex underlying themes and values of the game world. Their visual design, from their torn, soiled dresses to the haunting glow of their eyes, amplifies this emotional response. Their contrasting animations reinforce their duality: they whimper in fear and cower from the player, yet they display a disturbing nonchalance as they perform their grim task of harvesting ADAM.

Players are presented with moral choices as a way to express their agency and identity—whether to "harvest" the Little Sisters for more ADAM or "rescue" them at a potential cost to the player's power—that further deepen the emotional bond and complexity. The narrative context—the player's knowledge of the Little Sisters' forced servitude and the moral dilemma of whether to harvest or rescue them—adds a layer of complexity to the emotional connection. This potent combination of visual design, character animation, and narrative context results in a powerful emotional engagement that drives the player's decision-making process. These characters are ingeniously woven into the game's design, serving as focal points for its moral quandaries.

Next, we have Garrus Vakarian from the *Mass Effect* (Bioware) series. Garrus is a former law enforcement officer turned vigilante, and he's a member of an alien species known as Turians. His character is marked by a strong sense of justice, loyalty, and dry humor. These traits, combined with a backstory that reinforces themes of struggle and perseverance, create a figure that many players grow to respect and admire.

Garrus Vakarian is the quintessential loyal Companion—he's with the player's character, Commander Shepard, from the beginning to the end of the journey. His distinctive alien design, with his avian features and cool blue eyes, sets him apart visually, while his animations, often relaxed and self-assured, reflect his confident, sometimes cocky personality.

His backstory as a disillusioned C-Sec officer-turned-vigilante endears him to players as a figure striving for justice, albeit through unconventional means. Garrus's voice acting, delivered by Brandon Keener, also plays a crucial role in the character's charm, imbuing him with a characteristic dry wit and warm sincerity.

Throughout the series, players can engage in deep dialogue with Garrus, learning about his past, his values, and his fears. These conversations, combined with shared experiences in missions, allow trust and camaraderie to develop between player and

NPC, mirroring the in-game friendship between Shepard and Garrus. Throughout the series, the friendship and camaraderie (or even romance depending on player choices) between Garrus and the player's character, Commander Shepard, grow and evolve, making him a cherished companion in the *Mass Effect* universe.

Lastly, we'll examine Pikachu from *Pokémon* (The Pokémon Company). This electric Pokémon, the franchise's mascot, is synonymous with joy, friendship, and adventure. Pikachu's design is inherently appealing, invoking a sense of cuteness and familiarity that immediately strikes a chord with players of all ages. For many players, Pikachu sparks a mixture of joy, excitement, and nostalgia. The character's bright, simple design is immediately recognizable as a helpful Minion, and its high-pitched, chatty voice acting (which usually just involves the character saying its own name) is both adorable and emotive.

Pikachu's animations, from the delighted wiggle upon winning a battle to the sad slump when defeated, invoke an empathetic response from players. Pikachu's backstory isn't complex or fraught with the darker tones seen in *BioShock* or *Mass Effect*. Instead, Pikachu symbolizes friendship and loyalty in a manner consistent with the underlying themes and action in the game. The trust built between the character and the player stems from shared battles, victories, and even defeats.

Pikachu's design integration also leans heavily into the emotional bond between the player and their Pokémon. The game encourages training, nurturing, and even petting your Pokémon, which fosters a bond of virtual companionship that drives player engagement through interaction and agency. The emotional connection also deepens as players train and care for their Pikachu. In the *Pokémon* TV series, Pikachu is portrayed as the protagonist Ash Ketchum's loyal companion, further feeding into the player's emotional connection, reinforcing a bond that extends beyond the game itself, and enhancing the player's engagement with the wider Pokémon universe.

## CHARACTERS VERSUS CARICATURES

Because games have the opportunity to create new thought patterns in ways similar to teaching and learning (as we discussed in Chapter 5), it is vitally important that we as designers take care with how we represent characters in our games. In game designer Shawn Allen's GDC talk about creating characters, he emphasizes that we as designers must always "be specific about [our] characters, be detailed, and be deliberate" when making choices about representation and characterization.

As game developers, we need to evolve our character designs and look beyond the many one-dimensional characters of the past. The Lara Croft today is nearly unrecognizable from the original. We need to get past the idea of characters as titillating decoration at one end of the spectrum and long, overwrought lore dumps on the other, moving forward toward more meaningful systems integration. Does this mean we must put more work into researching and developing our characters? Of course. But if we want to create game brands that stand the test of time, like successful brands in other mediums, we need to put in that effort.

*Writing the Other* by Nisi Shawl and Cynthia Ward is a guide that helps writers create more diverse and inclusive stories. It emphasizes the importance of creating diverse and inclusive stories that reflect the complexities of the world we live in. By doing research, avoiding stereotypes, and being mindful of language and intersectionality, writers can create stories that are more authentic, respectful, and impactful.

Shawl and Ward highlight a few key best practices to consider when creating accessible characters.

## RESEARCH AND LISTEN

It is incredibly important to do your research and listen to members of the community you are writing about. This means attending cultural events, reading books by writers with the same background as your characters, and listening to this group's stories and experiences.

Developers of the game *Never Alone* (Kisima Ingitchuna) worked closely with Alaska's Iñupiaq community to create an authentic depiction of their culture and traditions. They consulted with community members to ensure that the game was respectful and accurate, and they even incorporated traditional stories and folklore into the game's narrative. This thoughtful approach resulted in an experience that was authentic, empathetic, and moving.

## AVOID STEREOTYPES

Avoid relying on stereotypes and generalizations when writing characters whose backgrounds differ from your own. Instead, create complex, nuanced characters that reflect the diversity of the world we live in.

In *Horizon Zero Dawn* (Guerrilla), the game features a diverse cast of characters who are not defined by stereotypes or tropes. The protagonist, Aloy, is a strong and capable female character who is not defined by her gender or sexualization. One only needs to examine gamers' outrage over her "peach fuzz" facial hair in *Horizon Forbidden West* to gain a deep understanding of the importance of making progress in this area of the medium.

## USE SENSITIVITY READERS

Consider hiring a sensitivity reader, someone from the community you are writing about, to read your work and offer feedback. They can help you identify stereotypes, cultural inaccuracies, and other issues that might arise in your writing.

In *Life is Strange* (Dontnod), which features a queer protagonist, the developers worked with consultants from the LGBTQ+ community to ensure that the game's portrayal of queer characters was accurate and respectful. As a result, the game explores themes of identity and acceptance in a nuanced and sensitive way.

## INTERSECTIONALITY

Recognize that people belong to multiple communities. Therefore, they have multiple identities that intersect and affect how they experience the world.

Consider how race, gender, sexuality, class, and other factors intersect in your characters and how this affects their experiences.

In *Gone Home* (Fullbright), the game explores the experiences of a young woman named Katie as she returns home from a trip abroad. The game touches on themes of sexuality, gender, and family dynamics in a way that acknowledges how these identities intersect and affect Katie's experiences.

As a queer dating sim, *Dream Daddy* (Game Grumps) really shines when it comes to intersectionality. Not only does the character creator support a wide variety of gender, racial, and cultural representations, but NPCs cover a wide range of datable dads. Players have the option of getting to know goth transgender dads, African American hipster dads, and athletic Asian American dads.

Questions to ask when creating characters

- Will a player understand this character in the context of the game world?
- Where am I pulling inspiration from for this character?
- What relationships does this character have with the cast?
- Do I understand this character's motivations, relationships, fears, and flaws?
- Does the character fit the setting and the world?
- How does the world react to the character?
- What does the character tell us about this world?
- Can I reinforce character traits through game mechanics?
- Does the character fit the game's core elements?
- Have I done enough research? Am I respecting the research I have done?
- Have I asked peers and subject matter experts for feedback?

The player's relationship with game characters can influence their attitudes and behaviors in the game, both positively and negatively. Video games are powerful tools and, like all tools, they carry a responsibility. Each design manipulates the player's emotional connection to their character in a different way, adjusting the lens through which the player perceives the game world and impacting their emotional journey. Let's take a look at how we can integrate characters into our game design with systems that drive and facilitate these relationships.

# RELATIONSHIP SYSTEMS

Effective relationship systems in games are a matter of intricate design and thoughtful mechanics that subtly seep into the fabric of gameplay, shaping not just the narrative but also the player's emotional investment. Too often, we ignore the potential of relationships and character progression as a facet of our meta layers. Characters are our game's best vehicle for emotional motivation, and relationship systems allow us to directly integrate that motivation into its progression and achievement vectors. They translate complex systems into digestible interactions, and more importantly, they emotionally engage the player. The player's attachment to characters, fear of negative outcomes, and satisfaction with successful interactions make for a more engaging, human experience.

## DESIGNING HEALTHY ROMANCE CHARACTER RELATIONSHIPS

As we discussed in Chapters 5 and 6, emotion and trust are potent social motivators—not just for in-person interactions, but also player-to-character interactions. They drive players to engage and explore, and ultimately shape the in-game experience. In doing so, players transform code and pixels into something that feels incredibly real and human. They live, love, fight, and connect in worlds far removed from our own that are somehow strikingly familiar. To achieve this and successfully use characters as metaphors for systems, designers must have a nuanced understanding of human interaction.

Without that understanding, the player will have shallow experiences with the game's characters at best and transactional experiences at worst. Sex (or sexual activities) in games has traditionally been an extrinsic reward akin to a stat boost or a new shield. This is a transgressive perspective that equates sex as a transactional interaction and neglects the rich narrative and design potential of romance and relationships.

Brenda Romero has voiced many insightful critiques of relationship systems in games. She also advocates for responsible and thoughtful depictions of sex and relationships, as reflected in her book *Sex in Video Games*.

Romero often points out the "gamification" of relationships as the source of this feeling of transaction. Many games reduce complex, intimate human interactions to simplistic cause-and-effect systems—give a gift, get a boost. This not only oversimplifies relationships, it promotes transactional views of relationships and objectifies characters, blurring the lines of consent. Consent should be at the forefront of every relationship, and the feedback should be crystal clear. Romero calls for more nuance and sensitivity, encouraging designers to avoid commodifying relationships. Video games, like many other mediums, sometimes portray idealized or sensationalized views of romance and sexual relationships. This can set unrealistic expectations and perpetuate harmful stereotypes such as hypersexualizing female characters or the expectation of sex as a reward.

*How do you Do it?* (Nina Freeman) is a game that playfully explores this space through the viewpoint of an adolescent girl playing with dolls. In the game, the player smashes together their dolls to emulate romantic and sexual acts, a commentary on the often awkward interactions explored in young adulthood, but also cleverly critiquing the actions available for exploring these themes in games.

There is also a general lack of diversity and inclusivity in video game relationships. Many games often default to heterosexual relationships and largely ignore other relationship types, including LGBTQ+. Relationship dynamics in games tend to be binary, leaving little room for the complex web of relationships humans can have, like polyamorous relationships, asexual relationships, or nontraditional family structures. Romero advocates for greater representation of diverse relationships and a more mature approach to sexual content, stepping away from sensationalism and toward a thoughtful, respectful portrayal.

Brenda Romero's critique is a call for games to grow up, shed simplistic and harmful portrayals, and embrace the full, beautiful complexity of human relationships. It's also a call for designers to treat their players with respect by offering them more than escapism—a mirror of their own experiences, struggles, joys, and desires. And given the profound impact games can have on our perceptions and our understanding of the world, it's a call that deserves to be heard.

Narrative designer Michelle Clough is one of the industry's primary advocates for answering this call, and her work often centers around emotional realism in games. She argues that characters should possess a level of depth and complexity that parallels the player's own emotional life, fostering a more intimate and profound connection. In her GDC talks, Clough emphasizes that to truly draw players into a narrative and generate genuine emotion, characters need to have the same emotional subtleties, flaws, and strengths found in real-life individuals. Nuanced systems that account for personality compatibility, chemistry, and communication can make relationships feel more authentic. When this happens, characters become more than just lines of code or well-drawn figures—they become emotional catalysts.

*Baldur's Gate 3* (Larian) uses strong relationship systems that are deeply integrated into the narrative to encourage repeated interactions with non-playable characters (NPCs). The interactions and choices create a mental model in which actions have consequences, often manifesting in changed character attitudes and plot developments. The player's dialogue choices can make or break relationships, and players can even develop romances. The player forms attachments to these characters, and those attachments incentivize them to interact with the world more, protect their in-game friends, or romance characters they've connected with. In essence, the player's emotions become a strong motivator.

Character relationships are measured through Companion approval, which is an essential mechanic in the game. This metric is measured in numeric segments that translate to ranges from Negative to Exceptional. This rating, combined with the actions the player chooses to make in the game, can have impacts ranging from witty banter to character death.

There are several systems that drive Companion approval in *Baldur's Gate 3*. The first is dialogue choice, which allows the player to express their own character as well as connect with others. These choices will have the potential to align with the values and desires of the characters around them in both subtle and impactful ways. Whether choosing a drink of choice in a celebratory moment or arguing against violent acts, each of these decisions can impact the approval of various characters. The game determines whether this dialogue influences characters by proximity, so if someone is standing too far away, they won't be affected (much like real life).

Actions speak louder than words, and players can also influence approval through their actions in the game. Who they attack or do not attack, what allies they choose, what skills they use, or how they choose to solve problems. A rogue may appreciate it when you make decisions around stealth or deception, whereas a mage prefers using wit or magic. These actions can unlock special dialogue or even additional quest content or items.

There is also a simple gifting system in the game that allows the player to give characters items from their inventory. Simple gifts have a small impact, and more meaningful gifts that reference specific character attributes or desires have a bigger impact.

The final vehicle for companion approval is completing favors or quests that are specifically associated with that character. Each companion has at least one unique storyline that allows players to dig deep into the backstory. These quests are entirely optional, but can have impacts on the main storyline, and often give the player opportunities to influence the morality and future of the associated companion.

| COMPANION APPROVAL IN BALDUR'S GATE 3 | HIGH | LOW |
|---|---|---|
| Impacting Systems | • Dialogue, decisions, or actions that align with the character's values, needs, or desires<br>• Complete favors for characters<br>• Make quest or moral choices that align with the character values<br>• Give appropriate gifts<br>• Empower characters to make their own decisions<br>• Support character choices and lifestyles | • Ignore characters<br>• Dialogue, decisions, or actions that run counter to the character's values, needs, or desires<br>• Act in a way that loses the respect of the character<br>• Ally with character enemies<br>• Try to control character's actions and decisions |
| Potential Results | • Character loyalty<br>• Unique items<br>• Unique quests<br>• Unique dialogue<br>• Character romance options<br>• Combat boosts | • Inter-character conflicts<br>• Character leaves party<br>• Character death |

Characters have their personalities, preferences, and even prejudices, and they respond dynamically to player choices. Building relationships is not always about saying the right things or presenting the right gift—it's about building a connection that aligns with the characters' beliefs, histories, and holistic selves. Relationships in *Baldur's Gate 3* extend beyond romance; they also explore the breadth and depth of human (and sometimes non-human) connections. These systems offer strong replayability and create a dedicated fan base.

The *Fire Emblem* series (Nintendo/Intelligent Systems) has another interesting approach to companion systems. It's a strategy game at heart, but the relationships between the characters can affect battle performance, influence story arcs, and even result in new characters being introduced. And this bond system is driven by the game verbs. This doesn't just apply between the player character and their surrounding NPCs, it also applies between the NPCs themselves. As allies work together on and off the battlefield, their bond deepens. These bonds in turn unlock support conversations—friendly chats the player can trigger under certain conditions—which can deepen their bond, which in turn affects their performance on the battlefield.

It is a fascinating system that marries tactical strategy with storytelling, grounding the high fantasy warfare in tangible, personal relationships. It beautifully simulates the way bonds are formed through shared experience. Players don't just send pawns to fight; they send friends, brothers-in-arms, even lovers. The mental model becomes a blend of strategy and interpersonal relations, and the stakes are often high—characters can permanently die, removing them from the player's pool of warriors and from the game's narrative.

This system varies from the one we've discussed in *Baldur's Gate 3* because it only increases bonds. There are very few choices or systems in place that negatively affect bonds.

Companion Bonds in *Fire Emblem: Three Houses*

| IMPACTING SYSTEMS | POTENTIAL RESULTS |
|---|---|
| • Choice of House<br>• Fighting together<br>• Cooking together<br>• Eating together<br>• Singing together<br>• Studying together<br>• Training together<br>• Returning lost items<br>• Giving gifts<br>• Having tea together<br>• Support conversations<br>• Dialogue choices that favor the character<br>• Completing unique character quests | • Character loyalty<br>• Unique items<br>• Unique quests<br>• Unique dialogue<br>• Character romance options (with select characters)<br>• Combat boosts<br>• Epilogue storylets |

*Coffee Talk*, by Indonesian indie developer Toge Productions, veers away from grandiose warfare and delves into the intimate confines of a late-night coffee shop. As the barista, the player listens to patrons' stories, brewing both beverages and relationships. The game introduces an intriguing mix of visual novel and a sort of "mixology" system. The player's role is not just about serving the right drinks—it's also about understanding customer preferences and emotions along with picking up on conversational cues. The game beautifully illustrates that a relationship isn't just about high points and dramatic turns; it's about the everyday interactions, the quiet moments of shared vulnerability over a cup of coffee.

| IMPACTING SYSTEMS | POTENTIAL RESULTS |
|---|---|
| • Drinks brewed | • Plot Changes<br>• Character relationships<br>• New recipes |

Each of the systems in these games explores the nuances of human behavior and relationships in interesting ways, but there is still room for the industry to improve. There's a lot to be said about the evolution of relationship mechanics in video games, with each of the aforementioned titles demonstrating the potential of video games as a medium for exploring human connections. Relationships in games aren't just about unlocking extra dialogue or boosting stats—they represent our innate desire for connection, intimacy, and understanding in a world that can often feel isolating. They add layers to the gaming experience, pushing the boundaries of interactive storytelling. The possibility space for relationship systems in games is still ripe for exploration, and we can only wait with bated breath to see where developers take us next.

That being said, exploring relationships in games should always be done with sensitivity and respect. Relationships provide avenues for players to experience various facets of human connection, but by including them, designers bear the responsibility of portraying these relationships accurately and without perpetuating harmful stereotypes. This balancing act is where the challenge lies—and the potential.

Characters embody our emotional journeys and represent our fears, hopes, and aspirations. They offer us opportunities to experience the world from different perspectives, allowing us to empathize and grow. They let us live a thousand lives and feel a thousand feelings—the heroic joy of victory, the sting of defeat, the heaviness of loss, and the relief of redemption. We as designers have an obligation to give them the time, energy, and attention they deserve when creating them.

# BIBLIOGRAPHY

Allen, Shawn. "Breaking Marginalized Character Narrative Molds to Write Better, Richer Characters." *GDC Vault*, 2017, https://www.gdcvault.com/play/1024133/Breaking-Marginalized-Character-Narrative-Molds. Accessed 4 July 2023.

Barrett, Lisa Feldman. "Opinion | What Faces Can't Tell Us." *The New York Times*, 2 March 2014, https://www.nytimes.com/2014/03/02/opinion/sunday/what-faces-cant-tell-us.html?_r=0. Accessed 4 July 2023.

Brathwaite, Brenda. *Sex in Video Games*. Brenda Brathwaite, 2013.

Brown, Fraser. "Marvel's Guardians of the Galaxy is the new king of party banter." *PC Gamer*, 2 November 2021, https://www.pcgamer.com/marvels-guardians-of-the-galaxy-is-the-new-king-of-party-banter/. Accessed 4 July 2023.

Clough, Michelle. "Desire Is Not a Dirty Word: Writing Healthy Fanservice in Games." *GDC Vault*, 2015, https://www.gdcvault.com/play/1021925/Desire-Is-Not-a-Dirty. Accessed 10 March 2024.

Diaz, Ana. "Thirst traps of Astarion on TikTok convinced me to play Baldur's Gate 3." *Polygon*, 20 August 2023, https://www.polygon.com/23835927/baldurs-gate-3-astarion-tiktok-bg3. Accessed 10 March 2024.

Eisner, Will. *Comics & Sequential Art*. Poorhouse Press, 1990.

Ekman, Paul, and Dacher Keltner. "Are Facial Expressions Universal?" *Greater Good Science Center*, 12 March 2014, https://greatergood.berkeley.edu/article/item/are_facial_expressions_universal. Accessed 4 July 2023.

Hummel, Claire, et al. "Creating Compelling Characters: Insights from a Panel of Character Concept Artists." *GDC Vault*, 2017, https://www.gdcvault.com/play/1024290/Creating-Compelling-Characters-Insights-from. Accessed 4 July 2023.

Khazan, Olga. "Why Do Russians Never Smile?" *The Atlantic*, 27 May 2016, https://www.theatlantic.com/science/archive/2016/05/culture-and-smiling/483827/. Accessed 10 March 2024.

King, Jade. "Gamers Complaining About Aloy Have Clearly Never Seen A Real Woman Before." *TheGamer*, 15 February 2022, https://www.thegamer.com/aloy-horizon-appearance-beard-beauty-ugly-woman/. Accessed 4 July 2023.

Koster, Raph. "The Trust Spectrum – Raph's Website." *Raph Koster*, 16 March 2018, https://www.raphkoster.com/2018/03/16/the-trust-spectrum/. Accessed 4 July 2023.

Machon, Josephine. *The Punchdrunk Encyclopaedia.* Edited by Josephine Machon, Routledge, 2019.

Mori, Masahiro, Karl F. MacDorman and Norri Kageki, The Uncanny Valley [From the Field], *IEEE Robotics & Automation Magazine*, 19:2, 98–100, June 2012, DOI: 10.1109/MRA.2012.2192811

Phillips, Tom. "Four months on, BioWare still patching Mass Effect: Andromeda facial animations." *Eurogamer*, 10 July 2017, https://www.eurogamer.net/four-months-on-bioware-still-patching-mass-effect-andromeda-facial-animations. Accessed 4 July 2023.

Rhimes, Shonda. "Writing Authentic Dialogue | Shonda Rhimes Teaches Writing for Television | MasterClass." *Masterclass*, https://www.masterclass.com/classes/shonda-rhimes-teaches-writing-for-television/chapters/writing-authentic-dialogue. Accessed 4 July 2023.

Salomaa, Heli. "Costume in Games: Integrating a Costume Designer into the ..." *GDC Vault*, 2019, https://www.gdcvault.com/play/1025997/Costume-in-Games-Integrating-a#close-modal. Accessed 4 July 2023.

Shawl, Nisi, and Cynthia Ward. *Writing the Other: A Practical Approach.* Aqueduct Press, 2005.

Tunru, Julian. All the game world's a stage: towards a model for asymmetric collaborative storytelling in persistent open world MMORPGs. *Diva Portal*, 2017. http://www.diva-portal.se/smash/get/diva2:1276877/FULLTEXT01.pdf

Yorke, John. *Into the Woods: How Stories Work and why We Tell Them.* Penguin Books, 2014.

Yorke, John, and Caroline Marchal. "How to Create Great Characters: Depth, Emotion and Player Agency." *GDC Vault*, 2018, https://www.gdcvault.com/play/1025156/How-to-Create-Great-Characters. Accessed 4 July 2023.

# Conclusion

Game narrative and UX share a deep, interconnected relationship. Narrative design gives a game its heartbeat while UX design ensures that this heart can beat without interruption. Hopefully, this book has helped you gain a greater understanding of these crafts and how their relationship enhances the player experience through their shared goals, tools, and methodologies. Game narrative should act as a vehicle for **player agency** and **interaction**. Game UX is driven by **immersive and playful interaction**.

Games are beautiful motivation engines. As we have explored the parallels between narrative and UX design together, we've covered the three key pillars that form the foundation of a player-centric system: **Context, Action**, and **Emotion**. These are the gears and pistons that power our motivational engine.

**Context** explores the foundational narrative decisions we make when crafting a game world to help guide and reinforce the player experience. In the Context section of this book, we first covered the foundational principles of game narrative and UX to get an overview, then dove into the iterative design process and how research can enhance this process, and ended with building our icebergs for our game world.

**Action** explores the verbs, inputs, and systems the player leverages to overcome the game world's challenges and rules. In the Action section of this book, we explored how game verbs intuitive design can create experiences focused on play and then took a close look at how players learn to craft experiences that guide them.

And **emotion** explores how we craft the game's stories and interactions to motivate and guide the player on their journey. In the Emotion section of this book we delved into what motivates our players and how emotion and story mapping can help map out and plan the best experiences for those motivations. We then looked at characters as vehicles for enhancing and reinforcing these emotional journeys.

Narrative designers support the game by creating narrative context, reinforcing action through storytelling, and using design and storytelling tools to evoke player emotion in the game experience. UX designers reinforce the context using an understanding of human perception and memory, guide the action by leveraging intuitive design principles and learning structures, and map out the emotions to ensure they fit within the story and player journey. By understanding the symbiotic relationship between these disciplines, we can create motivational engines that engage our players. The games highlighted in this book are just the tip of the iceberg when it comes to the wonderful experiences available to players, and I hope that you use the knowledge and insights you have gained from this text to add your own perspective and voice.

# Index

Printed in the United States
by Baker & Taylor Publisher Services